D0153228

National Income Theory
and Its
Price Theoretic
Foundations

ECONOMICS HANDBOOK SERIES

**McGRAW-HILL
INTERNATIONAL
BOOK COMPANY**

New York
St Louis
San Francisco
Auckland
Beirut
Bogotá
Düsseldorf
Johannesburg
Lisbon
London
Lucerne
Madrid
Mexico
Montreal
New Delhi
Panama
Paris
San Juan
São Paulo
Singapore
Sydney
Tokyo
Toronto

HB
171.5
,A53

W. H. LOCKE ANDERSON

*Professor of Economics
The University of Michigan
Ann Arbor, Michigan*

National Income Theory
and Its
Price Theoretic
Foundations

This book was set in Times Roman.

WITHDRAWN

INDIANA
PURDUE
OCT 2 3 1990
FORT WAYNE

Library of Congress Cataloging in Publication Data

Anderson, William Henry Locke, date
    National income theory and its price theoretic
foundations.

    (Economics handbook series)

    Bibliography: p.
    Includes index.
    1. Macroeconomics. 2. National income. I. Title.
II. Series: Economics handbook series (New York)
HB171.5.A53   339.3'2   78-27409
ISBN 0-07-001670-4

NATIONAL INCOME THEORY
AND ITS PRICE THEORETIC FOUNDATIONS

Copyright © 1979 McGraw-Hill Inc. All rights reserved.
Printed in the United States of America. No part of this publication may be reproduced,
stored in a retrieval system, or transmitted, in any form or by any means,
electronics, mechanical, photocopying, or otherwise,
without the prior permission of the publisher.

1 2 3 4 MPMP   81079

Printed and bound in the United States of America

CONTENTS

Although this is a graduate textbook, it does not serve the same function as, for instance, *Macroeconomic Theory* by Ott, Ott, and Yoo, which in some sense it complements. Whereas their effort surveys and catalogs a large literature, this book is much more selective in its coverage. Its main concern is with the unifying themes in macroeconomics and with its links to microeconomics. Because of this focus, some fairly standard material is omitted altogether. As one of the publisher's readers said, "This book suffers from excessive unity." If so, so be it. It does something important that other books do not do.

All the chapters other than 1 and 4 have been tested extensively in graduate courses at The University of Michigan. Chapters 2 and 3 provided the coverage of consumption and investment theory in a first-year macro course I taught several years ago. More recently, Chapters 5 through 7 have been used in a second-year course on the economics of interdependent markets, along with the general equilibrium surveys of Bent Hansen and Quirk and Saposnik.

Many of the students who have read these chapters have corrected errors and made suggestions for clarifying the presentation. The names that leap to mind are those of Jerry Caprio, André Chaib, Ann Hendricks, Dave Hughart, Carlyn Mitchell, and Lee Phillips, but there have been many others who have been equally gracious and helpful.

Kris Driscoll and Fran Patton are the most recent of the many kind people who have typed the various versions of the manuscript and tried to enforce upon it some measure of stylistic and notational unity.

Among my many colleagues who have helped me, I would like specifically to thank Professors John Cross, Alan Deardorff, and Robert Holbrook for general assistance, and Harold Shapiro for his careful reading of Chapter 5. Professor John Fitts of Carnegie-Mellon University made many contributions to Chapter 3, which I think is the best chapter in the book. Much of what is good in it reflects his contributions.

As for the many errors and omissions that remain despite all my efforts and all the help I have received, they are no one's fault in particular. Finding and correcting them are left as exercises for the reader.

My gratitude toward the people at McGraw-Hill who have helped me is heartfelt. First, there is J. Stephen Dietrich, who as economics editor somehow recognized that the audience for this idiosyncratic book might extend beyond my immediate circle of colleagues, students, friends, and relatives. Second, I must mention Albrecht von Hagen, publisher of the Advanced Books Division. I recognize the irrationality of slaying the messenger who brings bad news, but surely it is only human to love the bearer of a contract. Third, I want to say a word about my production editor and pen pal, Annette Bodzin, whom I have not met at the time of this writing. I am astonished that such a warm and charming friendship could spring up in the margins of galley and page proofs.

Finally, I would like to thank my colleague Professor Ann Anderson, not only for helping with the various versions of Chapter 1, but also for carrying a vastly disproportionate share of caring for our children while the book was being written. To her it is affectionately dedicated.

W. H. LOCKE ANDERSON

CHAPTER ONE

MACROECONOMIC MODELS

Some years ago the *Western Economic Journal* carried an article by Axel Leijonhufvud[1] entitled "Life Among the Econ." This witty and perceptive piece purports to be an anthropologist's account of a primitive tribe, dwelling in a "vast territory . . . appearing bleak and dismal to the outsider." Among other customs and foibles chronicled in the article is the tribal obsession with its totems, called "modls." Both the largest castes of the tribe, the micro and the macro, make modls that "could be roughly described as formed by two carved sticks joined together in the middle somewhat in the form of a pair of scissors." His accompanying figure presents them, with their labels S-D and IS-LM. Although allegiance to one of these totems or the other is the sole basis for caste membership, Leijonhufvud observes: "To the untrained eye, the totems of major castes will often look well-nigh identical."

If it were not obvious right from the start that the article is a spoof, the sentence just quoted would surely give it away. Anyone who has looked carefully at the syllabi of university courses labeled "Macroeconomics" and "Microeconomics" must be appalled by the lack of common content. Many students come to believe that the two branches of theory have nothing in common.[2] This is not simply a matter of differences in coverage. Micro theory describes the reactions of firms and households to changes in prices. Macro theory describes the reactions of these same firms and households to changes in quantities exchanged. These are two fundamentally opposed

---

[1] Leijonhufvud (1973).

[2] The author was recently informed by a student writing a Ph.D. thesis that the life-cycle model of consumption need not be reconciled with the theory of choice, since the one is macroeconomics and the other microeconomics.

pictures of economic life. Pity the poor graduate student who must master the two different languages and must always guard against speaking one in the province of the other. After passing general exams, he or she forgets one of them and settles down to speak the other, perpetuating the schism.

The split is not entirely or even mainly confined to instruction. Microeconomists generally hold the work of macroeconomists in contempt for its intellectual shoddiness, and the latter group views much of the work of the former as an elaborate and pretentious irrelevance. The general unpleasantness of this state of affairs is enough to make one cry "a plague on both your houses."

There have been, of course, a number of attempts to build bridges. Notable ecumenical contributions from the macro side are those of Patinkin, Clower, and Leijonhufvud.[3] Early contributions from the micro side may be found in the volume edited by Phelps.[4] The present work is an attempt to further the trend they have begun. It develops at some length the microanalytic analyses that form the basis of macro theory, explores the aggregation problem, and then reconstructs national income theory in a manner that relates it closely to its foundations in price theory.

Its point of departure is a critical examination of a well-known macro model, that of Modigliani.[5] This model was chosen for examination not specifically for its faults, but rather for its virtues. Although it is not especially new, it is surprisingly modern, and of all the macrostatic models known to the present author, it seems most clearly to rest on a consistent view of microeconomic behavior. The faults that can be found in traces in the Modigliani model appear in much richer lodes in the articles of other authors, and especially in the textbooks. The remainder of this chapter is devoted to an exegesis of Modigliani's model and to commentaries on its various shortcomings.

THE MODIGLIANI MODEL

The scope of the Modigliani model[6] is similar to that of the great majority of static macro models. It analyzes a closed economy with two "real" commodities, goods and labor, and two "paper" commodities, bonds and money. According to Modigliani, these commodities are exchanged in four markets. Perhaps it might have been more in the spirit of monetary economics to have talked in terms of three markets, in each of which demand is effected by means of money, but this is merely a quibble. In any case, the money value of the excess demand for one of the four commodities can be inferred from those of the other three. There are three independent prices in terms of current money; those of goods, of labor, and of a monetary unit for future delivery. Because of the purpose to which the model is put (the study of the monetary mechanism), the government exists only as a provider of outside money and bonds. All

[3] Patinkin (1956, 1963), Clower (1965), Leijonhufvud (1968).
[4] Phelps (1970a).
[5] Modigliani (1963).
[6] The model is set forth on pp. 79–83 of Modigliani (1963).

parties enter into the proceedings with "certainty, absence of money illusion, unit elasticity of price expectations, and independence of interest rate expectations from current prices."

For present purposes, there is no reason to discuss the government's part in what goes on. Therefore the version of Modigliani's model presented below incorporates neither government bonds nor government money. Bonds, if they exist, are obligations of private individuals and firms. Money is provided by competitive private banks, although its supply is exogenously determined.

In order to facilitate subsequent comparison, Modigliani's model is presented, not in his notation, but in the notation used in the rest of this book. Only the first twelve of his equations plus the definition of net worth are pertinent here. Of these, two have been dropped, along with two variables. The order in which the equations are presented has been changed. Modigliani's equation numbers are written in the right-hand margin.

Behavior of households

(1)
$$C = C\left(Y, L^d \frac{w}{p}, r, \frac{W_0}{p}\right)$$
(1)

(2)
$$L^S = L^S\left(\frac{w}{p}\right) \text{ if } L^d\left(\frac{w_0}{p}, K\right) > L^S\left(\frac{w_0}{p}\right)$$
(6)

$$w = w_0 \text{ if } L^d\left(\frac{w_0}{p}, K\right) \leqslant L^S\left(\frac{w_0}{p}\right)$$

Behavior of firms

(3)
$$I = I(r, Y, K_0)$$
(2)

(4)
$$Y^S = Y^S\left(\frac{w}{p}, K_0\right)$$
(4)

(5)
$$L^d = L^d\left(\frac{w}{p}, K_0\right)$$
(5)

Behavior of households and firms

(6)
$$\frac{M^d}{p} = \phi\left(r, Y, \frac{W_0}{p}\right)$$
(M.2)

Definitions

(7)
$$Y = C + I$$
(3)

(8)
$$W_0 = pK_0$$
(iv)

Equilibrium conditions

(9)
$$Y = Y^S$$
(7)

(10)
$$L^S = L^d$$
(8)

(11)
$$M^d = M_0$$

The eleven equations are respectively:

1. The consumption function
2. The labor supply function
3. The investment function
4. The goods supply function
5. The labor demand function
6. The money demand function
7. The definition of aggregate demand
8. The definition of net worth
9. The equilibrium condition in the goods market
10. The equilibrium condition in the labor market
11. The condition of equality between the demand for and supply of money

The last three conditions, if satisfied, imply equilibrium in the securities market, by Walras's law.[7]

The model consists of two distinct kinds of variables, predetermined and simultaneously determined. The predetermined variables are indicated by the following symbols.

W_0 = net worth of households
w_0 = initial money wage
K_0 = stock of capital
M_0 = supply of money

The simultaneously determined variables are indicated by these symbols.

C = real consumption
Y = aggregate demand
L^d = demand for labor
w = money wage
p = price level
r = rate of interest
L^S = labor supply
I = real investment
Y^S = supply of output
M^d = demand for money

---

[7]Since Modigliani's model is cast in terms of discrete time, transactions take place at distinct and separated moments, rather than continuously. In effect, they are all exchanges of stocks for stocks. Money balances, for instance, may be altered by buying commodities. In continuous time models, only the rate of change of money balances may be altered by buying commodities. The pattern of relationships among markets is materially affected by the choice between discrete and continuous time. For an exposition of Walras's law in continuous-time models incorporating both stocks and flows, see Chapter 5.

Such differences as exist between the model set forth above and the corresponding equations on page 80 of Modigliani's article stem entirely from changing notation and dropping variables that are not relevant in the present context.

THE DEFINITION OF NET WORTH

At least since the time of Walras, economists who have dabbled in general equilibrium theory have been counting equations and unknowns. It is well known that equality between the numbers of equations and unknowns is neither necessary nor sufficient for the existence of a solution, but inequality establishes a presumption that something is amiss. In the model above, there are ten simultaneously determined variables, but eleven restrictions. This suggests either an inconsistency or a functional dependency. Since there is no obvious dependency, one looks for an inconsistency.

The culprit is easily found. Equation (8) expresses an equality between the predetermined net worth and the money value of the predetermined capital stock. This, of course, ties down the price level at a value which may be inconsistent with the solution of the general equilibrium system. In Modigliani's article, net worth also includes outside money and bonds. Since they too are predetermined, his fuller formulation suffers from the same difficulty. This is obviously an inadvertent blunder, and not what he meant. The real and money values of net worth cannot both be predetermined.

This is so evident that it need hardly have been brought up, save for the fact that it brings to light a not-so-obvious blunder. In fact, the real value of net worth cannot itself be predetermined, even in an economy without outside wealth. If some inputs are momentarily fixed, increases and decreases in production must lead to corresponding variations in disequilibrium rents, or quasi-rents. These belong to the owners of the firms that receive them. Their present value, however capitalized, must be part of the net worth of the firms' owners. To ignore this is to oversimplify the static model by making real wealth a parameter rather than a simultaneously determined variable.

The stream of real property income is given by

$$(12) \qquad \frac{P}{p} = Y^S - \frac{w}{p} L^d - \delta K_0$$

where P is the money income of property owners and δ is the rate of depreciation. This can be rewritten as

$$(13) \qquad \frac{P}{p} = \left[Y^S - \frac{w}{p} L^d - (r + \delta)K_0 \right] + [rK_0]$$

The first term in brackets is the stream of rents. It may be positive, zero, or negative. The second term is the stream of return to the owners of the capital stock. If these two income streams are capitalized by the reciprocal of the interest rate, the result is

$$(14) \qquad \frac{W}{p} = \frac{1}{r}\frac{P}{p} = K_0 + \frac{1}{r}\left[Y^S - \frac{w}{p} L^d - (r + \delta)K_0 \right]$$

That is, real net worth equals the capital stock plus the capitalized value of real rents. It must rise and fall relative to the capital stock as the ratio of output to capital rises and falls. To say otherwise is to say that the value of firms is independent of their rate of operation.

The dependence of net worth, or wealth, on the general level of production, on the interest rate, and on the wage rate is a matter that is explored more fully in Chapters 5 and 6. Recognition of this dependence complicates general equilibrium theory considerably, and enriches Keynesian multiplier theory by tracing out an additional path through which changes in the rate of production lead to changes in demand. Furthermore, it considerably complicates the task of analyzing fully the labor market, since endogenous variations in wealth have potential effects on the supply of labor.

EQUILIBRIUM AND DISEQUILIBRIUM IN THE LABOR AND GOODS MARKETS

Although in some respects Modigliani's handling of disequilibrium in the labor market represents a distinct improvement over that in his earlier influential article,[8] it still is seriously flawed. The conditions governing the labor market are

$$
(2) \qquad L^S = L^S\left(\frac{w}{p}\right) \text{ if } L^d\left(\frac{w_0}{p},K_0\right) > L^S\left(\frac{w_0}{p}\right)
$$

$$
w = w_0 \text{ if } L^d\left(\frac{w_0}{p},K_0\right) \leqslant L^S\left(\frac{w_0}{p}\right)
$$

$$
(4) \qquad L^d = L^d\left(\frac{w}{p},K_0\right) \quad \text{and}
$$

$$
(10) \qquad L^S = L^d
$$

Apparently what is intended is that the money wage is rigid in the face of excess supply of labor, but fully flexible in the face of excess demand. Most economists would probably interpret the equations in that way. Yet a person trained in mathematics (but not in economics) would have real trouble with equations (2), (4), and (10), since the variable L^S is only defined by (2) under circumstances of excess demand at the predetermined money wage (w_0). Since it is undefined in other circumstances, it is hard to see how it can be set equal always to L^d, as in equation (10).

The formal way out of this difficulty is to replace (2) and (10), so that the restrictions on the labor market are

$$
(2a) \qquad L^S = L^S\left(\frac{w}{p}\right)
$$

[8]Modigliani (1944).

(4) $$L^d = L^d\left(\frac{w}{p}, K_0\right)$$

(10) $$L^d \leqslant L^S$$

(10a) $$w = w_0 \text{ if } L^d\left(\frac{w_0}{p}, K_0\right) < L^S\left(\frac{w_0}{p}\right)$$

The effect of this formulation is to ensure that employment is always equal to labor demand, but that labor supply is always defined, even when it exceeds demand.

Even with this correction made, Modigliani's treatment of the labor market leaves something to be desired. It is hard to see why a situation of excess demand for labor should be treated as though it were radically asymmetrical to a situation of excess supply. Modigliani, in effect, rules out excess demand altogether. The fact that this is traditional does not make it interesting. A much richer variety of results is available if it is admitted that disequilibria are possible in both directions. This is particularly the case if the object of analysis is the functioning of the monetary mechanism, Modigliani's main concern.

A final shortcoming in the treatment of the labor market is the assumption that that market is entirely isolated from the market for goods. Modigliani has assumed that goods prices always adjust instantaneously in the face of discrepancies between demand and supply. As a consequence, the price of commodities is always equal to its short-run supply price, and the real wage therefore is always equal to the marginal product of labor. If the commodity market were differently handled, a greater variety of problems in the labor market could be explored. Suppose, for instance, that the ruling price level could exceed the short-run supply price of the quantity demanded at that price. Then firms that produced so as to equate the marginal product of labor and the real wage could not collectively sell their entire output. Under such circumstances, might some of them not choose to restrict output rather than pile up unwanted inventories? If so, would not the demand function for labor have to account for this possibility? Modigliani's does not.

What shows up here as a defect, or rather a lack of generality, in the treatment of the labor market is really an asymmetry between the treatments of the goods and labor markets. Labor can be in excess supply; goods cannot. The only justification for such treatment is tradition. No body of empirical material supports such a position. To assume it is to restrict the realm of inquiry, and among other things to fail fully to appreciate the whole range of possible consequences of monetary changes. The analysis of Chapter 6, below, treats the goods market on all fours with the labor market and analyzes the consequences of both excess demand and excess supply in both markets. Price rigidity, both upward and downward, and upward wage rigidity are taken to be at least as interesting as downward wage rigidity.

THE IMPLICIT MICRO MODEL

A final respect in which Modigliani's model is less than satisfactory is that is seems not to derive from a fully consistent microanalytic foundation. The consumption function and the labor supply function presumably reflect the outcome of household choice. So, in part, does the demand function for money. Yet these equations, which summarize three dimensions of the same behavior, have quite different independent variables. Labor income appears separately in the consumption function, but not in the demand function for money. Wealth affects consumption and money demand, but not labor supply. The modeling of firm behavior is similarly inconsistent. The real wage rate affects the supply of output and the demand for labor, but not the demands for money and investment goods. The level of effective demand appears as an argument in the investment and money demand functions, but not in the equations for goods production or labor demand. Although it is not reasonable to expect every macro theorist to set forth his micro foundations at great length, it is reasonable to expect a bit more consistency than is apparent in Modigliani's model.

It is not entirely fair to hold Modigliani personally culpable for following precedent. The standard macro model has been pieced together over a number of years. Parts of it appear in Keynes's *The General Theory of Employment, Interest, and Money*, which is itself not very consistent. These parts have been modified and others grafted on. Usually, the modifiers and grafters have focused on one market at a time. The demand for money, for example, is usually modeled without much attention to the theory of the demand for goods, even though the same people who demand money also demand goods. Household and firm decisions are inherently simultaneous, and it is not very tidy or convincing to have unrelated theories about different facets of the same decision. Yet this is precisely what the market-by-market approach encourages. Inconsistencies of this sort are the natural outgrowth of a specialization and division of labor. Within a decade of the publication of the *General Theory*, Keynesianism had become a revolutionary movement, at least within the confines of the frog pond of academic economics. The Keynesian revolution, like many other revolutions, seriously underplayed the virtues of its prerevolutionary heritage. Consistency with the theory of choice ceased to be a crucial test for analytical innovations. Instead, ability to pass crude empirical tests became the main criterion for acceptability. The emphasis on empirical verification was healthy, and the tests soon became much more sophisticated, but one legacy of the piecemeal development of macroeconomics was a jumble of concepts not entirely consonant with one another or with the theory of choice.

Fortunately, it is possible to integrate microanalytic choice theory and macroeconomics without doing much violence to either one. The micro theory must be modified to reflect the fundamental Keynesian contributions to the theory of demand and supply in disequilibrium. The macro theory must be modified so as to incorporate explicitly in its demand and supply functions all the major variables suggested by the microanalysis of choice. These modifications not only integrate macro- and microeconomics, but also integrate the various pieces of the macro model.

The plan of the rest of the book is as follows. Chapter 2 develops the theory of household choice and derives from it the consumption function, the labor supply function, and the demand functions for money and securities. This is done in such a way that the households that appear in one market are recognizable as the same households that appear in another. It also is done so as to recognize explicitly the implications for all demands and supplies of a failure to realize planned employment. Chapter 3 does a parallel analysis of the choice problems of business firms, deriving the demand functions for labor, investment goods, and money and the supply functions for securities and goods. Again there is an emphasis on unity, and again there is explicit recognition of the effects on all demands and supplies of an inability to realize planned sales of output. These two chapters comprise the price theoretic foundations of the macro theory which follows.

Chapter 4 is an entr'acte, so to speak. It treats the problem of transition from individual supply and demand functions to aggregate functions.

Chapters 5, 6, and 7 comprise the macroeconomic portion of the book. Chapter 5 analyzes a model built from aggregate versions of the demand and supply functions of Chapters 2 and 3. Equilibrium is assumed in all markets. Chapter 6 relaxes the assumption of equilibrium and analyzes what is, in effect, an elaborately detailed version of the basic macro model. Chapter 7 introduces the fiscal activities of government and integrates them with the models of Chapters 5 and 6.

These last three chapters are sprinkled with sundry observations on the ideological content of macro theory. This theme is seldom addressed directly in the polite atmosphere of treatise and textbook writing, but there is much unspoken ideology in economics that cries out to be noticed. Even within the range of people who find standard macroeconomics useful, there is a startling diversity in nonanalytic perspective on the market system. This element of perspective exercises a subtle influence on the problems that economists choose to analyze, the assumptions which they make, the weights which they attach to varying pieces of evidence, and the findings which they emphasize.[9] An awareness of at least some of the ideological elements in theory is essential if one is to put competing bodies of thought in perspective.

[9] For a penetrating essay on this topic, see Joseph Schumpeter's Presidential Address to the American Economic Association, Schumpeter (1949).

CHAPTER
TWO

HOUSEHOLD DEMANDS AND SUPPLIES

Among the various criticisms that the previous chapter leveled at the conventional macroeconomic model was that its consumption, labor-supply, and money-demand functions do not reflect any unified theory of the behavior of the households that consume, work, and hold money. The present chapter is designed to remedy this deficiency. It treats within a single framework three kinds of choices: spending versus saving, working versus leisure, and holding money versus holding income-earning assets. Its point of departure is the so-called life-cycle model, but this model is modified and extended so as to encompass a broader range of choices than the spending-saving decision to which it is usually addressed.[1]

The chapter is divided into two main parts. The first develops the theory of life-cycle planning to an extent suffcient to provide a basis for a theory of household demands and supplies. The second examines the impacts of constraints and parameter changes on household plans, and studies the comparative properties of the demand and supply functions themselves.

I. THE THEORY OF HOUSEHOLD CHOICE

The fundamental premise of life-cycle theory is that when a household decides what to do in the present, it does so with full regard for the implications that its current

---

[1] The literature on consumer behavior in general and the life-cycle model in particular is staggeringly large. Notable contributions to the life-cycle literature and to the closely related permanent income model (see the appendix to this chapter) are Modigliani and Brumberg (1954), Brumberg (1956), Friedman (1957), Farrell (1959), Modigliani and Ando (1963), Yaari (1964), Modigliani (1966), and Mayer (1972). The extensions of the present chapter are the author's own, but they do not reflect any great originality and may well exist in various places in the literature.

choices have for the future. The inputs to its choice problem are current and expected future prices of commodities, labor, and assets, its current wealth, and its preferences. Given prices and wealth, the household attempts to plan its activities so as best to satisfy its preferences. The outcome of these deliberations is a set of current and planned future actions with regard to consumption, labor supply, and the purchase and sale of assets.

Planning on the basis of expectations is a sort of mental rehearsal of the future. For households whose preferences are stable, one should expect that if the expectations are fulfilled, the plans will be realized, making the performance look much like the rehearsal. Naturally, when unexpected changes in prices take place, or when unemployment or shortages prevent the fulfillment of plans, the household will have to rethink its opportunities and plan anew. This is the topic of the second part of the chapter. The first part is limited to the theory of the rehearsal. It begins by discussing the familiar two-period planning model of consumer choice, incorporating also the income, leisure choice. The model is then extended to longer time horizons, and sufficient complexities are introduced so as to provide a foundation for the theories of consumption demand, labor supply, and money demand.

A Simple Problem

It is easiest to introduce complicated problems by means of simpler ones. Imagine therefore a simple planning problem—the traditional two-period problem, whose parts appear in many standard micro texts, although not usually in combination. A household has a cardinal utility function whose arguments are consumption and labor supply over two periods. It is given by

$$(1) \qquad U = F(C_1, C_2, L_1, L_2)$$

The derivations with respect to the first two arguments are positive; with respect to the second two negative. The function is strictly concave. The household wishes to maximize it subject to the constraint that its terminal assets be nonnegative. Its initial assets are zero. Since terminal assets have no value, and since nonsatiety is assumed, terminal assets will be zero as well. In view of these considerations, the values of the C's and L's will satisfy

$$(2) \qquad C_1 + \frac{C_2}{1+r} = \frac{w}{p} L_1 + \frac{w}{p} \frac{L_2}{1+r}$$

where r is the real rate of interest and w/p is the (constant) real wage in terms of consumption goods. That is, the present value of the consumption plan will equal that of the planned real wage income.

The maximizing household will want to observe two kinds of marginalities. The first is that the marginal utility of consumption foregone in the first period be equal to the marginal utility of the consumption that may thereby be gained in the second. That is

$$(3) \qquad F_{C_1} = (1+r)F_{C_2} \qquad \text{or} \qquad \Delta F_C = -rF_C$$

where the F_C's are partial derivatives and Δ is the forward difference operator.[2] The second marginality is that in each period the marginal utility of additional consumption be equal to the marginal disutility of the work effort necessary to buy it. That is

$$(4) \qquad\qquad F_{L_i} = -\frac{w}{p} F_{C_i} \qquad \text{for} \qquad i = 1, 2$$

If the utility function is ordinal rather than cardinal, these marginalities should be replaced by obvious conditions on rates of substitution.[3]

Conditions (3) and (4) comprise three restrictions on the C's and L's, which will be assumed to be consistent and functionally independent. Any one of the four variables may therefore be taken as parametric to the other three. This parameter defines a member of a family of choices that are consistent with utility maximization. Among the members of this family, the one which satisfies the constraint (2) is the solution to the problem of choice.

If the household has marketable assets at the beginning of the planning period, the real value of these assets appears as an additive magnitude on the right-hand side of (2). The larger is this magnitude, the larger is the consumption bundle that can be bought at a given work effort, or the smaller the work effort necessary to procure a given consumption bundle. Since consumption is presumably a normal good and work a normal bad, the larger are the assets, the larger will be C_1 and C_2, and the smaller will be L_1 and L_2.

The effects of variations in w/p and r are beset with well-known complexities. The higher is w/p, the greater is the consumption that can be gotten by working harder. This induces a substitution of market goods for leisure. However, the greater is w/p, the greater is the consumption value of a given work plan. The income effect of a higher wage is therefore to reduce work effort and increase consumption. Income and substitution effects on work effort go in opposite directions. They both go in the same direction as they affect consumption.

A rise in the rate of interest has similarly conflicting effects. The higher is the rate of interest, the greater are the benefits in period 2 that can be garnered by deprivations in period 1. These intertemporal substitution effects call for a redistribution of consumption from period 1 to period 2 and of work effort from period 2 to period 1. However, there are also income effects to contend with. If the household plans to be a creditor, say at the end of period 1, a rise in the rate of interest increases the value of its planned saving, raising consumption and lowering work in both periods. If it plans to be a debtor, things go the other way. Taking income and substitution effects together, little can be said about the effects of interest rate changes, except that they all depend.

---

[2] The forward difference is defined such that

$$\Delta F_C(t) = F_C(t + 1) - F_C(t).$$

[3] Since the rate of substitution is inherently a marginal concept, it seems redundant always to include "marginal" as a modifier.

The above discussion contains in embryo much of what is contained in this section and the next. It constitutes the basis for the microanalytic theory of the consumption and labor-supply functions, which are seen to depend on the real wage, the rate of interest, and initial assets. The subsequent pages of this part of the chapter are devoted to a number of extensions of the theory, the most important of which are the consideration of longer time horizons and the incorporation of a theory of the demand for money.

Extension to Longer Time Horizons

It would not be very challenging to extend the two-period model to a three-period model, and the three-period model to an n-period model, in which n is the number of periods in an economic lifetime. Unfortunately, mathematical notation becomes formidable when the time horizon is extended in discrete-time analysis. This complexity can be avoided by viewing time as a continuous variable stretching from the present to the end of a planning horizon. This permits the clumsy trappings of period analysis to be replaced by the more graceful calculus.[4]

To get a foothold on the continuous analysis, consider the planning problem faced by a household with initial assets A earning a real rate of interest r. It wishes to consume them at an optimal rate over the rest of its life span. It has no source of income other than interest, and having no heirs, it plans to die with assets equal to zero. What consumption path $C(t)$ should it choose so as best to satisfy its preferences?

To answer this question, it is first necessary to find some way of characterizing preferences. One appealing way is to attach a utility index, say $F(C(t))$, to the rate of consumption of each date for which it is planning and then to value an entire plan by summing (i.e., integrating) the values at different dates. This leads to a valuation of the form[5]

$$(5) \qquad V(n) = \int_n^d F(C(t))\, dt$$

where $V(n)$ = value of a lifetime consumption plan as seen from date n
  n = "now," the planning date
  d = "death," the end of the plan

[4] Most of the life-cycle literature is cast in terms of discrete time. For examples of continuous-time models, see Yaari (1964) and Strotz (1956).
[5] This sort of integral performance index seems at first glance to be unduly restrictive. As it stands, it does not encompass the possibility of time preference ($F(C(t))$ depends on t only through $C(t)$). Furthermore, independence of utilities at different dates is implicit in the form of F, since the utility index at any particular date depends only on consumption at that date. These are not, however, disqualifying defects. Time preference will be introduced in a few pages. Nonindependence could be introduced by adding to F arguments that summarize previous consumption, but it hardly seems worthwhile. To say that a planner who is trying to value now consumption at a particular future date takes into account what he or she contemplates consuming at other future dates is to endow that person with a rare order of perspicacity.

$F(C(t))$ = the utility contemplated at time n of consuming at date t at a rate equal to $C(t)$

The problem it faces is that of choosing a time path $C(t)$ for all $t\epsilon\ [n, d]$ so as to maximize $V(n)$, the value of the plan as the household sees it.

Naturally, not all plans are open to it, for some will entail more consumption than the assets permit. Moreover, some will not exhaust this stock by death. The precise constraint that planned consumption path must satisfy is that its present value must equal the initial assets. To see this, note that if we measure real assets in terms of consumption units, and assume a constant price level

(6)
$$\frac{d\,A/p}{dt} = r\frac{A}{p} - C$$

The solution to this is

(7)
$$\frac{A(n)}{p} = \int_{n}^{d} e^{-r(t-n)}\,C(t)\,dt$$

The right-hand side is, of course, the present value of the consumption plan.

This is not much of a restriction. The family of consumption paths satisfying this constraint is a large one indeed, even if its membership is restricted to continuous, smooth functions of time. The problem calls for a marginal condition to restrict possibilities still further.

Imagine that the planner has found a path that satisfies (7), and is mentally rearranging consumption along this path so as to increase its value without violating the constraint. At what point will he or she decide that it is not worthwhile to lower consumption at t in order to increase it at some neighboring time point, say $t + h$? The natural marginalist answer, and the one proffered in the solution of the two-period problem, is that the planner should stop when the marginal utility of consumption foregone at t equals the marginal utility of the consumption gained at $t + h$. If the per annum interest rate is r, then the consumption to be gained at $t + h$ by foregoing one unit at t will be e^{rh}, which may be approximated by $(1 + rh)$. So he or she should stop rearranging between t and $t + h$ when

(8)
$$F_C(t) = (1 + rh)\,F_C(t + h)$$

where F_C is the marginal utility of consumption.

Now suppose that the interval over which the comparison is made shrinks. First, rearrange (8) so that it reads

(9)
$$\frac{F_C(t + h) - F_C(t)}{h} = -rF_C(t + h)$$

Letting h approach zero while obeying this marginality yields

(10)
$$\frac{dF_C}{dt} = -rF_C$$

This is the necessary marginal condition for optimal planning over continuous time. Compare it to Equation (3) above.

To see the sense of it, notice first its implications for optimal behavior with a zero rate of interest. Since the right-hand side of (10) is then zero, optimal planning requires that the marginal utility of consumption remain constant over the planning period. If F is independent of time

$$(11) \qquad \frac{dF_C}{dt} = F_{CC} \frac{dC}{dt}$$

Unless F_{CC} were zero, this would in turn imply that consumption ought to be constant. But F_{CC} must be negative (the marginal utility of consumption must diminish as consumption is increased) in order for any optimal plan to exist.[6] Therefore, it is best to consume the initial assets at a steady rate equal to $A(n)/p/(d - n)$ per unit of time. This satisfies optimality condition (10) as well as constraint (7).

If the interest rate is positive, (10) implies that F_C, the marginal utility of consumption, ought to decline over time at proportional rate r. Combining (10) and (11), C should follow

$$(12) \qquad \frac{1}{C} \frac{dC}{dt} = -r \left[\frac{F_C}{CF_{CC}} \right]$$

The quantity in parentheses on the right-hand side is the reciprocal of the elasticity of marginal utility with respect to consumption. Since this elasticity is negative, (12) implies that consumption should increase over the planning period. By departing from a path of steady consumption, the household may take better advantage of the market opportunities afforded by interest. Among those paths that satisfy constraint (7), it should choose that one that also satisfies (12).

Time Preference

Nothing in the derivation of (10) depends on the assumed time constancy of the utility function. If the spending unit values an increment to a given rate of consumption differently at different time points, this will affect its plans, to be sure, but not the marginal optimality conditions that they must satisfy. Suppose, for example, that a household has a pattern of time preference that is uniformly positive in Fisher's sense.[7] If it were forced to consume at a constant rate throughout its life span, it would place a relatively high marginal utility on consumption at early dates, a low marginal utility at later dates. If the interest rate were zero and it were free to choose its consumption, it would prefer a pattern with higher consumption early, lower consumption late. Such a pattern would make the marginal utility of consumption

---

[6] If F_{CC} were zero, all plans would be optimal at zero interest. If it were positive, a wild spending spree of short duration would be preferred to an equal rate of expenditure over the planning period, but an even wilder spree of shorter duration would be better still.

[7] See Fisher (1930, chap. IV).

the same at all dates in the planning period. With diminishing marginal utility ($F_{CC} < 0$), any rearrangement would worsen the plan.

Relations (11) and (12) must be modified to accommodate time preference. The appropriate adjustments are

$$(11') \qquad \frac{dF_C}{dt} = F_{CC}\frac{dC}{dt} + F_{Ct}$$

$$(12') \qquad \frac{1}{C}\frac{dC}{dt} = -\left[r + \frac{F_{Ct}}{F_C}\right]\frac{F_C}{CF_{CC}}$$

The second term in the parentheses on the right side of ($12'$) is the proportional rate of change in the marginal utility of consumption due simply to the passage of time. Suppose this were negative. This would imply that along a constant-consumption path the marginal utility of consumption would decline over time. Evidently this is an indication of positive time preference. A positive value of F_{Ct} would indicate negative time preference.

It is apparent from ($12'$) that interest and positive time preference war with one another in determining the best program of consumption. Positive interest encourages frugality early in life because of the higher total consumption that this makes possible. Positive time preference encourages prodigality early in life because of the improvement in allocation that this makes possible. The outcome of this war depends on the relative strengths of the forces at work. It may end in a standoff in which consumption is steady over the plan. A plan of rising consumption would be larger in total but more poorly allocated; a plan of falling consumption would be better allocated, but smaller.

Most economists, like Fisher, seem to associate positive time preference with impatience or shortsightedness. Consumption at a late date seems less valuable than consumption at an early date because remote pleasures loom less vividly in the imagination than immediate pleasures. This yields a utility index that is the product of a function of remoteness and a function of consumption. A typical example might be

$$(13) \qquad F(C, t) = e^{\lambda(t-n)} g(C)$$

where λ is a negative constant.[8] Under this formulation, what matters is remoteness, not calendar date. A person with constant tastes who continually replans will tend to value consumption at a given calendar date more highly as time passes, for it will become less remote as the planning date moves toward the calendar date.

If this were the only possible form of time preference, it would be hard to imagine what reasonable behavior might constitute negative time preference. A farsighted individual presumably imagines the remote future as vividly as the near future, but surely not more vividly. Yet there is an alternative approach to time preference in which negative rates make quite good sense.

Anyone who is attempting to plan his remaining life span sees not an undifferen-

---

[8] This is the example of constant discounting of future utility. See Strotz (1956) for the implications of this kind of time preference.

tiated stretch of time but a sequence of life-cycle stages. The children must be clothed and schooled and orthodontisted. When the children's dentist bills are finally ended, life will become simpler again, the way it was before they were born. To cope intelligently with the unfolding life cycle, expenditures will have to be heavy during some periods, lighter during others. For most people, time preference is probably negative early in the life cycle, positive later on. Along a constant consumption path, the marginal utility of consumption would first rise and then fall. Along an optimal path, therefore, consumpion will rise rapidly up to a point; then it will rise less rapidly or even fall.

In comparing this kind of time preference with the first, it should be noticed that calendar date is what counts. A remote wedding or bar mitzvah is accorded the same weight as one which is imminent. As time passes and the planning date approaches a life-cycle event, a planner with constant tastes will continue to value that event as he or she did before.

People who have time preference of the first sort must also always regret their past extravagances, for remote past pleasures must be discounted like those of the future. People whose time preferences are associated with the life cycle, by contrast, need not regret that they planned particularly large expenditures in particular periods.

Labor Supply

The continuous model just used to deduce the optimal rate of spending out of assets and accrued interest may be generalized so as to encompass variable labor supply and wage income. Assume that the integrand of the utility function includes labor supply as one of its arguments. The maximand of the choice problem is now

$$(14) \qquad V(n) = \int_n^d F(C, L, t)\, dt$$

The constraint is

$$\frac{d\, A/p}{dt} = r\frac{A}{p} + \frac{w}{p} L - C$$

where w is the money wage, p is the constant price of consumption goods, and A is the money value of assets. Assuming that F has the requisite concavity in C and L and that F_L is negative, it is possible to envision an optimal-consumption, labor-supply plan corresponding to any initial assets and expected prices. Such a plan will have to satisfy two optimality conditions and the budget constraint. The budget constraint in integral form is

$$(16) \qquad \frac{A(n)}{p} = \int_n^d e^{-r(t-n)} \left(C - \frac{w}{p} L \right) dt$$

That is, the present value of the differences between planned consumption and planned wages must equal initial assets. The first optimality condition is the static rule of Equation (4), which states that the marginal disutility of labor must equal the real wage times the marginal utility of consumption. If a plan does not satisfy this condition at any point, it should be changed by moving C and L in the same direction so as to leave A unaffected. This will make the plan better at that time without altering the choices that are available at other times. The second optimality condition is the intertemporal restriction (10). If it is satisfied, no rearrangement of consumption across time can improve the plan either.

Providing that the planning unit has no time preference and expects real wages to be constant over its remaining life span, it is possible to envision the plan with the aid of a diagram, Figure 2-1. The family of curves shown on this figure depicts combinations of consumption and work effort among which the household is indifferent. The straight lines have slopes equal to the real wage. Their tangencies to the indifference curves define an expansion path along which the condition

$$(17) \qquad\qquad F_L = - \frac{w}{p} F_C$$

is satisfied. Since the absence of time preference implies that tastes are expected to be stationary, the indifference curves pertinent to one date are pertinent to all dates. If the real wage is also expected to be constant, then the expansion path will apply to all dates. The planned life cycle may be depicted as a journey along this path. If the household has no initial assets and faces a positive rate of interest, it will want to begin its plan by saving, intending to dissave later on. Thus it will start out at some point such as α, at which earnings exceed consumption, intending to use its savings later on, augmented by interest. Thus it will plan to proceed toward the northwest along the expansion path, at a rate which satisfies intertemporal optimality, ending its days at some point such as γ.

Naturally, time preference and expectations of a varying real wage rate complicate the problem a good bit. If wages are expected to vary, the budget lines do not stay put; if time preference is present, the indifference map changes over time. Either afflic-

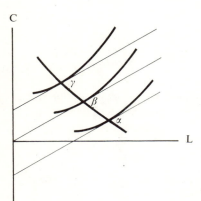

Figure 2-1 Optimal behavior in the absence of time preference.

tion destroys the usefulness of Figure 2-1. Nonetheless, the problem may still be partly analyzed by means of some differential equations. These differential equations derive from the optimality conditions (10) and (17). Straightforward expansion of (10) gives

(18)
$$F_{CC}\,\dot{C} + F_{CL}\,\dot{L} + F_{Ct} = -rF_C$$

Differentiation of (17) and substitution of (10) gives

(19)
$$F_{LC}\,\dot{C} + F_{LL}\,\dot{L} + F_{Lt} = -rF_L - F_C\,\frac{dw/p}{dt}$$

After a certain amount of rearrangement and other algebraical busy work, these may be rewritten

(20)
$$\dot{C} = a_{Ct} + a_{Cr}\,r + a_{Cw}\,\frac{dw/p}{dt} \quad \text{and}$$

(21)
$$\dot{L} = a_{Lt} + a_{Lr}r + a_{Lw}\,\frac{dw/p}{dt}$$

where $a_{Ct} = -\dfrac{1}{\Delta}(F_{Ct}F_{LL} - F_{Lt}F_{CL})$

$$a_{Lt} = -\frac{1}{\Delta}(F_{Lt}F_{CC} - F_{Ct}F_{LC})$$

$$a_{Cr} = -\frac{1}{\Delta}(F_C F_{LL} - F_L F_{CL})$$

$$a_{Lr} = -\frac{1}{\Delta}(F_L F_{CC} - F_C F_{LC})$$

$$a_{Cw} = \frac{F_C F_{CL}}{\Delta}$$

$$a_{Lw} = -\frac{F_C F_{CC}}{\Delta}$$

$$\Delta = F_{CC}F_{LL} - F_{CL}F_{LC}$$

These coefficients represent the effects of time preference, interest, and changing wages on the rate of change of consumption and labor supply.

The case of independence between C and L in utility (i.e., $F_{CL} = F_{LC} = 0$) is the easiest to analyze. In this instance, all the a coefficients are very simple

$$a_{Ct} = -\frac{F_{Ct}}{F_{CC}}$$

$$a_{Lt} = -\frac{F_{Lt}}{F_{LL}}$$

$$a_{Cr} = -\frac{F_C}{F_{CC}} > 0$$

$$a_{Lr} = -\frac{F_L}{F_{LL}} < 0$$

$$a_{Cw} = 0$$

$$a_{Lw} = -\frac{F_C}{F_{LL}} > 0$$

A shortsighted spending unit (for which $F_{Ct} < 0$, $F_{Lt} > 0$)[9] will choose declining consumption and rising labor supply at a zero rate of interest, although a sufficiently positive rate of interest could lead it to choose the opposite combination. Other patterns are also possible, however, for there is no real necessity that F_{Ct} and F_{Lt} have these signs, or even that they have unlike signs.

The general case is still less conclusive because F_{CL} has no clear-cut sign. Increased work effort probably raises the marginal utility of food, work clothes, and the like, but it also probably lowers the marginal utility of those forms of consumption that require inputs of time and energy. The overall effect is not clear.

Some restrictions are possible despite this ambiguity. The determinant Δ must be positive if the utility surface is to be concave. Thus a_{Lw} must be positive; a rising wage leads to a rising labor supply over time. The effect of rising wages on consumption is not clear, however. Further, a_{Cr} must be positive and a_{Lr} must be negative if consumption is a normal good and work effort a normal bad. This in turn implies that if F_{Ct}/F_C equals F_{Lt}/F_L, as it must if future utilities and disutilities are discounted at the same rate, then the signs of a_{Ct} and a_{Lt} are unambiguous. A shortsighted household facing a zero interest rate will choose declining consumption and rising labor supply just as in the case of independence. If time preference takes a more complicated form, however, nothing clear-cut about its effects can be said without restricting the sign of F_{CL}.

Household Demand for Money

Up to this point, the exposition of the theory of household choice has ignored the fact that households typically hold a portion of their wealth in the form of money, which yields no return, rather than in the form of income-earning assets. Since they must sacrifice consumption and leisure in order to do so, this practice calls for some explanation, some justification for what Patinkin has called "the peaceful coexistence of money and interest-bearing bonds."

The literature on the determinants of the demand for money[10] is a complicated one, unnecessarily so. Most households, one suspects, hold money simply because

---

[9] Shortsightedness or impatience presumably entails the discounting of remote work effort. If F_L, which is negative, is to become smaller in magnitude as it gets further from the planning data, F_{Lt} must be positive.

[10] Many models of the demand for money seem to be the products of the cartoonist Rube Goldberg, who created fantastic devices for achieving simple goals. For examples, see Tobin (1956, 1958) and Baumol (1952).

life is rendered more convenient and pleasant thereby. In order to hold wealth in forms that bear interest but are not widely accepted as means of payment, someone must be prepared to devote much time and effort to buying and selling assets so as to dispose of income receipts and finance commodity purchases. How much simpler to be sloppy, to keep a buffer fund of money so as not to have so relentlessly to maximize income.

Money brings a household a utility, therefore, that is not appreciably different from the utility of other inventories it holds.[11] If the timing of receipts and expenditures is uncertain, this may dictate the holding of more money than would be required if they were certain, but uncertainty is not really necessary to account for the demand for money. Nor is it necessary to adduce pecuniary transactions costs, as some writers have done. All that is required is to note that most consumers find incessant security or savings account transactions irksome.

This is most straightforwardly recognized by including money as an argument in the utility function. Since the convenience afforded by money depends on the extent of its command over commodities, the appropriate quantity to include is the real holding of money, M/p.[12] The maximand of the choice problem then becomes

$$(22) \qquad V(n) = \int_n^d F\left(C, L, \frac{M}{p}, t\right) dt$$

The new constraint is

$$(23) \qquad \dot{W} = rA + wL - pC \qquad \text{where}$$

$$(24) \qquad W = M + A$$

In integral form, it may be written as

$$(25) \qquad W(n) = \int_n^d e^{-r(t-n)} (pC + rM - wL) \, dt$$

This states that if the household's resources are to be exactly exhausted at the end of the planning period, it must choose L, C, and M so that the present value of its consumption plus the interest foregone by holding money less its wages equals its wealth as of the planning date.

---

[11]One of the first authors to treat money as a good conferring direct utility was Patinkin (1951). See also Friedman (1956).

[12]It may be objected that this formulation departs from neoclassical tradition, since the general price level appears as an argument of the preference function (as the denominator of the real money supply). An alternative that comes to much the same thing makes utility a function of consumption and leisure. Leisure, in turn, is determined by work effort, consumption, and real money holdings, for the reasons just adduced. This "destruction function" for leisure is a technical relationship, which may change as the institutions of payment change. Admittedly this is a superior formulation, but when the leisure function is substituted into the utility function, the result is not distinguishable from Equation (22). In effect, this method of handling the demand for money amounts to a variation on Lancaster's (1966) consumption model.

Along an optimal path of consumption, labor supply, and money holding, conditions (17) and (10) will still have to be observed. An additional optimality condition is called for to govern the amount of real money to be held. Naturally, the condition required is that the marginal utility of money be equal to the marginal utility of the consumption foregone in order to hold money, that is

$$(26) \qquad F_{M/p} = rF_C$$

Together with (17), this implies that

$$(27) \qquad F_{M/p} = -r\,\frac{p}{w}\,F_L$$

which states that the marginal utility of money must equal the marginal disutility of the work effort necessary to pay its opportunity cost.

It is possible to handle the grim mechanics of this three-variable choice problem by the same differential-equations technique used in the previous two-variable problem. Since the general case is quite cumbersome, not to mention dull, consider a simplified version in which the planner has no time preference and the marginal utilities of money and consumption are independent of the amount of labor supplied. Differentiation of (26) under these restrictions gives

$$(28) \qquad F_{M/pM/p}\,\frac{dM/p}{dt} + F_{M/pC}\,\frac{dC}{dt} = r\,\frac{dF_C}{dt}$$

Along an optimal consumption plan at positive interest, dC/dt is positive and dF_C/dt is negative. In order for there to exist a best plan, $F_{M/pM/p}$ must be negative. Furthermore, it is hard to believe that $F_{M/pC}$ is anything but positive.[13] It follows therefore that $d/dt\,(M/p)$ will be positive along a best money-holding plan. The farsighted household will not only work hard and consume little early in its life, but it will keep small money holdings as well. Gradually, as its consumption and leisure increase over time, so will its money holdings.

Bequests

Up to this point, the household has been treated as though it never wished to transfer assets to its offspring. Indeed, a good case can be made that the most frequent deliberately planned transfer of wealth from one generation to another takes the form of education. Parents forego other forms of spending in order to educate their children. Although this appears in national accounting systems as consumption expenditure, it might more appropriately be called a bequest of human capital. Moreover, a substantial proportion of those intergenerational wealth transfers that take the form of bequests, narrowly defined, must be the result of incorrect expectations about the life span. Untimely deaths terminate an economic life span before the planned-for date; assets that were expected to tide the decreased over the retirement span then

---

[13] Higher consumption must surely raise the marginal utility of money.

pass to his or her heirs. Nonetheless, there clearly exist bequests of nonhuman wealth that are deliberately planned, particularly in the upper reaches of the distribution of wealth. With very little difficulty they may be incorporated into the life-cycle planning model.

A utility function incorporating bequests may be defined in terms of the notation of the previous section. The overall utility of a plan could be written as

$$(29) \qquad\qquad U = U[V(n), W(d)]$$

where U is a concave utility function whose arguments are the value of the summed utility stream over the life span and the amount of assets remaining at the end of the plan to provide a bequest. The contours of U form a conventionally shaped family of indifference curves in V, W space. Presumably they exhibit a diminishing rate of substitution; the marginal amount of bequest necessary to compensate the planner for a loss of life-span utility increases as the amount of bequest increases and the amount of life-span utility declines. Furthermore, U is presumably shaped so that neither $V(n)$ nor $W(d)$ is an inferior good. Finally, the indifference curves intersect the $V(n)$ axis, so that corner solutions are possible.

The properties of the $V(n)$, $W(d)$ opportunity set may be seen from a formal statement of the maximization of

$$(30) \qquad\qquad V(n) = \int_{n}^{d} F\left(C, L, \frac{M}{p}, t\right) dt$$

subject to

$$W(n) - e^{-r(d-n)}W(d) = \int_{n}^{d} e^{-r(t-n)}(pC + rM - wL)\, dt$$

It is clear that the boundary of the set is negatively inclined: a rise in the planned bequest of course reduces the maximum life-cycle utility. It is also intuitively plausible, and is in fact the case,[14] that this boundary is concave; the further the bequest is increased, the more life-cycle utility is impaired by additional increases. Finally, it seems evident that if a household's wealth is increased, the slope of its opportunity frontier (with $W(d)$ on the vertical axis) as it hits the $V(n)$ axis will be increased in magnitude.[15]

These considerations lead to the situation shown in Figure 2-2.

Although nothing in the problem guarantees it, the changing slope of the oppor-

---

[14]This follows from the concavity of F and the linearity of (30). To see that it is so, differentiate (29) twice totally with respect to $W(d)$. The result is the integral of a negative definite quadratic form plus three odd terms. If (30) is differentiated twice with respect to $W(d)$ and the first order conditions for optimality are substituted, it is apparent that the three odd terms must integrate to zero, guaranteeing that $d^2V(n)/dW(d)^2$ is negative.

[15]This may be shown using the technique of footnote 14, but differentiating with respect to $W(d)$ and then with respect to $W(n)$.

W(d)

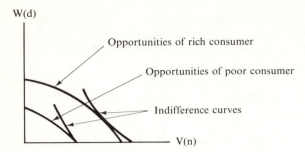

Figure 2–2 Bequests as a luxury good.

tunity frontier makes it likely that poorer households will find themselves at corner solutions and richer households at interior maxima.[16] This in turn implies that over the ordinary range of variations in wealth, bequests may be a luxury good.

Retirement

No discussion of the theory of household planning would be complete without some treatment of planning for retirement.[17] Retirement is one of the most important determinants of saving and spending decisions over the life cycle. In the interest of brevity, the present discussion is limited to cases in which the household's wage earner is bound by custom or law to retire at some known date.

Assume therefore that the household will receive no wage income beyond some date q, although it may be entitled to a retirement income at rate R during the time span from q to d. Assuming for the sake of simplicity that it plans to leave no bequest, its budget constraint is

$$(31) \quad W(n) = \int_n^q e^{-r(t-n)}(pC + rM - wL)\, dt + \int_q^d e^{-r(t-n)}(pC + rM - R)\, dt$$

The maximand is still given by (22).

Notice that R is a given, not a choice variable. The integral of its present value over the retirement span is therefore a fixed sum, and can be included as a part of wealth as of the planning date. Therefore it need not be discussed separately.

Maximization of (22) subject to constraint (31) does not differ greatly from the cases already considered. The marginal utility of consumption must still decline at proportional rate r over the entire life span. Since the utility function will not in gen-

---

[16] Some perfectly sensible utility functions necessarily produce this result. For example, suppose that U is given by $V(n) + g(W(d))$, where $g > 0$, $g'' < 0$, $g'(0)$ is finite. This function has contours that have a constant slope along the V axis. At some low enough V, they are steeper than the opportunity frontier.

[17] The early literature on the life-cycle model was mainly devoted to the implications of retirement. See Modigliani and Brumberg (1954).

eral exhibit independence, this will entail a discrete change in consumption at the retirement date, since L will abruptly drop at that date. Subsequent to the retirement date, (17) will no longer be one of the conditions of optimality, although (26) will continue to be. Otherwise the best plan is just like those previously discussed.

Whether or not $W(q)$ is positive or negative depends on the relative sizes of the retirement income R and the rate of consumption planned for during the same period. Ordinarily one would expect the former to be smaller than the latter and for the household to plan to supplement its retirement income out of assets accumulated prior to retirement. However, there is nothing inherent in the problem to keep a household from running up debts during its earning span that it repays after retiring. The possibility that this could in fact happen depends crucially on the "perfectness" of the capital market and the certainty of the death date, however.

Saving for retirement must account for a large part of the net household saving other than that done by the very rich. The cohorts in a growing population that are saving for retirement will be larger and may have higher wages than those dissaving during retirement. If so the rate of accumulation of assets by those working will exceed the rate of decumulation of those retired. Moreover, even in a stationary population with constant wages, the extent of saving for retirement will be a major determinant of the amount of wealth held by a cross section of households of various ages. Other things equal, the stronger is the retirement motive for saving, the larger is the equilibrium quantity of wealth that households will wish to hold. This quantity, in turn, is an important element in the neoclassical theory of income distribution.

This section completes the development of those aspects of planning and choice theory most relevant to a consistent treatment of the household sector in a macroeconomic model. Two things must be done to complete the derivation of household demand and supply functions. First, it must be recognized that households' plans are frequently circumscribed by disequilibria in the markets in which they buy and sell. Such circumscriptions, if they are binding, produce decisions which are materially different from those that the household would make if it were bound only by prices and the requirements of budgetary consistency. Second, the implications for planning of changes in parameters must be pursued in order to assess their effects on consumption, labor supply, and the demand for money. These two topics comprise the subjects of the following part of the chapter.

II. THE RESPONSE TO CONSTRAINTS AND PARAMETER VARIATIONS

The upshot of the discussion of the previous section is that a household's present and planned future values of consumption demand, labor supply, money demand, and security demand depend on current and expected future values of prices, wages, and the rate of interest, and on the household's asset position as of the date of planning. Like so much of economic theory, this discussion implicitly assumes that plans can be carried out unless the circumstances from which they arise are altered. Unfortunately, however, involuntary unemployment seems to be a characteristic feature of capitalism, and any theoretical structure claiming to explain its broad outlines must consider how the unemployed react to being out of work.

Most, if not all, of the life-cycle literature treats employment as though it were entirely determined by forces outside the control of the household.[18] This treatment of the matter is unduly simplistic; indeed, its only virtue is its simplicity. Any satisfactory analysis must recognize that the market sometimes will absorb all the labor that a household wishes to supply and sometimes will not. Thus its behavior is sometimes controlled by marginal conditions and sometimes by constraints. Before the household's behavioral functions may be developed, the effects of this off-again, on-again constraint must be looked at.

Unemployment and Planning

A household that is subject to market-imposed limitations on its employment operates under two different employment rules. It chooses the amount of labor it wishes to supply. Either the market will absorb this amount, in which case employment equals labor supply, or the market will not, in which case employment equals labor demand.[19] A few moments' reflection will convince the reader that in the former case, it will equate the marginal disutility of labor to the marginal utility of the wage, whereas in the latter, the disutility of work will fall short of the utility of consuming the wage at the margin.

If the household had a one-period horizon, the implications of unemployment for its planning would be simple. It would always consume its wage income, whether or not its work effort were subject to constraint. If it had initial assets, it would consume these as well, again quite irrespective of any labor market constraint.

In planning over a longer horizon, the problem is much more complicated. The household may choose to carry "buffer stocks" of precautionary assets so as to tide it over periods of unemployment. Such stocks will permit it to achieve greater consistency with the intertemporal optimality condition (10) than it would be able to achieve if it failed to anticipate unemployment and had to live on the proceeds of its restricted work efforts or to borrow necessitously.

The problem of optimizing under the constraint of a labor market that sometimes will not absorb the household's labor supply may be formalized in the following way. Maximize

$$V(n) = \int_n^d F\left(C, L, \frac{M}{p}\right) dt$$

subject to

$$W(n) = \int_n^d e^{-r(t-n)} [pC + rM - wL] \, dt$$

---

[18] This is true of all the references cited in the first footnote of this chapter.

[19] This statement ignores the possibility of "all or nothing" job offers, which induce households to work more than they would like rather than not to work at all. See Deardorff and Stafford (1976).

where $L \leqslant L^d(t)$ for $t \in [n, d]$. Over the entire optimal plan, the intertemporal condition (10) will be observed, as will the marginality condition (26) regulating the demand for money.[20] The marginal condition (17) on labor supply will hold except when it implies a violation of the labor market constraint.

Once the problem is posed in this way, it becomes evident that the household has some control over the extent to which it is constrained by unemployment. Suppose that it contemplates a plan with very high consumption and money holdings and very low work effort, satisfying always conditions (10) and (26). It may well thereby also be able always to satisfy (17), since the market may absorb all its limited supply of labor. Such a plan will be feasible if its initial assets are so high as to permit it to consume much and work little without violating its lifetime budget constraint. If its assets are not so high, it must plan to consume less, hold less money, and work harder, still satisfying (10), (26), and (17). The lower are its initial assets, the closer will it come to the market constraint. Ultimately there is a minimum asset level that will just permit it to follow an unconstrained plan. At any lower initial asset level, it will be led to offer a supply of labor that is ordinarily absorbed but that is sometimes greater than the market demand for its services. In effect, by choosing to work hard, it is choosing sometimes to be unemployed. It does so because a plan with some spells of unemployment is preferred to a more stringent regime that never comes up against the constraint. Such patterns of behavior are common in regions and industries with strong seasonal patterns. Feverish bursts of activity alternate with periods of prolonged idleness. A person living in such an environment who chooses never to be unemployed would thereby choose a lifestyle with too few goods and too much leisure.

It is important to notice that the life-cycle pattern of asset accumulation will be much more complicated in the presence of unemployment than in its absence. Superimposed upon the long swing of accumulation during the early years to provide for later years will be shorter bursts during full employment to provide stocks that may be decumulated during unemployment periods. The more frequent and devastating are the failures of the market in which the household sells its labor services, the more will this short-run pattern dominate its savings behavior.

This approach to the relationship between household behavior and unemployment presupposes that the household holds definite expectations about its future employability. Its implications can be approximated by a model incorporating less implausible assumptions about expectations, however. All that is necessary is that the household perceive the necessity for carrying precautionary assets to tide it over periods of unemployment. The perceived need for such assets will presumably be a function of its age, its own unemployment experiences, and general economic conditions. It will build up precautionary asset stocks during full employment periods and run them down when it is unemployed. Its employment will be less erratic than the demand for its labor, but more so than it would like it to be. Its consumption and money holding will be smoother than its labor income. If it makes adequate provision for

---

[20]Unless the utility function is additive, smoothness of marginal utilities over time need not be accompanied by smoothness in consumption or money holding. A discrete jump in employment may require a discrete jump in consumption to maintain consistency with (10).

its spells of unemployment, they need not imply any disturbance of intertemporal optimality of consumption.

The labor market is not the only possible source of disequilibrium constraints on household behavior, of course. Shortages of goods are an obvious alternative source of disturbance. However, neither tradition nor the needs of subsequent chapters call for much analysis of the consequences of shortages. They will therefore not be pursued here.

One additional matter does need to be mentioned, however. The fact that households adjust to labor market disequilibria by altering their sales and purchases does not, in itself, imply that they do not attempt also to cope with their problems by making wage adjustments. People who cannot find work when they would like to may make all kinds of efforts to obtain jobs.[21] Among these efforts may be wage concessions aimed at obtaining employment at the expense of those currently working. If times are sufficiently hard and the wage-concessions practice sufficiently widespread, the consequence will be a decline in the general level of wages. Yet even while they are declining, wages have a definite level at any moment; their level may for an extended period be incompatible with labor-market equilibrium, even though it is falling quite rapidly. Wages may be quite flexible in the face of disequilibria but may be nearly always at the wrong level. In fact, there may be no right level.

The Demand and Supply Functions

Because of the labor market constraint, the demand for a household's labor must be included along with the wage rate, the rate of interest, and wealth in the list of determinants of its behavior. Its behavioral relations may be written in the following way

$$(32) \qquad C = C\left(\frac{w}{p}, r, \frac{W}{p}, L\right)$$

$$(33) \qquad L^s = L^s\left(\frac{w}{p}, r, \frac{W}{p}\right)$$

$$(34) \qquad \frac{M^h}{p} = \phi^h\left(\frac{w}{p}, r, \frac{W}{p}, L\right)$$

$$(35) \qquad \frac{A}{p} = \psi\left(\frac{w}{p}, r, \frac{W}{p}, L\right) \qquad \text{where}$$

$$(36) \qquad L = \text{Min}\,(L^s, L^d)$$

These relationships are linked together by two identities

$$(37) \qquad W = M^h + A$$

$$(38) \qquad \dot{W} = rA + wL - pC$$

The structure of these relationships deserves several comments.

---

[21] The most pertinent literature is that relating to job search. See Holt (1970), McCall (1970), Mortensen (1970a, 1970b), Phelps (1970b), Whipple (1973), Lucas and Prescott (1974).

First, notice that all the behavioral relationships display zero degree homogeneity in money wages, prices, and the money value of assets. Thus money illusion is assumed away.

Second, notice that the labor supply function (33) is written in terms of the real wage, the rate of interest, and wealth. Thus it is what Clower calls a "notional" supply function,[22] expressing labor supply as a function of those variables that would be relevant if it could sell whatever labor services it wanted. The other behavioral functions include employment [which by (36) is the smaller of supply and demand] as an argument. Thus they represent what Clower calls "effective," or employment-constrained, demand functions. In subsequent analysis the employment variable will be suppressed whenever it is understood always to equal labor supply.

Third, all the behavioral relations ostensibly assume static expectations. Expected future time paths of w, p, r, and L^d are represented by their current values. This can only be done in a strict sense if the household expects that future values of these parameters will equal their current values. This assumption is surely not descriptive, particularly for labor demand. However, if expected values are all affected in the same direction by a change in the current value, their representation by the current value is a harmless simplification, provided that it is used with care.[23]

Fourth, notice that by virtue of (37) the asset demand function is not functionally independent of the money demand function. The derivatives of (35) may therefore be obtained from those of (34).

Compensating Variations and Income Effects

In the analysis of consumer choice among commodities, it is fruitful to break the response of a consumer's demand for a commodity to a fall in its price into two parts, an income effect and a substitution effect. The substitution effect occurs because the consumer will substitute the now cheaper good for others, even if his or her real income is held constant by a compensating variation in budget. The income effect occurs because if no compensating variation is made, the initial budget will buy a more highly valued commodity bundle, and it therefore constitutes a larger real income. The sign of the income effect is determined by the income-responsiveness of demand, and the magnitude is affected as well by the size of the implied real income increase.

In studying the matters at hand, this distinction between income and substitution effects is equally productive. The response of a household to a rise in the wage, for

---

[22] See Clower (1965).

[23] But it must be used with genuine care. Suppose that a variable y depended on the current and expected future values of another variable x, and that these expected values depended on the current value relative to past values. It might then be supposed that y could be written simply as a function of x. For comparing current variations in y to current variations in x, this would be perfectly legitimate, since the whole set of expected future values would, for the moment, depend on current x alone. However, the function relating y to x could not be expected to remain invariant over time. A given x value would imply different expectations at different dates, since there would be different pasts with which to compare it.

example, involves a substitution of work (and hence consumption) for leisure, but an income effect calling for more leisure as well as more consumption.

The key to understanding income effects lies in examining the lifetime budget constraint[24]

$$(39) \qquad W = \int_n^d e^{-r(t-n)} \left[rp\left(\frac{\dot{M}}{p}\right) + pC - wL \right] dt$$

where $L = \text{Min} [L^s, L^d]$.

Providing that variations in expected future values of w, p, r, and L^d are no more responsive to changes in current values than the current values themselves, outside limits on income effects may be established by assuming that expectations are genuinely static. Providing that no expected future value moves in a direction opposite to the current value, the signs of the income effects calculated on an assumption of static expectations will be correct in general.

The derivatives of the right-hand side of (39) with respect to p, w, r, and L^d [assuming that it is the binding argument of (36)], holding M/p, C, and L^s constant, give the Slutsky compensating variations in W that make an initially planned M/p, C, L^s combination still possible after a change in p, w, r, or L^d.[25] These derivatives are given by

$$(40) \qquad \frac{\partial W}{\partial p} = \int_n^d e^{-r(t-n)} \left[r\,\frac{M}{p} + C \right] dt$$

$$(41) \qquad \frac{\partial W}{\partial w} = - \int_n^d e^{-r(t-n)} L \, dt$$

$$(42) \qquad \frac{\partial W}{\partial L^d} = - \int_n^d e^{-r(t-n)} w \, dt$$

$$(43) \qquad \frac{\partial W}{\partial r} = \int_n^d e^{-r(t-n)} M \, dt + \int_n^d (t-n) e^{-r(t-n)} [wL - rM - pC] \, dt$$

The first three of these are readily interpretable. A rise in the price level can be compensated for by a wealth variation equal to the change in price times the present value of real consumption plus real consumption foregone to hold money. A rise in the wage rate can be compensated for by a negative variation equal in magnitude to the wage change times the present value of lifetime employment. This holds whether or

---

[24] This constraint might be modified to reflect bequests and retirement without affecting the substance of the argument in any but obvious ways.

[25] See Slutsky (1952). Recall that a plan consists of paths ranging from n to d for each of the choice variables. The parameters p, w, r, and L^d are in principle functions of time as well, but the simple model of expectations used here makes them scalar quantities.

not employment is constrained by labor demand. A rise in labor demand can be compensated for by a negative variation equal to the number of hours' change times the present value of an additional hour's wage at every date in the life span.

In each of these three cases, the compensating variation is equal to the present value of a change in either the costliness of a stream of outlays or the size of a stream of receipts. A price increase makes both market and imputed consumption more costly. A wage increase makes employment more rewarding. An employment increase converts a given wage into a higher income. Hence the first of the three is equivalent to a loss in current wealth and the last two are equivalent to gains.

The compensating variation to an interest rate change is also fairly straightforward, but this is not so obvious from Equation (43). It must be recast. To do this, put the first term in abeyance for the moment and turn to the second. Its integrand may be rewritten as follows

$$(44) \qquad (t - n)e^{-r(t-n)}(wL + rA - pC - rW) = (t - n)e^{-r(t-n)}(\dot{W} - rW)$$

Consider now the expression

$$(45) \qquad (t - n)e^{-r(t-n)}W(t)$$

Its time derivative is given by

$$(46) \qquad (t - n)e^{-r(t-n)}\dot{W} - (t - n)e^{-r(t-n)}rW + e^{-r(t-n)}W$$

Thus the integrand (44) is given by

$$(47) \qquad \frac{d}{dt}(t - n)e^{-r(t-n)}W(t) - e^{-r(t-n)}W(t)$$

Hence (43) may be rewritten as

$$(48) \qquad \frac{\partial W}{\partial r} = \int_n^d e^{-r(t-n)}(M - W)\,dt + \int_n^d \frac{d}{dt}[(t - n)e^{-r(t-n)}W(t)]\,dt$$

If we assume $W(d)$ equal to zero, the second integral is zero and $\partial W/\partial r$ may finally be written as

$$\frac{\partial W}{\partial r} = -\int_n^d e^{-r(t-n)}A(t)\,dt \qquad (49)$$

This states that the compensating variation per unit of interest rate change equals the discounted value of the initial plan of asset holdings.[26] If the discounted asset plan is

---

[26] The dimensionality of (49) initially looks puzzling, since the right-hand size is an integral of asset stocks. However, the units in which r is measured are hundreds of percentage points. A one-unit change is equal, say, to the difference between an interest rate of 6 percent and one of 106 percent. The compensating variation per percentage point is only 0.01 times the right side of (49). Clearly, then, (49) indicates the change in the present value of planned interest income per unit change in the interest rate.

Table 2-1 Income effects

Effects of increases in	Effects on		
	C	L^s	M/p
W	+	−	+
w	+	−	+
p	−	+	−
r	?	?	?
L^d	+	0	+

positive (the person plans predominantly to be a creditor), then a negative variation in wealth is required to leave the initial consumption, money holding, and employment plan exactly still attainable. If the planner expects mainly to be in debt, then a positive compensation is required. For some people, creditors, a rise in the interest rate is equivalent to a lump-sum increase in wealth, but for debtors, it amounts to a lump-sum loss.[27]

To determine the signs of the income effects, it remains only to discuss the effects of the lump-sum transfers themselves. Suppose that a household received an unforeseen increment to its wealth. If it were mindful of its needs over the remainder of its life cycle, it would presumably want to consume some or even all this increase (plus accrued interest) before the end of its life. But if it were to consume more at any one date, it would surely consume more at every date, for if it did not do so, it would not be allocating its consumption in an efficient way. Moreover, since leisure is a normal good, it would also want to consume some of the benefits of the transfer in the form of reduced work effort at every date in its life span at which employment was not constrained by labor demand. By the same argument, it would also like to take some of the benefits of its windfall in the form of the greater convenience that may be realized by increasing its money holdings at every life-cycle date.

Therefore, the signs of the effects of a positive lump-sum transfer must be those given in the first row of Table 2-1. The entries in the remainder of the table come from those of the first row. They are either the same or opposite in sign according to whether a change in the variable in question is equivalent (in its income effects) to an increase or decrease in current wealth. The question marks corresponding to changes in r reflect the ambiguity of its income effects.

Price Changes and Substitution Effects

Substitution effects in static consumer theory are calculated by supposing that the relevant compensating variation has been made and then examining how the consumer

---

[27]A rise in the interest rate will imply a capital loss for a creditor household that holds its wealth in the form of fixed-income securities. By the same token, a household that holds shares in a firm with outstanding fixed-income indebtedness will gain from the decline in the present value of its firm's obligations. These redistributive effects of interest rate changes will be ignored except when they concern the public debt, whose appreciation and depreciation is not purely a redistributive matter.

Table 2-2 Substitution effects

Effects on increases in	Effects on		
	C	L^s	M^h/p
w	+	+	+
p	–	–	–
r (atemporal)	+	–	–
r (intertemporal)	–	+	–

will react to new prices, his or her real income unchanged. The approach is similar here. Suppose, for example, that the money wage rate rises, and that the income effects are taxed away. Voluntary leisure is now more expensive relative to other goods. Although the household's life plan prior to the wage increase is still feasible, it is now inferior to another attainable plan involving more work, more consumption, and more money holding both immediately and throughout the remainder of the life span, except during periods of unemployment. The substitution effects of a rise in the commodity price level are mirror images of those of a rise in the wage. Money holding and consumption become more expensive relative to leisure. Providing the income effects are compensated for, the consuming unit will choose to work less, consume less, and hold less real money both immediately and throughout the life span.

The substitution effects of an interest rate increase are more complicated than those of wage and price increases. There is first the atemporal substitution away from money and toward consumption and leisure (i.e., less work effort), both immediately and throughout the unconstrained portion of the life span. In addition, a rise in the rate of interest changes the terms of trade between consumption today and consumption tomorrow, between leisure today and leisure tomorrow, and between money holding today and money holding tomorrow. The resulting intertemporal substitutions will lead to less consumption, less money holding, and less leisure immediately in exchange for still more consumption, money holding, and leisure in the future.

Since neither wealth nor labor demand is a price, neither can be said to have substitution effects. Hence the substitution effects on household planning are those summarized in Table 2-2.

Income and Substitution Effects Combined

The conclusions embodied in Tables 2-1 and 2-2 may be combined to indicate a pattern of overall effects. However, in keeping with the discussion early in this chapter, only the effects of changes in certain ratios are important, owing to an assumed homogeneity of the demand functions. Hence the combined income and substitution effects are those given in Table 2-3.

Since a certain amount of reorganization of Tables 2-1 and 2-2 has gone into the construction of Table 2-3, it seems well to mention explicitly the sources of its entries, which by column give the signs of the partial derivates of equations (32), (33), and (34) above. The first row contains the combined income and substitution effects

Table 2-3 Overall effects

Effects of increases in	Effects on		
	C	L^s	M^d/p
w/p	+	?	+
r	?	?	?
W/p	+	–	+
L^d	+	0	+

of a rise in the real wage. The income and substitution effects both go in the same direction in the case of consumption and money demand. They conflict in the case of labor supply; this is the source of the question mark. The second row gives the effects of an interest rate change; its question marks reflect a hopelessly conflicting tangle of incomes and substitution effects. The third row gives the income effects of a change in real wealth. The fourth row gives the income effects of a rise in the demand for labor.

Conclusion

Table 2-3, in effect, constitutes the message of the present chapter. It began with a complaint regarding the inconsistency with which various macro theorists treated the several aspects of household behavior incorporated in their models. It then developed in its first main section a unified model of household behavior. The second section undertook a comparative analysis of this model. The results form a unified basis for the treatment of the household sector in subsequent chapters.

TO CHAPTER TWO

THE PERMANENT INCOME MODEL
AND THE LIFE-CYCLE MODEL

The material that has just been presented is based on the life-cycle model of Modigliani and Brumberg. An alternative approach to many of the same issues is provided by Friedman's permanent income model.[28] Although Friedman's theory seems different from that of Modigliani and Brumberg, it really is much the same. This appendix is devoted to showing that the differences are small.

Friedman argues that in the absence of uncertainty and divergences between plans and their realization, a household's consumption may be written as

(50) $$C = k(r, u) \cdot Y^p$$

where Y^p is the household's "permanent income" and k, the proportion of permanent income consumed, is a function of the rate of interest and of a vector of other variables which reflect age, family composition, time preference, and the like. Permanent income is defined to be that which could be consumed while maintaining wealth intact.

Wealth, in turn, is defined as the sum of two parts: nonhuman wealth, or marketable assets, and human wealth, or discounted future earnings from work. Hence Friedman's wealth concept may be written

(51)
$$\frac{W^F}{p}(n) = \frac{W^N}{p}(n) + \frac{W^H}{p}(n)$$

$$= \frac{W^N}{p}(n) + \int_n^\infty e^{-r(t-n)} \frac{w}{p} L \, dt$$

----

[28] See Friedman (1957).

where W^N corresponds to the wealth concept used above in this chapter.

Friedman takes wealth to be a given, and therefore implicitly treats labor income as exogenous. To find out what permanent income consists of, it suffices therefore to differentiate (51) with respect to time (n), treating w/pL as a given. The result is[29]

$$(52) \qquad \frac{dW^F/p}{dn} = \frac{dW^N/p}{dn} + r\,\frac{W^H}{p} - \frac{w}{p}L$$

Setting the left-hand side equal to zero and remembering that the rate of change of nonhuman wealth is equal to wage and property income minus consumption, it is seen that the rate of consumption that would keep wealth intact is given by $r\,W^F/p$, that is, by the interest on nonhuman and human wealth combined. This comprises a household's permanent income.

The household's consumption is then k times permanent income. That is

$$(53) \qquad C = k(r, u) \cdot r \cdot \frac{W^F}{p}$$

The quantity k varies with age, presumably increasing over the life span. In the early years it may be less than one, as households accumulate nonhuman wealth at a rate greater than that at which their human wealth is declining. However, it is likely to be greater than one late in the life span, especially for those households that have no motive to leave bequests.

In the life-cycle model, if both the wage and the lifetime employment path are exogenously determined (as they are for someone who expects never to be able to find as much work as he or she would like), the present value of lifetime consumption as of date n plus the discounted value of any bequest is predetermined and equal to Friedman's wealth. Since employment is predetermined, the wage rate affects consumption only as a component part of W^F/p. Therefore, consumption at any date in the life cycle depends only on W^F/p, r, and the date. Under the assumed circumstances, therefore, the life-cycle model implies that consumption can be written

$$(54) \qquad C = C\left(r, \frac{W^F}{p}, t\right)$$

This is almost indistinguishable from Friedman's consumption function (53), which is really just a special case of (54) in which consumption is assumed to be proportional to wealth.

[29] Those who are not familiar with the differentiation of integrals should consult the relevant portion of an advanced calculus book. See "Leibnitz's rule" in its index.

THREE
BUSINESS DEMANDS AND SUPPLIES

This chapter does for the business sector what the previous chapter did for the household sector. That is, it first sets forth the generally accepted theory of the behavior of business firms, then studies the way this behavior may be expected to change in the face of constraints and parameter changes. The ultimate aim of this analysis is to derive functions that describe the supply of commodities and demands for capital goods, labor, and business bank accounts, all on a consistent basis.

I. THE BEHAVIOR OF THE FIRM

There are several models of managerial behavior in the literature on the theory of the firm. The traditional, neoclassical model depicts the manager as the conscious, willing agent of the firm's owners, perhaps even himself the supplier of risk capital. He acts at all times so as to maximize the market value of the shareholders' equity. More recent treatments have suggested that managers may have interests of their own, different from and in conflict with those of the stockholders.[1] For example, they may wish to maximize the rate of growth of the resources they control, subject to some upper bound on the risk that their firms will be taken over by new owners who will employ different managers.

---

[1] The obvious reference is to Berle and Means (1933). See also Berle (1959). There seems to be no good published summary of contemporary literature on the subject. For references, see Fitts (1978).

Since the aim of this book is to set forth the structure and workings of traditional theory, no effort will be made here to develop the more recent literature. Firms' managers are thought to act always so as to maximize the wealth of the stockholders of the moment. There is no uncertainty and no taxation. Moreover, the participants in the securities market view the prospects of business in the same way as do the managers, so that market values in fact register the calculations of the managers. This is not to say that the managers and the market are always right about the future, but merely that their views coincide, whether right or wrong.

The Market Value of the Firm's Securities

In a world in which there is general agreement about the future and no risk, all securities, whether bonds or shares, have the same prospective yields. Security transactions take place because firms need to finance their investment and households wish to turn a portion of their saving into income-earning securities.[2] The securities held by households have value because they promise future income, and because this promise ensures marketability.

In such a world there are no prospects for capital gain other than those anticipated by all parties, so that the demand price (and supply price) for a security is given by the present value of the income payments stream to which ownership of the security gives title. In the case of the shares of a firm, the value of those outstanding at time n is given by

$$(1) \qquad S(n) = \int_n^\infty e^{-r(t-n)} H(t) \, dt$$

where $S(n)$ denotes the market value of the outstanding shares, $H(t)$ the rate at which the firm is expected to make dividend payments in the future, and r the rate of interest.[3] Similarly, in the case of bonds the value of those outstanding at time n is given by

$$(2) \qquad B(n) = \int_n^\infty e^{-r(t-n)} R(t) \, dt$$

[2] In addition, securities pass from households that want cash in order to dissave to other households that want to turn their surplus cash into securities. Also, banks buy and sell securities, creating or destroying money in the process (see Chapter 5).

[3] To write the value of S in this way involves an implicit assumption that shareholders expect the rate of interest to remain forever constant. If they expect it to vary over time, the correct expression is somewhat more complicated. Since nothing crucial in the argument of this chapter depends on whether or not the interest rate is expected to vary, generality has been foregone in favor of simplicity.

where $B(n)$ is the market value of the stock of outstanding bonds and $R(t)$ is the rate at which the firm has promised to make interest and redemption payments to the holders of its outstanding bonds.[4,5]

The stream of future income represented by $R(t)$ is a claim on the firm's resources that must be met prior to the payment of future dividends, $H(t)$. It might seem that the future financing decisions of firms would therefore have to be considered along with its production decisions in determining the value of its shares. This would complicate the model of firm behavior, since it would be necessary to study the optimal choice of share and bond issue and income retention, as well as optimal factor purchase and production decisions. Fortunately, the value of a firm's shares is independent of its financing in a certain, tax-free world, as the next section will show. This will permit subsequent portions of the chapter to concentrate on theory of production and factor purchase choices unfettered by any worries about the way in which they are financed.

Financing and Share Valuation

To see that current share valuation must be independent of financial plans, consider the following problem. A firm produces a single product using only labor and investment goods as inputs. Its managers expect a constant interest rate over the indefinite future. They plan to finance their future investment through some combination of retained earnings and bond financing.[6] Their planned rate of dividend payment for any date in the future is therefore given by

$$(3) \qquad H(t) = p(t)\,Q(t) + \dot{B}(t) - w(t)\,L(t) - p_K(t)\,I(t) - rB(t)$$

where $p(t)$ = expected price of what the firm sells
$\quad Q(t)$ = planned quantity to be sold
$\quad w(t)$ = expected wage rate that the firm will have to pay its employees
$\quad L(t)$ = firm's planned level of employment
$\qquad r$ = yield on securities (expected to be constant)
$\quad B(t)$ = market value of the firm's outstanding bonds

---

[4] Quite obviously, the total value of all firms' securities (whether stocks or bonds), the rate of interest (which equals the yield on shares), and the stream of expected or promised payments to share and bondholders are not independent magnitudes. Chapters 5 and 6 describe how the value of securities and their yield are determined in neoclassical and Keynesian theoretical systems.

[5] The upper bound of integration in Equations (1) and (2) may seem objectionable, since neither the issuers of securities nor their owners (not to mention capitalism itself) can be expected to last forever. In the case of the firms, this poses no problems at all. If all payments are expected to end after some date, the values of the integrands will be zero thereafter, and the values of the integrals completely unaffected by integrating way beyond the last necessary upper point. In the case of the owners, those who expect to truncate their income streams through the sale of securities can always realize at the time of sale the remaining portion of the integral from someone who will then pay the present value of the subsequent income.

[6] If future investment is to be financed partly through new equity issue, the mathematics of the problem is somewhat more complicated. Its solution is consistent with the general rule, however.

$p_K(t)$ = expected price level of investment goods that the firm buys

$I(t)$ = quantity of investment goods that the firm plans to buy

Equation (3) states that the planned dividend is equal to the receipts from selling output and borrowing less the payments for labor, investment, and interest.

If the managers' expectations are shared by the market and their intentions are known, the market value of the firm's shares will be given by[7]

$$(4) \qquad S(n) = \int_n^\infty e^{-r(t-n)} \left[pQ + \dot{B} - wL - p_K I - rB \right] dt$$

which comes from the substitution of (3) in (1). This can be rewritten as

$$(5) \qquad S(n) = \int_n^\infty e^{-r(t-n)} \left[pQ - wL - p_K I \right] dt + \int_n^\infty e^{-r(t-n)} \left[\dot{B} - rB \right] dt$$

The first term on the right side of (5) is the present value of the firm's production decisions; in the rest of the chapter it will be indicated by the symbol $V(n)$, and called simply "the value of the firm." The second term on the right may be written as

$$(6) \qquad \int_n^\infty e^{-r(t-n)} \left[\dot{B} - rB \right] dt = \int_n^\infty \frac{d}{dt} \left[e^{-r(t-n)} B(t) \right] dt = e^{-r(t-n)} B(t) \Big]_n^\infty$$

If the firm is to have a finite market value, it must be that

$$(7) \qquad \lim_{t \to \infty} e^{-r(t-n)} B(t) = 0$$

Therefore (5) may be rewritten as

$$(8) \qquad S(n) = V(n) - B(n)$$

The value of a firm's shares equals the value of the firm [as defined by the first term on the right side of (5)] less the value of its bonds. Its financing plans for the future have no bearing on its current share value.

What is going on here? Why must things work out this way?

The answers to these questions can only be seen once the relationship between outside financing and capital gains is understood. Picture two firms which are identical in all respects at some moment of time. Over an interval subsequent to this moment, Firm 1 pays a low dividend and finances its investment out of retained earnings. Firm 2 pays a high dividend and must therefore borrow to finance its investment. If both firms follow the same production and investment plans, both will have the same value at the end of the interval. However, Firm 2 will have the larger debt and the less valuable shares. Its stockholders will have paid for their higher dividends by receiving smaller capital gains.

The implications of this can best be appreciated if it is worked out a bit more com-

---

[7] Whenever clarity does not suffer from the omission of time arguments, they will be left out.

pletely. Equation (2) is of the form

(9)
$$S(n) = \int_n^\infty f(n, t)\, dt$$

The derivative with respect to n of an integral of the form of the right side of (9) is given by

(10)
$$\frac{d}{dn} \int_n^\infty f(n, t)\, dt = \int_n^\infty \frac{\partial f}{\partial n}\, dt - f(n, n)$$

In the particular case at hand, this comes down to saying that

(11)
$$\frac{dS(n)}{dn} = rS(n) - H(n) \quad \text{or}$$

(12)
$$S(n) = \frac{1}{r}\left[H(n) + \frac{dS(n)}{dn}\right]$$

Since $dS(n)/dn$ constitutes the capital gains accruing to the stockholders as of time n, Equation (15) states in effect the following proposition: if the shares of two firms have the same value, any difference between the dividend flows being paid by the two firms must be exactly offset by differences in the rates at which the share prices are changing.

If the owners of Firm 1 prefer the larger dividend incomes implicit in Firm 2's financial policy, they can always realize their capital gains by selling shares, effecting their own outside financing despite the policies of the firm's managers. If the owners of Firm 2 prefer the capital growth implied by Firm 1's financial policy, they can always buy the bonds that their firm sells to finance its investment, thus effectively internalizing the financing. Since the extra dividends equal the outside financing, which equals the foregone capital gains, the two firms are equivalent from the shareholders' viewpoint. The value of their shares could hardly be different.[8]

The capital gains in question here arise, it should be stressed, from the steady progress of the present toward the future. If two certain income streams differ at some particular time, their relative market values will change as the time approaches. Thus capital gains can accrue even in the absence of surprises.

The upshot of this discussion is that a firm's managers should maximize the value of the firm if they wish to serve the interests of its current stockholders. Their share is equal to the value of the firm less the value of its bonds, which is given, so that their wealth and the firm's value move hand in hand. In turn, the value of the firm depends only on decisions about production and factor purchases, and not on financial decisions. The remainder of this chapter will therefore focus on the choice of policies to maximize the value of the firm.

[8] These results have been derived under assumptions of certainty, full information, uniformity of opinion, and absence of taxation. These are effectively the assumptions of the celebrated article of Modigliani and Miller (1958), owing to their peculiar treatment of uncertainty. For references to more general treatments of the determination of share values, see Fitts (1978).

Capital Accumulation: A Simple Problem

The value of the firm is the integral of the discounted proceeds from production net of discounted costs. Production is dependent, in part, on inputs (such as labor) whose costs are registered contemporaneously with the output to which they contribute.[9] However, it is also dependent on capital inputs that must be accumulated before they may be used. Current production is tied to past accumulation; current accumulation is tied to future production. This interdependence of activities across time complicates considerably the problem of choosing optimum levels of output and factor purchases. In order to develop the threads of its solution in an orderly way, the complexities associated with irreversibilities and costs of change are deferred until later sections. This section sets forth a much simplified model that is sometimes (confusingly) referred to as the "neoclassical" model of investment.[10]

Consider therefore the problem faced by the managers of a firm who are trying to maximize its value under the following circumstances.[11]

1. They hold with certainty expectations about $p(t)$, $w(t)$, $p_K(t)$, and r; the first two are expected to be continuous functions of time, the third is expected to have a continuous first derivative, and the fourth is expected to be constant. None of these variables is affected by the firm's own actions.
2. The firm produces its output $Q(t)$ according to a production function with two inputs, capital $K(t)$ and labor $L(t)$. Capital and labor have positive marginal products in any combinations, but the marginal product of each diminishes as its quantity is increased, holding the input of the other factor constant. The production function exhibits increasing returns to scale at low production rates but diminishing returns at high rates. Its isoquants are convex.
3. Capital goods can be bought or sold at any finite rate of gross investment $I(t)$. Capital goods in place wear out at constant proportional rate δ. Labor can be hired or fired at will.
4. At the date of planning, the firm has a stock of capital goods that is optimal for its current conditions. The criterion for optimality will be developed below.

The problem and the conditions surrounding it imply that the managers must plan to maximize

---

[9] Throughout this chapter and the rest of the book the value of raw materials purchased and used in the production process is to be thought of as having been netted out against the value of output. Thus pQ is the gross value of output less the value of raw materials used up. Investment should be thought of as accounting for any changes in the value of inventories of raw materials as well as of finished goods.

[10] The person most responsible for advocating the neoclassical model is Jorgenson [see Jorgenson (1967), Hall and Jorgenson (1967), Jorgenson (1974)]. For a perceptive earlier treatment, see Haavelmo (1960). See also the critical analyses of Eisner and Nadiri (1968) and Ackley (1978).

[11] These conditions are the weakest restrictions under which the neoclassical model is either consistent or complete. Their restrictiveness will be discussed in subsequent sections.

(13)
$$V(n) = \int_{n}^{\infty} e^{-r(t-n)} \, [pQ - wL - p_K I] \, dt$$

subject to

(14)
$$Q = F(K, L)$$

and

(15)
$$\dot{K} = I - \delta K$$

The variables directly within the managers' control are L and I. They control the rate of growth of K through I, but not its current level.

One rule that governs the optimum-factor purchase plan is simply derived, since L is always within the momentary control of the managers. If they are trying to maximize the integral (13), they should choose L so as to maximize its integrand at every moment. The first-order condition for this maximization is

(16)
$$p \frac{\partial Q}{\partial L} - w = 0$$

or

(17)
$$F_L = \frac{w}{p}$$

This is, of course, the familiar equation of the marginal product of labor to the wage measured in terms of output. Since F_L depends on K, in general, Equation (17) is not sufficient to determine the whole time path of L,[12] but is only one condition which must be observed.

The other rule for determining the optimum-factor purchase plan is not so simple as the first. Since the integrand of (16) is linear in I, there is no choice of I that will maximize it. Even if there were a finite I that would do the job, it would do the wrong job, since future values of K are dependent on current values of I. Clearly the choice of the rate of investment rests on some intertemporal optimality calculation.

Such a rule is the following: the firm ought always to maintain equality between the market price of investment goods and the internal shadow value of capital. The shadow value of capital is made up of two parts: the present value of having at some later date, $t + h$, what remains of it after depreciation, and the money to be made by using it in the meantime. According to this formulation, the shadow value of capital $\lambda(t)$ is given by[13]

(18)
$$\lambda(t) = [1 - (r + \delta) h] \, \lambda(t + h) + hp F_K(t)$$

---

[12] It is sufficient, however, to determine $L(n)$, since $K(n)$ is completely determined by past investment. At moment n, labor is the only variable input.

[13] In this formulation, $[1 - (r + \delta) h]$ approximates $e^{-(r + \delta)h}$.

This may be written as

$$\text{(19)} \qquad \frac{\lambda(t + h) - \lambda(t)}{h} = (r + \delta) \lambda(t + h) - pF_K$$

As h approaches zero, this reduces to [14]

$$\text{(20)} \qquad \dot{\lambda} = (r + \delta) \lambda - pF_K$$

If this shadow price is always set equal to the market price of investment goods, p_K, then the marginal product of capital will have to obey

$$\text{(21)} \qquad F_K = \frac{p_K}{p} \left(r + \delta - \frac{\dot{p}_K}{p_K} \right)$$

Since p_K/p is the cost of a unit of investment goods measured in units of output, the right-hand side of (21) equals the interest and depreciation cost of owning capital less any capital gains or losses accruing to its owners due to changes in its price. Thus (21), like (17), involves an equation of a marginal product to a real factor cost. Together they imply an optimum plan of factor purchases for the future and therefore a production plan. If the firm has an optimal capital stock at time n, as assumed, it should hire the labor force that goes with it and thereafter obey the differential equations obtained by time differentiation of (17) and (21). They are

$$\text{(22)} \qquad F_{LL}\dot{L} + F_{LK}\dot{K} = \frac{d}{dt} \left(\frac{w}{p} \right) \qquad \text{and}$$

$$\text{(23)} \qquad F_{KL}\dot{L} + F_{KK}\dot{K} = \frac{d}{dt} \left[\frac{p_K}{p} \left(r + \delta - \frac{\dot{p}_K}{p_K} \right) \right]$$

In matrix notation these are written as

$$\text{(24)} \qquad \begin{bmatrix} F_{LL} & F_{LK} \\ F_{KL} & F_{KK} \end{bmatrix} \begin{bmatrix} \dot{L} \\ \dot{K} \end{bmatrix} = \begin{bmatrix} \dot{\pi}_L \\ \dot{\pi}_K \end{bmatrix}$$

where $\dot{\pi}_L$ and $\dot{\pi}_K$ are the time rates of change of the real factor prices.[15]

Because capital has a ready resale market, the firm will not stay in business if its price falls short of average total cost. From the description of the production function, the long-run average cost function is U-shaped. If the firm operates at all, therefore, it operates in the region of increasing average cost, and therefore, in a strictly concave region of its production function. Since that is so, the determinant of the Hessian on the left side of (24) is positive. Solving (24) for the time derivatives of K and L gives

---

[14]The validity of this limit taking depends crucially on the firm's ability to maintain continuity in λ. If parameters were discontinuous, it would require discontinuous policies to do so. This point will recur later in the chapter.

[15]The real price of capital, π_K, is the cost of owning it (in terms of units of product). The symbol p_K/p denotes the price (also in terms of product) of buying a unit.

$$\dot{L} = \frac{1}{D}\,[F_{KK}\,\dot{\pi}_L - F_{LK}\,\dot{\pi}_K]$$

(25)

$$\dot{K} = \frac{1}{D}\,[F_{LL}\,\dot{\pi}_K - F_{KL}\,\dot{\pi}_L]$$

where D is the Hessian determinant. If these are substituted in the total time derivative of the production function, the result is

$$(26) \qquad \dot{Q} = \frac{1}{D}\,[(F_L F_{KK} - F_K F_{KL})\,\dot{\pi}_L + (F_K F_{LL} - F_L F_{LK})\,\dot{\pi}_K]$$

From (25) and (26), a number of propositions can be derived about the behavior of a firm following rules (17) and (21).

1. If the real price of a factor is rising, the use of that factor will be falling. This follows from the assumption of diminishing marginal productivity, which guarantees the negativity of the own second partial derivatives of F.
2. If the real price of one factor is rising, the use of the other factor will be rising or falling according to whether the cross partial derivative of the production function is negative or positive.
3. A positive cross partial derivative is sufficient to ensure that if either real factor price is rising, output will be falling. However, there exists a much weaker sufficiency condition for this, the normality of both factors. This will always be assumed.

Thus the problem considered in this section is quite productive of results. Unfortunately, it is based on a very restrictive model. In particular, the assumed continuity of parameters and resalability of capital goods must be abandoned if any generality is to be achieved.

Irreversible Investment[16]

Rather than assuming that capital goods can be resold at their purchase price (less wear and tear), assume the opposite polar case, that they have no resale value whatever. If this is true, there is a practical lower bound on gross investment of zero, since firms cannot get rid of capital goods short of dumping them in the sea. Firms will not do this if they ever expect to use the goods again, since they are "free goods" once they have been purchased.

In order to focus closely on the problem of investment, picture a firm whose only input is capital. Its managers are trying to follow the rule of Equation (21) while facing a constant r and p_K. As long as p is rising, the firm must invest so as to raise K and thereby lower F_K. If p stops increasing, investment must be lowered to match depreciation (δK). If p falls slowly, it may still be possible to follow (21), providing that

---

[16] This section owes a considerable debt to Bosworth (1969).

the implied rise in F_K does not call for a rate of decline in K greater than δ. If prices are falling rapidly, however, observance of (21) may not be possible, since it may not be possible to decumulate capital fast enough to keep F_K in step with the rising π_K.

The decision rule (21) belongs to the class of rules that are called "myopic." Even though it solves a problem with an infinite planning horizon, it contains only currently dated parameters. This remarkable result stems from assumptions 1 and 3, which let a firm invest or disinvest at any finite rate, and ensures that it would never want a discontinuous jump in its stock of capital facilities. It provides incomplete guidance for the firm that can disinvest only by allowing its capital to decay through age.

As a first step towards solving the problem of the firm that cannot sell capital goods, the following theorem must be proved.

Theorem: If a firm is optimizing under the above stated assumptions, one or the other of the following two things must be true over any portion of its optimal plan:

1. $F_K = \pi_K$ and $I \geqslant 0$ or
2. $F_K \neq \pi_K$ and $I = 0$

The proof is short and proceeds in part by contradiction.

Proof: Assume that an optimal plan of capital accumulation is known and that a part of it covers the small time interval (t_0, t_1). If $F_K > \pi_K$ and $I > 0$, the plan could be improved by raising I early in the interval and lowering it later in the interval, rejoining the remainder of the plan with the same $K(t_1)$ and increasing profitability over (t_0, t_1). Similarly, if $F_K < \pi_K$ and $I > 0$, the plan could be improved by lowering I early and raising it later, again returning to the optimal path at t_1 and again improving profit in the meantime. Thus inequality between F_K and π_K is ruled out for all portions of the path for which $I > 0$.

The same argument cannot, however, rule out portions of an optimal path for which $F_K \neq \pi_K$ and $I = 0$. On such portions reductions in investment early in the interval are impossible and increases early in the interval cannot be offset by reductions later on so as to rejoin the remainder of the plan with the same $K(t_1)$. Nothing, of course, rules out portions over which $F_K = \pi_K$ and $I = 0$.

The upshot of this theorem is that the firm's planned path of capital accumulation will consist of portions that obey the myopic rule of Equation (21) interspersed with portions during which gross investment equals zero and capital is declining at proportional rate δ. The theorem does not, however, provide guidance as to when the firm should shift from one course of action to the other. The answer to that question can only be found by taking a closer look at the internal shadow value of capital.

Equation (20) may be rewritten in the following form

(27) $$e^{-(r+\delta)(t-n)}\dot{\lambda} - (r+\delta)\,e^{-(r+\delta)(t-n)}\lambda = -e^{-(r+\delta)(t-n)}pF_K$$

The left-hand side is the time derivative of $e^{-(r+\delta)(t-n)}\lambda$. Integrating both sides from n to ∞ gives

(28) $$\int_n^\infty \left[\frac{d}{dt}e^{-(r+\delta)(t-n)}\lambda(t)\right]dt = -\int_n^\infty e^{-(r+\delta)(t-n)}pF_K\,dt$$

The expression whose derivative appears as the left-side integrand of (28) is the value as of n of the shadow price of a unit of capital purchased at n and depreciated until t. To see this, think of it as

$$(29) \qquad e^{-r(t-n)} [e^{-\delta(t-n)}\lambda(t)]$$

where $\lambda(t)$ is the shadow price of a whole, undepreciated piece of capital at time t. If we assume that this goes to zero as t gets indefinitely large,[17] (28) and therefore (20) have the solution

$$(30) \qquad \lambda(n) = \int_n^\infty e^{-(r+\delta)(t-n)}p(t)\, F_K(t)\, dt$$

This says simply that the shadow price of a unit of capital bought at time n is the present value of its stream of marginal products in its future uses.[18]

Suppose that the managers of a firm forgot for the moment that capital goods could not be resold, and drew up a plan on the assumption that they could always follow the myopic rule of Equation (21). Suppose further that their plan looked like $\hat{K}$ in Figure 3-1, containing a portion (t_2, t_3) over which the sale of capital goods would be contemplated. Upon being reminded that the sale of capital goods would not be possible, they would recognize that if they were in fact to follow the myopic rule until t_2, they would have to follow $\tilde{K}$ (along which $I = 0$) from t_2 to t_5.

Question: Would they still plan to follow the myopic rule up until t_2? Answer: No. Why not?

If the firm were always able to follow the path $\hat{K}$, it would always be able to equate F_K and π_K through adjustments in K. Thus it would always be true that

$$(31) \qquad \lambda(n) = \int_n^\infty e^{-(r+\delta)(t-n)} [(r+\delta)p_K - \dot{p}_K]\, dt$$

By integrating, it is easy to see that (31) implies constant equality between $\lambda(n)$ and $p_K(n)$.[19]

However, if the firm were forced to follow $\tilde{K}$ from t_2 to t_5, it would have an excessive capital stock over this period, and as a consequence the marginal product of capital would fall short of its real price. From this and (31) it follows that $\lambda(t_2)$ must fall short of $p_K(t_2)$ if the firm is forced to follow $\tilde{K}$. Thus if the firm followed the myopic path up until t_2, it would then find that the shadow value of capital was smaller than its market price. Indeed, if it followed the myopic rule until t_2, it would for some considerable interval be paying for capital goods a price which exceeded their shadow value to the firm. The only way to ensure that it never invests when the shadow value of capital is smaller than its market price is always to look ahead. The

[17]If the shadow price is expected to rise faster than a new unit of capital loses present value through depreciation and interest, the firm had better stock up!

[18]$F_K(t)$ is the marginal product of a new unit of capital at date t. Hence the depreciation factor $e^{-\delta(t-n)}$ is necessary to convert to the marginal product of a $(t-n)$-year-old unit of capital.

[19]Note that the integrand of (31) is an exact differential.

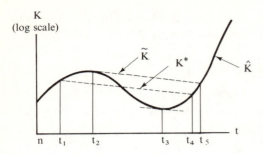

Figure 3-1 Alternative paths of accumulation.

managers must evaluate always the shadow price of capital along a path of zero invest-ment. At some date, say t_1, the discounted accumulated excess of F_K over π_K early on the path of zero investment will just match the discounted accumulated deficiency later on, leaving $\lambda(t_1)$ just equal to $p_K(t_1)$. If it continues to invest beyond t_1, it will pay more for capital goods than they are worth to the firm and so to its owners. It must be therefore that the best path of accumulation is to follow $\tilde{K}$ until t_1, to cut across by way of K^* until t_4, and to follow $\hat{K}$ thereafter.

It may be instructive to see what is happening over (t_1, t_4) to the marginal product of capital relative to its real price (π_K) and to the shadow value of capital goods rela-tive to their market price (p_K). In the intervals preceding t_1 and following t_4, F_K matches π_K and λ matches p_K. However, the relationships between t_1 and t_4 are given in Figure 3-2.

The top panel shows the discounted excess of the marginal product of capital over the real cost of using it. This is positive at first, for the optimal path of accumulation falls below the myopic path initially. Later on it is negative. The curve in the bottom panel shows the difference between the shadow price and the market price. At any date it is simply the integral under the top curve from that date onward. It is zero at t_1 and t_4, and everywhere in between it is negative. No investment is taking place pre-cisely because it is negative.

Suppose that investment had been carried on until t_2. The corresponding diagram would be Figure 3-3.

Since the entire area under the top curve is negative from t_2 to t_5, the shadow

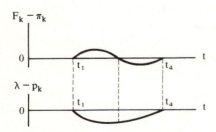

Figure 3-2 Price configurations when zero investment is optimal.

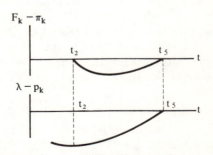

Figure 3-3 Price configurations when in-vestment is excessively prolonged.

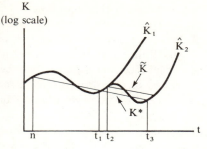

Figure 3-4 The required horizon.

price is smaller than the market price at t_2, and indeed before t_2. Investing under these circumstances is clearly a mistake.

One question remains to be answered before the argument is complete. How far into the future along a path of zero investment must the firm's managers look in making their calculation of the shadow price of capital? The answer may be developed with the aid of Figure 3-4. Suppose that as of planning date n the managers expect the next recession (as measured by the optimal K along a strictly myopic path) to be the worst that their firm will ever have to go through again. Thus they expect $\hat{K}$ to follow some future course such as $\hat{K}_1$ in Figure 3-4. Clearly, if they stop investing at date n, they will start again at t_1, since the shadow price at t_1 could not possibly be smaller than the market price.[20] Since the shadow price at t_1 will then equal the market price, the present value of the marginal products of new capital at that date will also equal the market price. In this case, (30) can be rewritten as

$$(32) \qquad \lambda(n) = \int_n^{t_1} e^{-(r+\delta)(t-n)} pF_K \, dt + e^{-(r+\delta)(t_1 - n)} p_K(t_1)$$

All that is necessary is to compare $\lambda(n)$ (calculated along K^*) with $p_K(n)$ and to stop investing at the point of equality between the two. Since the right side of (32) contains only data over the period $[n, t_1]$, this is the only span of time for which the managers must have very definite expectations in order to make decisions that are the best they can make at that time. What happens to $\hat{K}_1$ beyond t_1 is immaterial, provided only that successive recessions are not worse than that taking place between n and t_1.

Suppose, alternatively, that the managers expect $\hat{K}$ to follow $\hat{K}_2$. Then they must calculate the shadow price of capital at t_1 by using

$$(33) \qquad \lambda(t_1) = \int_{t_1}^{t_3} e^{-(r+\delta)(t-t_1)} pF_K \, dt + e^{-(r+\delta)(t_3 - t_1)} p_K(t_3)$$

[20] Recall the argument of the previous few pages. The shadow price at t_1 could only fall short of p_K if a resumption of investment at t_1 would *force* the firm into a situation of excess capital at some later date. If $\hat{K}$ follows path $\hat{K}_1$, this will not be the case.

where F_K is calculated along K^*. Assuming that the recession that occurs between t_1 and t_3 is the worst that they expect their firm ever to encounter, they will want to resume investment at t_1 provided that the shadow price calculated from (33) is not smaller than the market price of that date. They will then plan to stop investing at some later date, say t_2, and to follow $\tilde{K}$. If the second recession is expected to be very serious, the shadow price calculated by (33) will be smaller than $p_K(t_1)$. If so, they will want to ride out the preceding boom with a capital stock given by K^* in order to avoid having too big a stock during the deep recession.

Notice that whether the firm has to look as far ahead at t_3 depends crucially on the depreciation rate δ. If the firm's capital wastes away very rapidly, then it will not have to look beyond t_1, even if the second recession is worse than the first. A firm that uses very long-lived capital will have to look much further ahead.

The foregoing discussion applies only to the case in which the resale price of capital is zero. If the resale price is positive, but smaller than the purchase price, the firm must choose among buying, holding, and selling; this is a rather messy problem.

Discontinuities in Parameters and Costs of Change

In the development of the simple model of accumulation it was assumed that the component parts of the real price of capital are continuous functions of time, so that the myopically optimal stock of capital is continuous as well. This assumption is not only counterfactual, but very limiting to inquiry. In order to derive an investment demand function, it is necessary to consider alternative sets of parameter values at a moment in time. Since only one point in the parameter space at a given moment can be continuous with the immediate past, the drawing of a demand function involves discontinuities in an intrinsic way.

Suppose that a firm has a capital stock that is optimal for a particular parameter configuration and then one of the parameters, say the price of the good it sells, changes in a discrete fashion, so that its existing capital stock is no longer optimal for the new situation. What should it do? If the price has fallen and capital cannot be sold, it should simply stop investing until its capital stock shrinks to fit the new situation. But what if p has risen? Should it invest at a moderate rate for an extended period until it has achieved an appropriate capital stock? Or should it invest at a faster rate for a shorter period? The grim mathematics of the simple accumulation model indicate that a short burst of rapid investment is always inferior to a shorter burst at a more rapid rate. Pushed to its limit, this suggests that the optimal response to a rise in the output price of any magnitude at all is an undefinedly large rate of demand for investment goods. Small wonder that several authors have claimed that neoclassical thought has no theory of investment at the firm level.[21]

One response to this problem is to argue that indeed a rise in price by itself would

[21]The problem seems first to have been appreciated by Lerner (1944, chap. 21) and is clearly spelled out in Ackley (1961, chap. 17). Jorgenson seems not to have understood their argument very fully.

produce an infinite demand for investment goods. The investment goods industry, of course, cannot supply an infinite demand, and the price of investment goods must jump high enough to eliminate the discontinuity in π_K, and hence moderate the desired rate of change of the capital stock. Although there is no theory of investment on a firm level, the problem can be handled in a general equilibrium context.

This response is at once both resourceful and lame, indeed something of a swindle. It tries to take away the problem rather than to supply an answer. Alternatives are available that provide conventional demand functions at the firm level. Since these are more satisfactory from the viewpoint of richness of analytical results, it seems appropriate to develop them here.[22]

One alternative is to argue that firms must pay a market premium for rapid construction, delivery, and installation of capital goods. A given amount of accumulation costs more if it is done in a hurry. If this is true, then the value of the firm is written as[23]

$$(34) \qquad V(n) = \int_n^\infty e^{-r(t-n)} \left[pF(K) - p_K(I) I \right] dt$$

where $p_K(I)$ gives the supply price of capital goods to the firm as a function of its rate of investment. The cost of investing is now given by

$$(35) \qquad p_I = p_K + I \frac{dp_K}{dI}$$

If we assume that p_K is a uniformly increasing function of I, it may be seen that the integrand of (34) is strictly concave in I, whereas that of (13) is linear in I. Because of this concavity, a premium is placed on a smooth path of investment. No such premium is implied by (13); this is the source of the infinite investment demand in the face of sudden, finite rise in output price.

Another formulation traces the smoothness premium to the disruptiveness of investment. A plant of a given size can produce less when it is growing than when it is stationary, since the installation of new facilities interferes with the normal operation of old facilities. In this case the value of the firm is written as

$$(36) \qquad V(n) = \int_n^\infty e^{-r(t-n)} \left[pF(K,I) - p_K I \right] dt$$

The cost of investing is given by

$$(37) \qquad p_I = p_K - pF_I$$

[22] Some of the major contributions to this literature are Eisner and Strotz (1963), Lucas (1967a, 1967b), Gould (1968), and Treadway (1969, 1970). The adjustment-cost literature, which provides most of the alternative treatments, may be traced back to Penrose (1955, 1959).

[23] Again for the sake of simplicity, capital is taken to be the only factor of production.

where F_I is the (negative) marginal productivity of investing. Concavity of the integrand of (36) is imparted through concavity of F. The increasing marginal cost of investing comes from higher revenue foregone rather than a higher price paid. Otherwise there is no difference between these two models, the so-called pecuniary and real adjustment cost models. For the remainder of this discussion the symbol p_I will be used to denote the cost of investing without always specifying whether it is defined by (35) or (37).

Suppose that a firm that is subject to adjustment costs were to try to derive the shadow price of investment goods. It would go through the same line of thought used to justify the derivation of (20), which must therefore serve to guide its actions as well as those of a firm that need draw no distinction between the cost of capital and the cost of investing. However, its cost of investment is in part within its own control. If its managers try to keep the cost of investment equal to its shadow price, they must try to follow

$$(38) \qquad \dot{p}_I = (r + \delta)\, p_I - p F_K$$

This provides less obvious guidance than (21), the solution to the simple problem, since (38) does not specify an optimum investment rate, but only its rate of change. Emanating from a given initial capital, $K(n)$, there are any number of paths of K and I that satisfy (38) for some given set of parameters and satisfy as well the dynamic constraint $I = \dot{K} + \delta K$. To find an optimal policy, it is necessary to examine the properties of this family of paths.

Solely for the sake of expositional simplicity, assume that p_I is independent of K[24] and that p_K and p are expected to remain constant. These assumptions permit (38) to be written as the autonomous[25] differential equation

$$(39) \qquad \dot{I} = \frac{1}{\partial p_I / \partial I} \left[(r + \delta)\, p_I(I) - p F_K(K) \right]$$

Additionally, of course, the relationship between I and K is restricted by

$$(40) \qquad \dot{K} = I - \delta K$$

which is also autonomous. Owing to this autonomy, the properties of the system (39) and (40) may be examined on a diagram, Figure 3-5.

Equation (40) divides the K, I plane into two halves, that in which K is increasing and that in which K is declining. The dividing line is indicated on Figure 3-3; it is positively inclined. Similarly, if p_I is kept equal to the shadow price of investment, (39) serves to divide the K, I plane into two halves with increasing and decreasing I. Since p_I increases with I, and F_K declines with K, this dividing line is negatively inclined.

When I is higher than that required to make $\dot{K}$ equal to zero, K increases. When

---

[24]When p_I is defined by (37), to say that p_I is independent of K is also to say that F_K is independent of I.

[25]That is, the functions are invariant over time.

I is higher than that required to keep the cost of investment equal to the shadow price at a constant rate of investment, it must be that the shadow price is increasing, and that the cost of investment should increase. Investment should increase as well. Therefore the arrows in Figure 3-5 indicate the direction of movement of K and I as they move in various regions of the plane, subject to (39) and (40). The only stationary point for a firm that is keeping its investment cost equal to the shadow value of investment is given by point A, at which investment matches depreciation, and the shadow value of investment is constant and equal to the cost of investment.

Assume that a firm is initially at rest at point A, with capital stock $K(n)$, and that the price of the goods it sells increases suddenly. The increase is expected to be permanent. It shifts the line along which $\dot{p}_I = 0$ to the right, so that the new rest point is A* in Figure 3-6. Naturally the new equilibrium capital stock K^* and the associated rate of replacement investment I^* are greater than the corresponding magnitudes at A.

Immediately following the increase in p, the array of possible actions open to the firm's managers is given by the vertical line at $K(n)$ in Figure 3-6. Which initial level of investment should the managers choose?

The choice of an initial rate of investment, together with a commitment to follow (39) and (40), is really a choice of a whole path of investment over the indefinite future. The general characteristics of the family of paths were developed in Figure 3-5 and the surrounding text. If the managers choose to start investing at a rate as high as or higher than that indicated by α in Figure 3-6, they thereby choose a path which leads ultimately to an ever-rising cost of investment and an ever-failing marginal product of capital. This could hardly be their best choice. If they choose to start at β, they would be picking a path which curved back around, revisiting $K(n)$ at some later date, say t_1. But it could not be optimal to be at β at date n and δ at t_1. One or the other of the two rates of investment would have to be wrong, since they both accompany the same capital stock. Finally, it could hardly be optimal to go to a point like δ at date n, since this would entail starting off in the direction of extinction in response to good news.

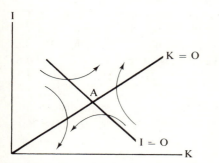

Figure 3-5 Properties of equations (39) and (40).

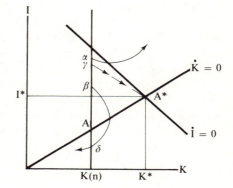

Figure 3-6 Alternative investment paths following a price increase.

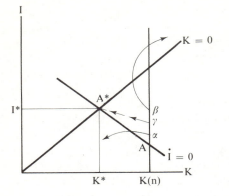

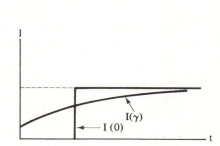

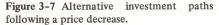

Figure 3-7 Alternative investment paths following a price decrease.

Figure 3-8 Optimal and nonoptimal decumulation.

The above arguments rule out all possibilities other than γ, which lies on the dashed line separating paths that swing up and away from paths that curl down and back. This line leads to the new rest point. It corresponds to a time profile in investment that is initially high, that subsides, and that approaches I^*, the rate necessary to maintain K^*; $K(t)$ itself approaches K^*.

Suppose that the price of output drops, so that the firm at rest would be smaller, although still in business. What rate of investment should its managers choose? The answer may be seen with the aid of Figure 3-7, whose labeling corresponds to that of Figure 3-6. A point such as β is ruled out because it implies that two rates of investment might be optimal at a given capital stock. The point δ is ruled out because it implies an indefinite expansion in response to adverse changes. The point α is ruled out by the assumption that the price drop is not sufficient to drive the firm out of business.[26] This leaves only γ, the dividing line between paths that curl up and away and paths that swing around and down.

Why should the firm not stop investing temporarily, letting its capital stock decay until $K(t) = K^*$, at which point $I(t)$ would rise to I^*? The answer to this cannot be seen from Figure 3-7, which lacks a time dimension. Instead, turn to Figure 3-8. The path marked $I(\gamma)$ is the investment path along the dashed line joining γ and A^*. The path marked $I(0)$ is the alternative of zero investment until K^* is reached. Because of the concavity of the investment cost function, the present value (as of n) of investment cost along $I(0)$ is higher than it is along $I(\gamma)$. Thus $I(0)$ is inferior even though it achieves the rest-point capital stock sooner.

There is, however, one circumstance in which the managers might wish to stop investing altogether even though they wished to remain in business. The price level

---

[26]If it does want to go out of business, the shadow value of investment is below its cost at a zero rate of investment. In this case the firm should invest nothing and allow its capital stock to wear out.

might fall far enough so that the point γ was situated below the I axis. This would mean that the shadow value of investment was below its cost at a zero rate of investment. In this case all investment would cease until the shadow value rose, at which point the firm would pursue that remaining portion of the path toward A* lying above the I axis. There would be no planned discontinuities in investment, and therefore no planned discontinuities in the cost of investment.

Anticipated Changes in Parameters

All the discussion just completed was based on the premise that any parameter change was unanticipated, and that all parameters were expected to remain constant in the future. Without this assumption, Equations (39) and (40) would not be autonomous, and the diagrams would not be useful. Most problems involving anticipated changes in parameters are therefore very difficult unless the functional forms of the production and cost functions are explicitly specified. Since this is the case, and since most of the rest of the book will be concerned with static expectations, no extensive analysis of anticipated parameter changes will be undertaken here. Instead, the following list of comments is offered in the hope of sketching some of the dimensions of the problem and solution.

1. If output and input prices are expected to vary at the same rate, then a firm at rest will have no incentive to move.[27] What matters are real prices.

2. Myopic behavior cannot be optimal. Changes must be anticipated in order to avoid extreme fluctuations in the rate of investment.

3. If the rest-point capital stock is expected to fluctuate cyclically because of changes in output prices, planned investment will fluctuate with it. However, the fluctuations in investment will be less marked than in the simple model of accumulation because of the penalty that attaches to uneven investment.

4. If the rest-point capital stock is expected to go up and down because of opposite fluctuations in capital goods prices, planned fluctuations in investment will be more marked than they would be if the changes in rest-point capital came from goods prices. Investment will be high when investment goods are cheap.

5. A discontinuous jump in output prices or a fall in the rate of interest will be anticipated by rising investment, so that investment and therefore the cost of investment is continuous.

6. A discontinuous fall in capital goods prices will not be so fully anticipated. A discontinuous fall in price accompanied by a discontinuous increase in investment produces a continuous cost of investment.

7. A zero rate of planned gross investment will be rare if bad times are expected to be followed by good times. The penalty attached to uneven investment precludes zero investment unless the bad times are expected to last a long while.

---

[27]If the adjustment costs are pecuniary, the phrase "at given levels of investment" should be inserted after the word "rate." Similar modifications must be made in subsequent comments, where appropriate.

Labor in the Adjustment Cost Model

In the last two sections, the argument was simplified by assuming that capital is the only productive factor. In principle, it is not particularly difficult to reintroduce current as well as capital inputs, although this complicates somewhat the mechanics of the solution.

For the sake of example, consider the real adjustment cost model, in which the maximand is

$$(41) \qquad V(n) = \int_n^\infty e^{-r(t-n)} \left[pF(K,L,I) - wL - p_K I \right] dt$$

Capital and labor have positive marginal products, investment a negative marginal product. The production function is concave in the relevant region. The parameters p, w, p_K, and r are subject to abrupt changes, but are expected to remain constant following such changes.

By the force of previous argument, the optimizing rules are (17), (37), (38), and (40), which are reproduced here

$$(17) \qquad F_L = \frac{w}{p}$$

$$(37) \qquad p_I = p_K - pF_I$$

$$(38) \qquad \dot{p}_I = (r + \delta) p_I - pF_K$$

$$(40) \qquad \dot{K} = I - \delta K$$

Since F is assumed to be concave, (17) implicitly defines L as a function of the real wage and of K and I

$$(42) \qquad L = \theta\left(K, I, \frac{w}{p}\right)$$

The derivatives of (42) are given by

$$(43) \qquad \frac{\partial \theta}{\partial K} = -\frac{F_{LK}}{F_{LL}}; \quad \frac{\partial \theta}{\partial I} = -\frac{F_{LI}}{F_{LL}}; \quad \frac{\partial \theta}{\partial w/p} = \frac{1}{F_{LL}}$$

The first of these is usually thought to be positive; the third is surely negative. There exists no particular preconception regarding the second. Since it is convenient to take it to be zero, this will be done here.[28]

The right-hand side of (42) may be inserted in place of L where it appears as an argument of F_I in (37) and F_K in (38). This produces a system that is indistinguishable in form from that whose properties were studied in Figures 3-3, 3-4, and 3-5, save that it has an additional parameter, the money wage. Any change in the money wage will

---

[28] This amounts to assuming that F is additively separable into a production function of K and L and an adjustment cost function of K and I.

have a direct effect on employment whose magnitude may be determined from (42). In addition, a change in the wage will alter the rest-point capital stock. As the capital stock moves from its initial position toward its new equilibrium, further adjustments in employment will be appropriate. These and other responses to parameter changes will be explored more fully later in the chapter.

Money as a Factor of Production

Firms, like households, must as a practical necessity hold some quantities of the exchange medium simply because of the imperfect synchronization of their sales receipts and their factor purchases. However, they have latitude concerning the frequency with which they transfer funds between bank balances and income-earning assets (which may be their own securities). During periods in which they have a net inflow of funds from production, they can allow their balances to build up, making a few large purchases of securities. Alternatively, they can make many small purchases and avoid thereby holding large balances. Similarly, during periods of net outflow, they can sell securities either in large lots infrequently or in small lots frequently.

If the purchase and sales of securities were costless, the firm's managers would always serve their stockholders' interests by making many small transactions, minimizing their cash balances and thereby the interest cost of holding these balances. Presumably, however, transactions are costly to the firm just as they are to the household. The household that keeps small money balances pays for it by spending much of its time rushing to and from the savings and loan. The firm that keeps small money balances must employ many financial officers, accountants, clerks, and computers to handle its frequent securities transactions. Alternatively, it must hire some outside financial specialists to do the same job. In either case, the optimum choice of cash holding involves a balancing of the interest cost of holding money against the wage and capital cost of avoiding doing so.

One particularly convenient way to recognize these matters is to treat money as a factor of production.[29] The larger are a firm's money balances (relative to the prices of the things it buys and sells), the larger will be the output of its labor and capital. With large balances, the labor and capital inputs can be devoted more to production and less to financial management than would be the case if balances were small. Treating the function of money in this way leads to a production function of the form[30]

$$(44) \qquad Q = F\left(K, L, \frac{M}{p}, I\right)$$

---

[29] A similar treatment of business demand for money may be found in Levhari and Patinkin [1968]. This article also treats household demand for money as deriving from the presence of real balances in the utility function.

[30] It is clearly necessary to normalize the money holding by some sort of deflation. When prices are low, a given nominal money stock will handle many real transactions and therefore substitute for many other factors. However, the choice of the output price rather than some combination of input prices as the deflator is an oversimplification. In a more extensive treatment of the matter, the production function would be written as $F(K, L, I, M, p, p_K, w)$, homogeneous of degree zero in its last four arguments.

in which the first three arguments have positive marginal products and the fourth a negative marginal product. As usual, F is assumed to be concave in the region in which the firm operates.

The maximand of the managers' choice problem is given by

$$(45) \qquad V(n) = \int_n^\infty e^{-r(t-n)} \left[pF\left(K, L, \frac{M}{p}\right) - wL - p_K I - rM \right] dt$$

Money, like labor, is strictly a current input. The amount held at one moment in no way restricts the choices open to the firm in subsequent periods. Therefore, the marginal condition for maximization with respect to M/p comes from maximization of the integrand of (45) at all times. It is[31]

$$(46) \qquad\qquad\qquad\qquad F_{M/p} = r$$

The marginal product of real money must be kept equal to the rate of interest.

The marginal product of money, like the marginal product of labor, is potentially a function of all inputs. The determination of the optimal money stock may depend, therefore, on all the parameters within which the firm operates. Moreover, as the firm proceeds along a path of capital accumulation, the optimal money holding for any given set of parameters may change. The relationships between parameter values and factor purchases will be more fully explored later in the chapter.

The Value of the Firm

The previous section completes the basis for a derivation of the demand and supply curves of the firm. Before turning to this derivation, however, it seems useful to pick up the thread of analysis that served to introduce this part. Early on it was shown that the managers of a firm ought in the interest of stockholders to maximize its value as a producer. This value is given by

$$(47) \qquad\qquad V(n) = \int_n^\infty e^{-r(t-n)} \left[pQ - wL - rM - p_K I \right] dt$$

As a little rearrangement will show, this value is equal at all times to the present value of the firm's future rents plus the value of its capital stock at current market prices. To see that this is so, rewrite (47) as

$$V(n) = \int_n^\infty e^{-r(t-n)} \left[pQ - wL - rM - p_K(r+\delta)K \right] dt$$

$$(48) \qquad\qquad\qquad\qquad + \int_n^\infty e^{-r(t-n)} \left[p_K(r+\delta)K - p_K I \right] dt$$

---

[31]The marginal product of money measured in commodity units is the derivative of a flow of commodities taken with respect to a stock of commodities. It therefore conforms dimensionally to the interest rate, which is the ratio of a flow of money to a stock of money.

The first term is the present value of the receipts less payments and imputations to the factors of production. It is therefore the present value of rents. The integrand of the second term may be written as

(49)
$$e^{-r(t-n)} p_K [rK - \dot{K}] = \frac{d}{dt}[-e^{-r(t-n)} p_K K]$$

If we assume that $\lim_{t \to \infty} e^{-r(t-n)} p_K K = 0$, which is surely true for a competitive firm, the second integral on the right side of (48) is therefore equal to $p_K K(n)$, the spot value of the firm's capital stock.

If the firm's technology entails real costs of adjustment to investment, the value of the capital that a firm has already in place exceeds its current market price by the amount of the adjustment cost embodied in it. Similarly, the value of its current activities exceeds the value of its output by the value of the adjustment costs currently being embodied in the stock of capital. To see the implications of this, rewrite (47) as

$$V(n) = \int_n^\infty e^{-r(t-n)} [pQ + (p_I - p_K) I - wL - rM - p_I(r + \delta - \dot{p}_I/p_I) K] \, dt$$

(50)
$$+ \int_n^\infty e^{-r(t-n)} [p_I(r + \delta - \dot{p}_I/p_I) K - p_I I] \, dt$$

where

(51)
$$p_I = p_K - pF_I$$

The integrand of the second term on the right side of (50) may be rearranged to give

(52)
$$e^{-r(t-n)} [rp_I K - \dot{p}_I K - p_I \dot{K}] = \frac{d}{dt}[-e^{-r(t-n)} p_I K]$$

If we assume that $\lim_{t \to \infty} e^{-r(t-n)} p_I K = 0$, this means that the value of the firm is given by

$$V(n) = \int_n^\infty e^{-r(t-n)} [pQ + (p_I - p_K) I - wL - rM - p_I(r + \delta - \dot{p}_I/p_I) K] \, dt + p_I K(n)$$

(53)

The integral on the right of (53) is the present value of the firm's rents measured in a particular way. Its productive activities embrace not only the output of goods but also the putting in place of capital goods. The costs of current inputs are conventionally treated, but the costs of capital input are not. The capital stock is valued at the price of having it in place rather than at its market price. Interest and depreciation on this value include a deduction for the rate of capital gains and losses arising from changes in the cost of installing capital goods, which arise in turn from changes in the rate of growth of capital.

The value of the firm, as measured in (53), also includes the value of its capital stock, priced at its installed price, p_I, rather than its market price, p_K. In the presence of real adjustment costs, the installed price exceeds the market price. Hence $p_I K$ exceeds $p_K K$. Since the left-hand sides in (48) and (53) are equal, this means that the rents as measured in (48) exceed the rents as measured in (53). This excess arises from the lower valuation that (48) places on capital costs. When capital is valued in place, as in (53), the result is a high capital value and a low rental stream as compared with those based on a market-price valuation of capital.

II. THE RESPONSE TO CONSTRAINTS AND PARAMETER VARIATIONS

In keeping with the parallelism between this chapter and the previous one, this part examines the implications of disequilibrium constraints for the maximizing firm and derives the effects of changes in both prices and nonprice constraints. Given the complexity of present-value maximization under fairly general conditions, it seems best for expositional purposes first to explore the implications of price changes and then to introduce disequilibrium constraints. The first four sections are therefore devoted to parameter variations and the fifth to modifications necessary to cope with disequilibrium. The final two sections deal with other related matters that are prefatory to later chapters.

The Comparative Statics of Rest Points

The most convenient starting point for analyzing the effects of parameter changes is a comparison of alternative steady states. This may be done by examining those responses to parameter changes that maintain consistency with the following definitional and optimality conditions, derived in the previous part

$$(54) \qquad\qquad I = \delta K$$

$$(55) \qquad\qquad \frac{p_I}{p} = \frac{p_K}{p} - F_I$$

$$(56) \qquad\qquad (r + \delta)\frac{p_I}{p} = F_K$$

$$(57) \qquad\qquad \frac{w}{p} = F_L$$

$$(58) \qquad\qquad r = F_{M/p}$$

The first of these is the condition for a constant capital stock. The second defines the real price of investment. The third is the condition under which the shadow price of investment remains constant over time. The fourth and fifth are marginal conditions guiding the choice of current inputs.

In order to limit to manageable size the range of possible responses, assume that all adjustment costs take the form of foregone output, and that the production function can be written in the following separable form

$$(59) \qquad F\left(K, L, \frac{M}{p}, I\right) = G\left(K, L, \frac{M}{p}\right) + H(K, I)$$

where G is strictly concave and H is linearly homogeneous and concave. These assumptions make F_L and $F_{M/p}$ independent of I, and F_I invariant between rest points.[32]

With these assumptions, the total differentials of (56), (57), and (58) may be written as

$$(60) \qquad \begin{bmatrix} F_{KK} & F_{KL} & F_{KM/p} \\ \\ F_{LK} & F_{LL} & F_{LM/p} \\ \\ F_{\dot{M}/pK} & F_{M/pL} & F_{M/pM/p} \end{bmatrix} \begin{bmatrix} dK \\ \\ dL \\ \\ d\dfrac{M}{p} \end{bmatrix} = \begin{bmatrix} \dfrac{p_I}{p}\,dr + (r+\delta)\,d\,\dfrac{p_K}{p} \\ \\ d\,\dfrac{w}{p} \\ \\ dr \end{bmatrix}$$

This expresses the dependence of rest-point inputs on variations in the rate of interest, the real price of capital goods, and the real wage. The nine derivatives determined by (60) are given below by (61)–(69). In each expression the symbol D stands for the determinant of the Hessian on the left side of (60). It is necessarily negative, by the concavity of F.

$$(61) \qquad \frac{dK}{dr} = \frac{1}{D}\left[\frac{p_I}{p} \begin{vmatrix} F_{LL} & F_{LM/p} \\ F_{M/pL} & F_{M/pM/p} \end{vmatrix} + \begin{vmatrix} F_{KL} & F_{KM/p} \\ F_{LL} & F_{LM/p} \end{vmatrix}\right]$$

$$(62) \qquad \frac{dK}{dp_K/p} = \frac{(r+\delta)}{D} \begin{vmatrix} F_{LL} & F_{LM/p} \\ F_{M/pL} & F_{M/pM/p} \end{vmatrix}$$

$$(63) \qquad \frac{dK}{dw/p} = -\frac{1}{D} \begin{vmatrix} F_{KL} & F_{KM/p} \\ F_{M/pL} & F_{M/pM/p} \end{vmatrix}$$

$$(64) \qquad \frac{dL}{dr} = -\frac{1}{D}\left[\frac{p_I}{p} \begin{vmatrix} F_{LK} & F_{LM/p} \\ F_{M/pK} & F_{M/pM/p} \end{vmatrix} + \begin{vmatrix} F_{KK} & F_{KM/p} \\ F_{LK} & F_{LM/p} \end{vmatrix}\right]$$

$$(65) \qquad \frac{dL}{dp_K/p} = -\frac{(r+\delta)}{D} \begin{vmatrix} F_{LK} & F_{LM/p} \\ F_{M/pK} & F_{M/pM/p} \end{vmatrix}$$

$$(66) \qquad \frac{dL}{dw/p} = \frac{1}{D} \begin{vmatrix} F_{KK} & F_{KM/p} \\ F_{M/pK} & F_{M/pM/p} \end{vmatrix}$$

[32] The ratio of I to K is δ at all rest points. If H is linearly homogeneous, its first derivatives depend only on I/K.

$$(67) \qquad \frac{dM/p}{dr} = \frac{1}{D} \left[\frac{p_I}{p} \begin{vmatrix} F_{LK} & F_{LL} \\ F_{M/pK} & F_{M/pL} \end{vmatrix} + \begin{vmatrix} F_{KK} & F_{KL} \\ F_{LK} & F_{LL} \end{vmatrix} \right]$$

$$(68) \qquad \frac{dM/p}{dp_K/p} = \frac{(r+\delta)}{D} \begin{vmatrix} F_{KK} & F_{KL} \\ F_{M/pK} & F_{M/pL} \end{vmatrix}$$

$$(69) \qquad \frac{dM/p}{dw/p} = -\frac{1}{D} \begin{vmatrix} F_{KK} & F_{KL} \\ F_{M/pK} & F_{M/pL} \end{vmatrix}$$

Of these nine expressions, only two, (62) and (66), have signs that are determined by the theory of production. Each of them gives the slope of the demand curve for a factor of production written as a function of its own price. Each is negative.[33]

Expressions (63), (65), (68), and (69) all describe the demand for one factor as a function of the price of one other factor. Why are they ambiguous?

The answer lies in conflicting scale and substitution effects, which are quite similar to the income and substitution effects of consumer demand theory. If all factors are normal, then a rise in the price of any one of them makes the firm want to reduce production. The reduced production will lead to a reduced demand for all factors; this is the scale effect. Further, if the price of a factor goes up, the firm will want to substitute other factors for it. This substitution effect reduces still more the demand for the factor whose price has risen. However, it increases the demand for other factors, running counter to the scale effect. This is the source of the ambiguity in the four expressions just cited.

The resolution of the ambiguity rests on the signs of the cross partial derivates of the production function. Consider any two factors of production. They might be competitive if a rise in the use of one lowered the marginal product of the other. They would be cooperative, or cooperating, if increased use of one raised the marginal product of the other. Between competitive factors, the cross partial derivative is negative. Between cooperative factors, it is positive.[34]

Suppose, for example, that money is competitive with labor and capital, which are cooperative with one another. Thus $F_{KM/p}$ and $F_{LM/p}$ are negative and F_{KL} is positive. As an examination of (68) and (69) will show, this pattern determines that a rise in either the real wage or the real price of capital raises the demand for real money. This means a rise in the price of one factor raises the demand for a competitive factor. By contrast, (63) and (65) indicate that a rise in the real price of capital goods lowers the demand for the cooperative factor labor, and a rise in the real wage lowers the demand for the cooperative factor capital.

Expression (64) is an interesting case. The interest rate is part of the prices of both money and capital. If money is competitive with labor and capital, which are cooperative with one another, then the sign of (64) is ambiguous. A rise in r raises the

---

[33] Remember that D must be negative and that the two-by-two principal minors on the right sides of (62) and (66) must be positive if G is to be concave.

[34] The parallel with substitutes and complements in Hicksian demand theory should be evident.

price both of a cooperative factor and a competitive factor. However, if all factors are cooperative then the sign of (64) is necessarily negative.

Expressions (61) and (67) are also interesting. Since the rate of interest is part of the price of both money and capital, it serves a dual role in these expressions. Any increase constitutes a rise in one factor's own price and also in the price of another factor. If all factors are cooperative, there is no problem. Both influences go in the same direction, and (61) and (67) are surely negative. But if money is competitive with the other two factors, there remain ambiguities.

It is hard to know what to do in the face of the richness of possibilities. Examining all of them is tedious to the point of tears. Asserting that all factors are cooperative is dogmatic, for it has no justification in production theory, however much it simplifies things. The best course of action seems to be to avoid the issue wherever possible, to follow tradition where it exists, and to choose the most interesting assumptions wherever choice is necessary and neither analysis nor tradition offers any guidance.

For the rest of this discussion the following rules are in effect:

1. A rise in the interest rate lowers the rest-point demand for both money and capital, whatever it does to the demand for labor.
2. A rise in the real wage lowers the rest-point demand for both labor and capital.
3. A rise in the real price of capital goods lowers the rest-point demand for capital, whatever it does to the demand for other factors.

The Demands for Money and Labor

When a firm is at rest, or in equilibrium, its stock of capital has been determined by the parameters of the firm's environment. However, at any moment the capital stock is a given, a product of past investment rather than of present parameters. Only current inputs are currently determinable. Since this is so, labor and money inputs can be chosen for the moment without regard for the optimum capital. If the separability assumption embodied in Equation (59) is true, then they can be determined without regard for the current rate of investment as well. All that matter are the real wage, the rate of interest, and the existing stock of capital. The relations that guide the managers are

(70)
$$F_L\left(K, L, \frac{M}{p}\right) = \frac{w}{p} \quad \text{and}$$

(71)
$$F_{M/p}\left(K, L, \frac{M}{p}\right) = r$$

If these relations are differentiated, the resulting relationships are given by

(72)
$$\begin{bmatrix} F_{LL} & F_{LM/p} \\ \\ F_{M/pL} & F_{M/pM/p} \end{bmatrix} \begin{bmatrix} dL \\ \\ d\dfrac{M}{p} \end{bmatrix} = \begin{bmatrix} d\dfrac{w}{p} - F_{LK}\, dK \\ \\ dr \ - F_{M/pK}\, dK \end{bmatrix}.$$

The derivatives implied by (72) are listed below. As usual, the symbol D denotes the determinant of the Hessian on the left, which is in this case positive.

$$(73) \qquad \frac{dL}{dw/p} = \frac{F_{M/pM/p}}{D}$$

$$(74) \qquad \frac{dL}{dr} = -\frac{F_{LM/p}}{D}$$

$$(75) \qquad \frac{dL}{dK} = \frac{F_{M/pK}\,F_{LM/p} - F_{LK}\,F_{M/pM/p}}{D}$$

$$(76) \qquad \frac{dM/p}{dw/p} = -\frac{F_{LM/p}}{D}$$

$$(77) \qquad \frac{dM/p}{dr} = \frac{F_{LL}}{D}$$

$$(78) \qquad \frac{dM/p}{dK} = \frac{F_{M/pL}\,F_{LK} - F_{LL}\,F_{M/pK}}{D}$$

As one might expect, the only determinate quantities are (73) and (77), each of which measures the response of the demand for one factor to changes in its own price. All other quantities depend on the relationships of competition and cooperation among factors. Thus the following rules, to be added to those listed above, rest in part on assumption.

4. A rise in the interest rate lowers the momentary demand for money, whatever it does to the momentary demand for labor.
5. A rise in the real wage lowers the momentary demand for labor, whatever it does to the demand for money.
6. A rise in the capital stock increases both the demand for labor and the demand for money.[35]

These lead immediately to the formulation of labor and money demand functions of the form.

$$(79) \qquad L^d = L^d\left(\frac{w}{p}, r, K\right) \quad \text{and}$$

$$(80) \qquad \frac{M^b}{p} = \phi^b\left(\frac{w}{p}, r, K\right)$$

where L^d is labor demanded and M^b/p is the business demand for money. Rules 4, 5, and 6 restrict some but not all the derivatives of (78) and (80).

---

[35] This assumes cooperation between factors.

The Demand for Investment Goods

In order to develop a demand function for investment goods, two questions must be answered. How is the rate of investment influenced by changes in the rest-point capital stock? How is it influenced by changes in the actual capital stock? The answers to these questions, in conjunction with the conclusions reached earlier concerning the determinants of rest-point capital, provide the basis for the investment function.[36] Once the investment function has been specified, it may be combined with (79), (80), and the production function to give a supply function for output.

Both questions about investment may be answered by means of diagrams similar to Figures 3-6, 3-7, and 3-8 of this chapter. Those particular diagrams were based on a very special case, however. The only arguments in the production function were I and K, and the cross partial derivative was assumed to be zero. This section requires analysis of a somewhat more general character.

One conclusion reached earlier was that an optimal investment path would have to satisfy

$$(81) \qquad \dot{p}_I = (r + \delta) p_I - p F_K$$

where p_I is defined by (55) above. Substituting (55) and the production function (59) into (81) and reorganizing gives

$$(82) \qquad \dot{I} = \frac{1}{H_{II}} \left[G_K + H_K - (r + \delta) \left(\frac{p_K}{p} - H_I \right) \right] - \frac{H_{IK}}{H_{II}} (I - \delta K)$$

This must be set equal to zero to find the I, K combinations for which investment is temporarily stationary along a path of optimal investment.

Setting (82) to zero and reorganizing gives

$$(83) \qquad G_K + H_K = (r + \delta) \left(\frac{p_K}{p} - H_I \right) + H_{IK} (I - \delta K)$$

If this is totally differentiated with respect to K, the result is

$$(84) \qquad \frac{dI}{dK} \bigg]_{\dot{I}=0} = \frac{(I - \delta K) dH_{IK}/dK - dG_K/dK - H_{KK} - (r + 2\delta) H_{IK}}{(r + \delta) H_{II}}$$

Nothing of great generality can be said about this rather unappealing expression. However, in a neighborhood of the locus on which $I = \delta K$, it simplifies considerably. Three substitutions may be made: $I = \delta K$, $H_{KK} = H_{IK}^2/H_{II}$, and $H_{IK}/H_{II} = -\delta$. The first is a property of the neighborhood in question, the second is a consequence of linear homogeneity, and the third combines the first with another consequence of linear homogeneity. After the substitutions are made, (84) reduces to

$$(85) \qquad \frac{dI}{dK} \bigg._{\dot{I}=0} = \left[\frac{\delta}{r + \delta} \right] \left[\frac{dG_K/dK}{H_{IK}} \right] + \delta$$

---

[36]This two-stage analysis is not entirely rigorous, since it assumes that a knowledge of K and K^* is sufficient to determine I. However, it has great heuristic value.

The total derivative of G_K with respect to K, which appears in (85), is given by

$$(86) \qquad \frac{dG_K}{dK} = G_{KK} + G_{KL} \frac{dL}{dK} + G_{KM/p} \frac{dM/p}{dK}$$

If (75) and (78) are substituted in (86), the result can be reorganized to give

$$(87) \qquad \frac{dG_K}{dK} = \frac{\begin{vmatrix} G_{KK} & G_{KL} & G_{KM/p} \\ G_{LK} & G_{LL} & G_{LM/p} \\ G_{M/pK} & G_{M/pL} & G_{M/pM/p} \end{vmatrix}}{\begin{vmatrix} G_{LL} & G_{LM/p} \\ G_{M/pL} & G_{M/pM/p} \end{vmatrix}}$$

By the concavity of G, this is negative. An increase in the capital stock lowers the marginal product of capital when current inputs are adjusted in an optimal way.

There is a presumption that capital and investment are cooperative factors.[37] The bigger is a plant, the less destructive to current production is a given amount of investment.[38] Therefore H_{IK} is positive, and the sign of (85) is ambiguous. For sufficiently small H_{IK}, the first term on the right dominates, and dI/dK is negative. In this case, Figure 3-9 may be used to analyze the influences of rest-point and actual capital on the rate of investment.[39] Suppose a firm has a capital stock equal to K_0 and is investing at rate I_0 along a path of optimal accumulation leading to rest point A_0. Since all paths in the quadrant to the left of A_0 are downward sloping, the optimal path slopes downward. If a small parameter change were to shift the rest point from A_0 to A_1, increasing the equilibrium capital stock, the optimum rate of investment would increase from I_0 to I_1. If the firm's actual capital stock were to increase instead, say from K_0 to K_2, the optimum rate of investment would fall. No surprises here.

What if H_{IK} is sufficiently large that the locus of constant optimal investment slopes up from left to right? The answer may be seen in Figure 3-10, whose labeling corresponds to that of Figure 3-9. The path leading from an initial position to a rest point is upward sloping.[40] Therefore investment is increased not only by a rise in the rest-point capital, but also by a rise in the actual capital stock.

The reason for this seemingly peculiar result is the following. When H_{IK} is positive, investment is more costly at a low capital than at a high capital. If this influence is strong enough, investment and capital will move together despite the incentive to move quickly to an optimal stock.

Between the cases shown in Figures 3-9 and 3-10 is an obvious third possibility.

---

[37] Besides, it is a corollary to Euler's theorem that H_{IK} must be positive if H_{II} and H_{KK} are negative.

[38] That is, a rise in K makes F_I less negative. Thus F_{IK} is positive.

[39] The Figures 3-9 and 3-10 depict only modest-sized neighborhoods in which monotonicity may be assumed, and not necessarily the entire K, I space.

[40] The region above the constant-investment locus is always the region of increasing investment, however.

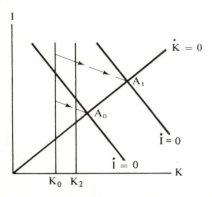

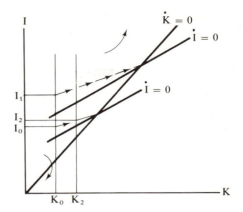

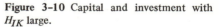

Figure 3-9 Capital and investment with H_{IK} small.

Figure 3-10 Capital and investment with H_{IK} large.

The locus of constant investment could be horizontal.[41] If so, it coincides with the path to the rest point. An increase in the rest-point stock raises investment, but an increase in the actual stock leaves it unaffected.

In all three possible cases, a rise in the equilibrium stock raises investment. Further, a rise in the actual stock in each case lowers the ratio of investment to capital and therefore the rate of growth of capital, as an examination of the diagrams will show. Nonetheless, there remains an ambiguity about the effect of increasing capital on the level of investment. In what follows, it will always be assumed that Figure 3-9 depicts the true state of affairs. Moreover, it will be assumed that dI/dK is negative everywhere and not simply in a neighborhood of rest.

Several strands of thought must be pulled together to complete the discussion of investment demand. In the section on the determinants of rest-point capital, it was concluded that an increase in the interest rate, the real price of capital goods, or the real wage would lower the rest-point capital stock. These relationships, together with those decided upon in the previous paragraph, determine an investment demand function of the form

$$(88) \qquad I = I\left(\frac{w}{p}, r, \frac{p_K}{p}, K\right)$$

All four derivatives are negative.

The Supply of Output

Equations (59), (79), (80), and (88) provide the raw materials for the construction of a commodity supply function

---

[41] From inspection of (87), verify that its slope could never be greater than δ no matter how large the value of H. This rules out any further possibilities.

$$Q^s = Q^s \left(\frac{w}{p}, r, \frac{p_K}{p}, K \right) \qquad (89)$$

Its first derivatives come from the marginal products of the production function and the derivatives of the input demand functions. They are

$$\frac{\partial Q}{\partial w/p} = F_L \frac{\partial L^d}{\partial w/p} + F_{M/p} \frac{\partial \phi^b}{\partial w/p} + F_I \frac{\partial I}{\partial w/p} \qquad (90)$$

$$\frac{\partial Q}{\partial r} = F_L \frac{\partial L^d}{\partial r} + F_{M/p} \frac{\partial \phi^b}{\partial r} + F_I \frac{\partial I}{\partial r} \qquad (91)$$

$$\frac{\partial Q}{\partial p_K/p} = F_I \frac{\partial I}{\partial p_K/p} \qquad (92)$$

$$\frac{\partial Q}{\partial K} = F_K + F_L \frac{\partial L^d}{\partial K} + F_{M/p} \frac{\partial \phi^b}{\partial K} + F_I \frac{\partial I}{\partial K} \qquad (93)$$

Two of these are clear-cut, (92) and (93), which are both positive. It might seem that the rule about the effect of a rise in the price of a normal factor could be applied to the other two. However, the dynamics of adjustment costs preclude this. A rise in the rate of interest reduces the level of investment; a rise in the wage may do so as well. Any diminution in investment will increase the output to be gotten from a given combination of inputs. Thus the third terms in (90) and (91) are positive. Even through labor and real balances are normal factors, the transitory output response to increases in their prices may be positive in principle. In practice, this nicety will be ignored. The influence of the wage will be assumed to be strong and negative; that of the interest rate to be negligible, whatever its sign. Commodity supply is therefore an increasing function of the capital stock and the real market price of capital goods, and a decreasing function of the real wage.[42]

The Response to Disequilibrium

Up to this point the optimal behavior of the firm has been analyzed against a backdrop of markets that are always cleared. No mention has been made of the possibility that a firm might not be able to sell all that it would like to supply at the ruling price configuration. The neoclassical approach to competition is to suppose that any firm can sell all that it chooses to supply at the ruling price, and nothing at all at any higher price. If a firm fails to sell its supply, this is a signal that its price is out of line with the market. It must therefore lower its price. If we assume that its supply curve is normally sloped, it will contract its output. All this happens with sufficient precision that no firm ever makes sales at any price other than the market equilibrium.

---

[42] The attention paid here to the market price of capital goods has little relevance to matters discussed in subsequent chapters, in which the ratio p_K/p is taken always to equal one. The reason for allowing it to vary in this chapter is to provide a fairly complete treatment of this kind of investment theory.

Although Keynes implicitly incorporated this view of commodity markets in much of the *General Theory*, many of his followers have supposed that "excess capacity," a concept without meaning in the neoclassical model, is a common market phenomenon. By this they mean that firms routinely engage in sales transactions at rates smaller than those determined by their supply curves.

Several arguments have been advanced to account for excess capacity.[43] Some explanation is needed of a firm's ability to make disequilibrium sales at all. One possibility is that all firms are charging too high a price, so that no one firm is out of line with the market. A second is that a firm's customers lack the information that better prices are available elsewhere. Additionally, the firm's willingness to tolerate excess capacity rather than to lower price must be rationalized. One possibility here is that the firm does in fact lower its price in an attempt to stay on its supply curve, but it is frustrated by the similar price cuts of its competitors. The industry as a whole stops short of the market-clearing price cut. A second possibility is that it believes price cuts to be ineffective, perhaps because they may induce matching cuts by competitors,[44] perhaps because they may not be perceived by potential customers. A third possibility is that firms may be deterred from lowering price in the face of temporary drops in demand because of the cost of change itself—the expenses of putting on new price tags and issuing new catalogs.

All these issues are important, but quite outside the scope of the book, which is mainly concerned with comparative statics. For the matters at hand it is sufficient simply to admit that goods markets do not always clear, and that exchanges manage to take place at prices above (and indeed below) those necessary to keep all firms on their supply curves.

What must be faced squarely is the response of firms to disequilibrium. Suppose, for instance, that a firm's demand falls short of the level given by (89), its supply schedule. Will it produce to meet demand, or will it equate marginal cost to price? In business cycle theory it is common to suppose that when a firm suffers an unexpected fall in demand, its production manager either does not get the message right away or is prevented by rigid production schedules from responding to it.[45] The result is an excess buildup of inventory stocks. Ultimately the drop in demand is confronted, and production is adjusted, or even overadjusted so as to eliminate the earlier stock buildup. Although this approach may be appropriate to a dynamic analysis of the price, production, income system, it is not suitable for a comparative static analysis.[46] For that purpose it seems best to focus on sustainable rates of production and therefore to suppose that firms do not produce more than they can sell, even though price

---

[43] Among the relevant papers on this topic are those of Phelps and Winter (1970) and Gordon and Hynes (1970).

[44] This argument is more persuasive in a context of undifferentiated oligopoly than it is in one of competition.

[45] Of the many articles written on inventory investment, probably the best is Lovell (1961).

[46] To the author's knowledge no reasonably complete dynamic analysis has ever been written. The business cycle models so far developed do not incorporate any recognizable model of the maximizing firm or household.

exceeds marginal cost. However, it also seems best to assume that they never produce at a rate at which marginal cost exceeds price. Hence production will be taken to be the smaller of the two magnitudes, supply and demand. This leads to the specification of a supply function more general than (89), such that

$$(94) \qquad Q = \text{Min} \, (Q^s, Q^d)$$

Supply, Q^s, is determined by (89); demand, Q^d, is outside the firm's control.

Failure of a firm to sell all that its managers would choose to sell must influence their factor purchase decisions. Therefore (79), (80), and (88), which hold in equilibrium, must be replaced by

$$(95) \qquad L^d = L^d \left(\frac{w}{p}, r, K, Q^d \right)$$

$$(96) \qquad \frac{M^b}{p} = \phi^b \left(\frac{w}{p}, r, K, Q^d \right)$$

$$(97) \qquad I = I \left(\frac{w}{p}, r, \frac{p_K}{p}, K, Q^d \right)$$

whenever there is deficient demand.[47]

Suppose, for instance, that the deficient demand is expected to persist forever. Then the rest-point capital stock will be lower than that which firms would choose if they could sell all that they wished. At a given actual capital stock, the lower is the rest-point stock, the lower is investment. Current input requirements are also reduced both by the curtailment of production and the the reduction of investment. Therefore the derivatives of (95), (96), and (97), with respect to Q^d will all be positive whenever Q^d is less than Q^s.

If the deficient demand is expected to be temporary, there is no stationary rest point toward which the firm is moving. Nonetheless, near-term input requirements will be reduced and both current factor purchases and investment will be adversely affected. The extent of this influence depends on the expected duration of deficient demand in much the same way that the impact of unemployment on consumption depends on its expected duration. This can only rigorously be treated in a discussion that takes account of the dynamics of expectations. Providing, however, that no expected future demand is increased by a fall in current demand, the derivative of investment with respect to current demand must be nonnegative.

In addition to the problem of deficient demand for a firm's output, there are also problems of deficient input supplies. Firms may be unable to hire all the labor or buy all the investment goods they would like, given the ruling set of prices. The reasons that this might happen are basically similar to those explaining the existence of excess

---

[47]Equations (95)–(97) result from solving a present-value maximization problem in which Q is a constant parameter, Q^d, rather than a variable that the firm can control. If Q^d is a time-dependent parameter, the maximization problem is very complicated, well beyond the level of difficulty of this book.

supply—insufficiently rapid price adjustment or incomplete information. In a careful examination of the theory of the firm in disequilibrium, these problems would have to be dealt with in detail. In a treatise on aggregate economics, a number of niceties can be sidestepped. In later chapters, no distinction will be drawn between investment and consumption goods from a production viewpoint. In view of this, a shortage of investment goods is evidence of a shortage of goods in general, that is, of excess demand. Similarly, a shortage of labor implies a shortage of goods, and again an excess demand. Since no particular importance will be attached to the amount of the unsatisfied demand, no thorough analysis of the consequences of factor shortage is necessary. But it is necessary to recognize explicitly the constraint that labor shortages impose on production. This requires the introduction of an additional behavioral relationship[48]

$$(98) \qquad Q^L = Q^L \left(L^s, \frac{w}{p}, r, \frac{p_K}{p}, K \right)$$

where Q^L is the optimum rate of production given that the firm is constrained to employ a labor force L^s that is smaller than the L^d determined by (95). Recognition of the possibility of labor shortage also requires that (94) be replaced by

$$(99) \qquad Q = \text{Min}\, (Q^s, Q^d, Q^L)$$

That is, the firm's output is the smallest of three quantities: that which it would choose if it were unconstrained, that which it could sell in the face of deficient demand, and that which it could produce with a limited supply of labor.

Rents and Capital

This chapter and the previous one have been devoted to analysis of the individual household and firm. Chapters 5, 6, and 7 comprise the macroanalytic portion of the book, built upon the foundations laid in Chapters 2 and 3. The problems of proceeding from microanalytic foundations to macroeconomic theory are discussed in a general way in the next chapter, Chapter 4, which covers aggregation. However, there is one important aspect of aggregation that fits better into this chapter on the behavior of firms than it does in the general treatment of aggregation. This concerns problems of disequilibrium and the instability of relations between inputs and output.

Suppose that a competitive industry is initially in equilibrium. The demand curve then shifts up. Entry is not immediately forthcoming, so existing firms expand their plants to a size in excess of that which yields minimum average cost. When new firms do enter the industry and equilibrium is reestablished, all firms will be of least-cost size. Total factor cost may be smaller than that incurred by the overexpanded initial firms, even though output is larger.

To see this, consider Figure 3–11. The horizontal HH' is the long-run industry

---

[48] Equation (98) results from solving a maximization problem in which L is a fixed quantity, L^s, rather than a controllable variable. Again, the problem of a time-variant constraint is a much more difficult one.

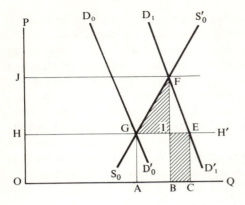

Figure 3-11 Entry and factor cost.

supply curve. The rising curve $S_0 S_0'$ is the long-run supply curve without entry; it is the horizontal sum of the long-run marginal cost curves of the initial firms. The initial and shifted demand curves are $D_0 D_0'$ and $D_1 D_1'$. At the outset, the industry is in equilibrium, producing output OA at total cost OAGH. The demand curve shifts and existing firms expand so as to produce output OB. The increment to factor cost is the trapezoid ABFG under the summed marginal cost curves, so that the cost of producing OB is the pentagon OBFGH, and rents are given by the trapezoid HGFJ. These rents attract entry until price falls back to OH, the minimum cost of production in an efficient-sized firm.[49] The ultimate cost of producing the equilibrium output OC is the rectangle OCEH.

The difference in cost between producing OB inefficiently and OC efficiently is the difference between the areas of the triangle GIF and the rectangle BCEI. If $S_0 S_0'$ is sufficiently steep, then this difference will be positive. A rise in output will be accompanied by a fall in cost. Since factor prices are assumed unchanged and since factor proportions may be the same at both levels of production, a rise in output may accompany a fall in all inputs. Thus an industry could have positive disequilibrium rents accompanying a capital stock that was above its long-run equilibrium level. In the rest of the book, this possibility will be dismissed by assuming that entry takes place with sufficient rapidity that existing firms never become greatly overexpanded. Thus positive rents always signal an incentive for accumulation and negative rents an incentive for decumulation.

Calculation and Animal Spirits in Investment Theory

Most of the preceding discussion has centered around capital spending decisions, which are the most complex factor purchase choices that a firm's managers must make. Unless capital goods can be costlessly installed and resold willy-nilly, decisions to buy them entail some assessment of the future, perhaps the very distant future. By

---

[49] The figure implicitly assumes that expansion of the industry does not increase factor prices.

contrast, decisions regarding the rate of purchase of current inputs may be made on the basis of current data alone, once the rate of investment has been chosen.

Current data must provide some of the raw material from which managers' views of the future are formed. Throughout most of this book it is assumed that they expect the future always to be much like the present. Yet many different futures could emanate from any given present. Though hard data for choosing among them may not exist, the choice must be made. Hunch and whim—what the Keynesians like to call "animal spirits"—must serve as a basis for decisions when rational calculation is impossible.

The material developed in this chapter cannot constitute in any sense a complete model of investment behavior. It focuses on one particular aspect of the problem: the relationship between current prices and the decisions that shape the firm's future. There is nothing wrong or irrelevant about this; it is only incomplete.

Moreover, it is doubtful that any complete model exists or ever will exist. The names of the variables influencing the optimism and pessimism of investors probably change faster than the survey researchers can catalog them. It must therefore be that the relationship between the rate of investment and its known determinants will always be a loose one. Models of national income determination are necessarily open rather than self-contained.

FOUR

THE AGGREGATION OF MICROECONOMIC RELATIONSHIPS

The two previous chapters have been concerned almost exclusively with the behavior of individual households and firms. The main emphasis of the chapters that follow is on the relationships among broad aggregates such as national income, total wealth, and the like. This chapter treats some of the problems encountered in trying to deduce the nature of the relationships among aggregates from a knowledge of the behavior of individual households and firms.

On the whole, the tale that it tells is not a happy one. Proceeding from the part to the whole is not easy. In the main, macro textbooks tend to underemphasize this fact. They proceed almost entirely by analogy from theories of individual behavior to discussions of the links among aggregates. The main focus of the present discussion is to show how fantastically restrictive the underlying modes of behavior would have to be if this were to be a valid procedure.

The literature on aggregation is both extensive and difficult. Although the topic has only been a major interest of economic theorists for forty years or so,[1] it has in this period occupied the attention of some of the most technically gifted people in the profession.[2] There is no possibility of surveying the literature in a single chapter, and all that is attempted here is to bring out a few major aspects of the problem.

---

[1] Price aggregates, or index numbers, have been in use since the eighteenth century [see Fisher (1922), Appendix IV]. Interest in the economic theory of index numbers dates back at least as far as Pigou (1912), but it was not until the middle 1930s [Staehle (1935), Allen (1935), Frisch (1936), Leontief (1936)] that the subject came to occupy a prominent place in the literature.

[2] The list of contributors reads like a who's-who of the Econometric Society. Some of the major contributions have been made by Klein (1946a, 1946b), Samuelson, (1947, chap. 6), Leontief (1947a, 1947b), Nataf (1948, 1967), Theil (1954), Solow (1956), Strotz (1957, 1959), Gorman (1959, 1968), F. Fisher (1965, 1968a, 1968b), F. Fisher and Shell (1972), Samuelson and Swami (1974).

In order to keep the coverage within bounds, the discussion is focused mainly on the aggregation of household behavior. In part, it entails a critical examination of the analysis of Chapter 2. In that chapter, considerable implicit aggregation was swept under the rug. It was assumed that rational planning could be done in terms of aggregates such as total consumption, the general level of prices, and so forth, and further that changes in planned aggregates could be expressed as functions of changes in the individual and market aggregates underlying the formulation of plans. The legitimacy of these assumptions is treated in the first two sections that follow. The third describes the conditions that permit the aggregation of individual consumption functions into a market demand function. The fourth discusses conditions that are sufficient for deriving a supply function in terms of the same aggregates that appear in the demand function.

All these sections deal with the circumstances in which aggregation poses no problems. There exist exact relationships among aggregates, and a knowledge of detail adds nothing to the understanding of movements in aggregates. The conditions required for this are very, very restrictive. The final section deals with the sources of error in the aggregation of relationships that do not meet these conditions.

PLANNING IN TERMS OF AGGREGATES[3]

Consider a household that consumes several kinds of goods:

$$C_1, C_2, \ldots, C_i, \ldots, C_u$$

and supplies several kinds of labor services:

$$L_1, L_2, \ldots, L_j, \ldots, L_v$$

In a very general form, its utility index might be written[4]

(1) $$V(n) = H[C_1(t), \ldots, C_u(t), L_1(t), \ldots, L_v(t); n, d]$$

This expression is a "functional," that is, a function of functions of some independent variable, in this case time. Utility maximization involves finding functions $C_1(t), \ldots, C_u(t)$ and $L_1(t), \ldots, L_v(t)$ that maximize (1) subject to the constraint[5]

(2) $$W(n) = \int_n^d e^{-r(t-n)} \left[\sum_{i=1}^{u} p_i(t) \, C_i(t) - \sum_{j=1}^{v} w_j(t) \, L_j(t) \right] dt$$

in which the p's and w's are the prices and wage rates for the various goods and labor services.

---

[3] This section, like the rest of the chapter, owes a great deal to Green (1964).

[4] The omission of time preference and real balances is deliberate. To include them would introduce complexities without adding insights into the aggregation question. Bequests have been omitted for the same reason.

[5] As in previous chapters, the rate of interest is taken to be a constant simply to limit notational problems.

This maximization problem, as posed, is so general that nothing can be said about the nature of the solution. The commonest way out of this unhappy state is to assume that the utility functional has a particular form

$$V(n) = \int_n^d \phi(C_1(t), \ldots, C_u(t), L_1(t), \ldots, L_v(t)) \, dt \tag{3}$$

In effect, this asserts that the utility of a consumption, work-effort plan can be written as a linear aggregate. The integral (3) is, so to speak, a sum of utility indices at an infinity of different moments. This is quite a strong assumption. It implies, for instance, that the marginal utility of false teeth at age 60 is taken to be independent of amounts spent on dental hygiene at age 30. It is essential to the analysis of Chapter 2, since without it one could not deduce the conditions of intertemporal optimality from an assumption of atemporal diminishing marginal utility.[6]

The assumption that expected lifetime utility is a linear aggregate is not, obviously, the only aggregation assumption underlying the analysis in Chapter 2, since consumption and work effort were both expressed in terms of aggregates. Under what conditions might this aggregation be valid, not approximately, but exactly?

A rather plausible sufficient condition is the following: future consumption and future work effort must be "composite" goods and bads, respectively.[7] A composite is a collection of goods and/or bads whose relative prices do not change. It is quite reasonable to suppose that a household that is planning its future has definite views about general price and wage movements but no expectation of change in relative prices and wages. That is, the expected values of prices and wages may be given by

$$(4) \qquad \begin{aligned} p_i(t) &= \bar{p}(t) \cdot p_i(n) \qquad \text{and} \\ w_j(t) &= \bar{w}(t) \cdot p_j(n) \end{aligned}$$

where $\bar{p}(t)$ and $\bar{w}(t)$ are indices of the general level of prices and wages, with $\bar{p}(n) = \bar{w}(n) = 1$.

To see why this helps, consider the following problem

$$(5) \qquad \begin{aligned} &\text{Maximize } U(t) = \phi(C_1(t), \ldots, C_u(t), L_1(t), \ldots, L_v(t)) \\ &\text{subject to } \sum p_i(t) \, C_i(t) = X_C(t) \qquad \sum w_j(t) \, L_j(t) = X_L(t) \end{aligned}$$

This entails the maximization of utility subject to the stipulation that specified amounts must be spent on goods and raised through work. The solution to this problem is a set of functions expressing the C_i and L_j as functions of X_C and X_L and the p_i and w_j. These functions may be substituted into the maximand of (5) so as to express utility as a function of the same variables that determine the C_i and L_j. That is

$$(6) \qquad U(t) = f(X_C(t), X_L(t), p_1(t), \ldots, p_u(t), w_1(t), \ldots, w_v(t))$$

---

[6] See page 13, footnote 5.

[7] The term "composite good" in this sense is due to Hicks (1939). The "composite bad" is a natural extension of the concept.

However, in view of the assumption of composites (4), the prices and wages of (6) may be replaced by the indices $\bar{p}(t)$ and $\bar{w}(t)$ in combination with the detailed prices and wages of time (n). Since the latter are givens, independent of t, they may be suppressed for notational convenience, and the "indirect utility function"[8] may be written

$$(7) \qquad U(t) = g(X_C(t), X_L(t), \bar{p}(t), \bar{w}(t))$$

That is, utility depends only on the amounts spent on consumption and earned through work, and on the general levels of prices and wages.

Further simplification is possible. The constraints of (5) are unaltered by equiproportional changes in prices, wages, and corresponding sums of money. This in turn implies that

$$g(\lambda_C(t) X_C(t), \lambda_L(t) X_L(t), \lambda_C(t) \bar{p}(t), \lambda_L(t) \bar{w}(t))$$

is independent of the λ's. Choosing $\lambda_C(t) = 1/\bar{p}(t)$ and $\lambda_L(t) = 1/\bar{w}(t)$, (7) may be rewritten

$$(8) \qquad U(t) = F \left[\frac{X_C(t)}{\bar{p}(t)}, \frac{X_L(t)}{\bar{w}(t)} \right] \qquad \text{or}$$

$$U(t) = F(C(t), L(t))$$

where $C(t) \equiv \dfrac{X_C(t)}{\bar{p}(t)} = \sum p_i(n) C_i(t)$ and

$$L(t) \equiv \frac{X_L(t)}{\bar{w}(t)} = \sum w_j(n) L_j(t)$$

The variables $C(t)$ and $L(t)$ are fixed-weight indices of the C's and L's, and $\bar{p}(t)$ and $\bar{w}(t)$ are indices of prices and wages. They satisfy

$$(9) \qquad \bar{p}(t) \cdot C(t) = \sum p_i(t) \cdot C_i(t) \qquad \text{and}$$

$$\bar{w}(t) \cdot L(t) = \sum w_j(t) \cdot L_j(t)$$

so that constraint (2) may be written

$$(10) \qquad W(n) = \int_n^d e^{-r(t-n)} [\bar{p}(t) \cdot C(t) - \bar{w}(t) \cdot L(t)]\, dt$$

and the entire intertemporal maximization problem is to maximize

$$(11) \qquad V(n) = \int_n^d F(C(t), L(t))\, dt$$

subject to (10).

---

[8]It is called indirect because utility is expressed as a function of the parameters of choice rather than of the direct sources of utility.

The maximization of $V(n)$ may be done in the following way. Suppose that the total sum $X(t) = X_C(t) - X_L(t)$ were specified and $U(t) = F(C(t), L(t))$ were maximized. The choice of C and L would depend on the parameters $X(t)$, $\bar{p}(t)$, and $\bar{w}(t)$. An appropriate marginal condition would be

(12)
$$\frac{F_C}{\bar{p}} = -\frac{F_L}{\bar{w}}$$

If satisfaction of this condition were assured, still another indirect utility function could be written

(13)
$$F(C(t), L(t)) = G(X(t), \bar{p}(t), \bar{w}(t))$$

Finally, the overall planning problem could be written

(14)
$$\text{Maximize } V(n) = \int_n^d G(X(t), \bar{p}(t), \bar{w}(t))\, dt$$

$$\text{subject to } W(n) = \int_n^d e^{-r(t-n)} X(t)\, dt$$

The intertemporal optimality condition for this problem is[9]

(15)
$$\frac{d}{dt}\left(\frac{\partial G}{\partial X}\right) = -r\left(\frac{\partial G}{\partial X}\right).$$

The choice of an $X(t)$ which satisfies both (15) and the budget constraint is, in effect, a choice of an optimal saving plan, since

(16)
$$\text{saving} \equiv S(t) = \dot{W}(t) = rW(t) - X(t)$$

Since the choice of X determines $\dot{W}$ for all t, it determines W for all t subsequent to n, and therefore saving for all t.

The upshot of this whole discussion is that if expected utility[10] is intertemporally additive and relative prices are not expected to change, the lifetime planning problem may be solved in three stages, the first two of which are cast in terms of aggregates:[11]

1. Choose a saving plan.
2. Given the saving plan, choose the best aggregate consumption and work effort consistent with it.
3. Given the chosen aggregates, allocate them optimally among the detailed categories of consumption and work.

---

[9] See Chapter 2, pages 14–15.

[10] The term "expected" is used in the sense of ordinary discourse rather than in that of probabilistic utility theory.

[11] The validity of this three-stage procedure depends on the concavity of the indirect utility functions. Although it can be shown that they are indeed concave, this will not be done here because of the lengthiness of the derivations. See Green (1964, pp. 28–32).

The beauty of this three-stage process is that optimal current saving can be determined without a detailed examination of the precise goods and labor services to be bought and sold in the future. All that is needed is some notion of the future marginal utility of X.

AGGREGATE DEMAND AND SUPPLY FUNCTIONS FOR THE INDIVIDUAL HOUSEHOLD

It might seem that the conditions which make it possible for a household to plan in terms of aggregates would make it possible to write its current demand and supply functions in terms of the same aggregates. This is not so, however. The compositeness assumed in the previous section applied to projections, not to the present. The structure of relative prices at time (n) is an implicit parameter of the indirect utility functions (7) and (13). Any change in current conditions will change these relative prices. To assume otherwise is to assume effectively that there is only one kind of commodity and one kind of labor. This simply ducks the problem of aggregation rather than solving it. What is needed is some set of conditions under which current prices and wages may be reduced to index numbers that, along with current wealth, the interest rate, and expected rates of price and wage increase, determine current aggregates of consumption and labor supply.[12]

Consider then the problem of maximizing

$$(17) \qquad V(n) = \int_n^d \phi(C_1(t), \dots, C_u(t), L_1(t), \dots, L_v(t))\, dt$$

subject to a lifetime budget constraint. Suppose that ϕ is decomposable in a particular way, such that

$$(18) \qquad \phi(C_1(t), \dots, C_u(t), L_1(t), \dots, L_v(t)) = \Psi(C(t), L(t))$$

where $C(t) = f^C(C_1(t), \dots, C_u(t))$
$\qquad L(t) = f^L(L_1(t), \dots, L_v(t))$

Suppose further that the functions f^C and f^L are linearly homogeneous. Suppose finally that goods and labor are composites in the sense that any change in relative prices at time n is expected to affect in the same proportion all relative prices subsequent to n. Under such circumstances, demand and supply functions may be written in terms of aggregate quantities and price indices, with well-defined relationships between quantities and prices.[13]

---

[12]The basic literature on this aspect of the aggregation problem is to be found in Leontief (1947a, 1947b), Strotz (1957, 1959), and Gorman (1959). Much of this literature is summarized in Green (1964, Chaps. 2–4). Its extension to the problem of planning over time is due to the present author.

[13]In effect, the subsequent argument outlines only the sufficiency of these conditions. However, they are also necessary. See Green (1964, pp. 25–27).

For any date t, let total expenditures on consumption and amounts raised through work be given by X^C and X^L, as in (5) above. Define price and wage indices p and w by

$$p(t) = \frac{X^C(t)}{f^C(t)},$$

$$= \frac{\sum p_i(t) \cdot C_i(t)}{f^C(t)};$$

(19)

$$w(t) = \frac{X^L(t)}{f^L(t)},$$

$$= \frac{\sum w_j(t) \cdot L_j(t)}{f^L(t)}$$

Assume that relative prices are fixed through time and given by (4). Because of the homogeneity of f^C and f^L, the weights of the price and wage indices are also invariant through time.[14] Therefore, the indices may be rewritten as

$$p(t) = \frac{\bar{p}(t) \sum p_i(n) \cdot C_i(n)}{f^C(n)} = \bar{p}(t) \cdot p(n)$$

(20)

$$w(t) = \frac{\bar{w}(t) \sum w_j(n) \cdot L_j(n)}{f^L(n)} = \bar{w}(t) \cdot w(n)$$

Each of these indices is the product of a homogeneous function of prices or wages at the planning date and of an expected trend in prices or wages. Moreover, from the definitions of the indices

(21)

$$X^C(t) = p(t) \cdot C(t) \qquad \text{and}$$

$$X^L(t) = w(t) \cdot L(t)$$

so that

(22)
$$\dot{W}(t) = rW(t) + w(t) \cdot L(t) - p(t) \cdot C(t)$$

or

(23)
$$W(t) = \int_n^d e^{-r(t-n)} \left[p(n)\bar{p}(t) C(t) - w(n)\bar{w}(t) L(t) \right] dt$$

Optimum planning can be achieved by maximizing

(24)
$$V(n) = \int_n^d \Psi(C(t), L(t)) \, dt$$

---

[14] Because of the homogeneity of f^C, a representative weight may be written as $1/f^C(C_1/C_i, C_2/C_i, \ldots, C_u/C_i)$. Homogeneity and fixity of relative prices implies that the ratios C_j/C_i will remain fixed over time.

subject to (23). The resulting values of X^C and X^L may then be allocated in a second stage of optimization using obvious marginal criteria. For example, the allocation problem for goods is

(25)
$$\text{Maximize } f^C(C_1(t), \ldots, C_u(t))$$
$$\text{subject to } \sum p_i(t)\, C_i(t) = p(t) \cdot C(t)$$

The marginal condition for each good is

(26)
$$f_i^C = \lambda p_i$$

where λ is a Lagrange multiplier. Multiplying by C_i and summing over i gives

(27)
$$\sum C_i f_i^C = f^C = \lambda \sum p_i C_i$$

If we use Euler's theorem, it follows that $\lambda = 1/p$ and

(28)
$$f_i^C = \frac{p_i}{p}$$

for all i and t. These conditions determine the relative sizes of the C_i's. Their absolute sizes are determined by the constraint of (25) and the conditions of optimality governing $X^C(t)$. Similar conditions determine the L_j's.

The essential feature of the multi-stage maximization process described in this section is the presence in the budget constraint of wage and price indices that are functions of the separate wages and prices at the planning date. Any change in a wage or price is reflected in the corresponding index, and therefore registers a change in the constraint (23). In turn, it must be reflected in changes in the optimum paths for $C(t)$ and $L(t)$. The latter are therefore functions of these price and wage indices, and in particular their values at time n may be written

(29)
$$C(n) = F^C(p(n), w(n), W(n), r)$$
$$L(n) = F^L(p(n), w(n), W(n), r)$$

Given the assumption that expected prices and wages move in proportion to current values,[15] these functions are homogeneous of degree zero in their first three arguments, and may therefore be rewritten as

(30)
$$C(n) = C\left(\frac{w(n)}{p(n)}, r, \frac{W(n)}{p(n)}\right)$$
$$L^S(n) = L^S\left(\frac{w(n)}{p(n)}, r, \frac{W(n)}{p(n)}\right)$$

These are, of course, the consumption and labor supply functions of Chapter 2. Their validity rests on three conditions:

---

[15] The expected trends $\bar{p}(t)$ and $\bar{w}(t)$ are, recall, taken as given. They are implicit parameters of (29) and therefore (30).

1. The comparability of utilities at different dates, in this instance their additivity.
2. The proportionality of expected prices and current prices.
3. The separability of the utility functions into a function of homogeneous functions.

These are, of course, highly restrictive conditions. Moreover, their imposition only guarantees the existence of aggregate demand and supply functions at the individual level. The existence of aggregate functions at the market level is even more tenuous.

AGGREGATION OF HOUSEHOLDS

Consider a group of households, each of which satisfies the conditions of the previous section. Under what conditions is it possible to express the aggregate consumption of the group as a function of price and wage indices and of the group's total wealth?

The individual consumption functions are given by[16]

$$(31) \qquad C(1) = C^1 \left(\frac{w(1)}{p(1)}, r, \frac{W(1)}{p(1)} \right)$$

$$\cdot$$

$$\cdot$$

$$\cdot$$

$$C(h) = C^h \left(\frac{w(h)}{p(h)}, r, \frac{W(h)}{p(h)} \right)$$

It is tempting to think of aggregate consumption as given by

$$(32) \qquad C = \sum_{i=1}^{h} C(i)$$

Notice, however, that according to the previous section, each individual household's aggregate consumption is given by the part of its utility function that is homogeneous in the individual consumption goods; that is

$$C(i) \equiv f^{C,i} (C_1(i), \ldots, C_u(i))$$

$$(33) \qquad = \sum_{j=1}^{u} \frac{\partial f^{C,i}}{\partial C_j} \cdot C_j(i)$$

and that, therefore

$$(34) \qquad C = \sum_{i=1}^{h} \sum_{j=1}^{u} \frac{\partial f^{C,i}}{\partial C_j} \cdot C_j(i)$$

[16]The time variable has been dropped since it is unchanged throughout the present argument. It has been replaced by a variable denoting the houshold in question.

According to (28), for each household,

$$\frac{\partial f^{C,i}}{\partial C_j} = \frac{p_j}{p(i)}$$

where $p(i)$ is the individual's overall price index. Therefore

$$(35) \qquad C = \sum_{i=1}^{h} \sum_{j=1}^{u} \frac{p_j}{p(i)} C_j(i)$$

Since different households will, in general, form different indices from the same set of prices, (35) makes it evident that a given collection of individual consumption goods can constitute differing aggregates according to how it is distributed among people. Only if all households form identical indices from a given set of prices will aggregate consumption be independent of the distribution of the goods of which it is made up. Similarly, since

$$(36) \qquad L = \sum_{i=1}^{h} L(i) = \sum_{i=1}^{h} \sum_{j=1}^{v} \frac{w_j}{w(i)} L_j(i)$$

a given bundle of labor services will comprise more or less total labor according to the distribution of effort among households.

It would, of course, be possible to define aggregate consumption and labor supply as more or less arbitrary fixed-weight indices of the total amounts of the separate consumptions and labor supplies, that is

$$\overline{C} = \sum_{j=1}^{u} \alpha_j \sum_{i=1}^{h} C_j(i) \qquad \text{and}$$

$$(37) \qquad \overline{L} = \sum_{j=1}^{v} \beta_j \sum_{i=1}^{h} L_j(i)$$

However, every quantity index implies a price index,[17] and there is no assurance that the price and wage indices implied by (37) would correspond to any of the indices appearing in individual demand and supply functions.

The problem of the dependence of aggregates on their distribution would disappear if every individual's utility function could be written as

$$(38) \qquad U(i) = \psi^i(f^C(C_1(i), \ldots, C_u(i)), f^L(L_1(i), \ldots, L_v(i)))$$

In this formulation, the homogeneous parts of the utility functions are the same for all households, although different households weight them in different ways. If the utility functions meet this condition, then all households form the same price and wage indices from a given collection of detailed price and wage data. This makes the

[17]Students of aggregation at least since the time of Fisher (1922) have insisted that price and quantity indices that are used together must have a product equal to the value index of the aggregate whose quantity and price they purport to measure.

weights in (35) and (36) independent of i, and therefore makes the aggregates independent of the distribution of the detailed quantities. It has the added advantage of simplifying the individual demand and supply functions, and very nearly clearing up the aggregation problem. The aggregate demand and labor supply functions under this condition may be written

$$C = \sum_{i=1}^{h} \sum_{j=1}^{u} \frac{p_j}{p} C_j(i) = \sum_{i=1}^{h} C^i\left(\frac{w}{p}, r, \frac{W(i)}{p}\right)$$

$$(39) \qquad\qquad L = \sum_{i=1}^{h} \sum_{j=1}^{u} \frac{w_j}{w} L_j(i) = \sum_{i=1}^{h} L^i\left(\frac{w}{p}, r, \frac{W(i)}{p}\right)$$

The only remaining problem is that the wealth variables in (39) continue to be indexed according to household, so that C and L depend on the distribution of wealth. This must be so even if all households have identical utility functions, if for no other reason than that a redistribution from the young to the old will raise both consumption and work effort.

This remaining problem can be solved if individual levels of wealth vary in proportion to the total so that

$$(40) \qquad\qquad W(i) = \gamma_i W$$

where $W \equiv \sum_{i=1}^{h} W_i$ and $\sum_{i=1}^{h} \gamma_i = 1$

This would be true if, for instance, all property incomes were funneled through one giant mutual fund whose shares were all identical. Then any change in profit levels or the rate of interest would affect the value of the holdings of all individuals in the same proportion. If some such institutional arrangement were in effect,[18] then $W(i)$ in (39) could be replaced by $\gamma_i W$, and there would be exact functional dependences of C and L on w/p, r, and W/p.[19] The partial derivatives of these functions with respect to wages and prices would be simple sums of the corresponding derivatives of individual functions. The partial derivatives with respect to wealth would be weighted sums, reflecting the γ's as well as the derivatives of the individual consumption and labor supply functions. Both relationships would be stable so long as both individual behavior and the parameters of the wealth distribution remained stable.

The conditions that make it possible to write a market demand for goods and a supply of labor are the following:

1. The conditions for the existence of individual demand and supply functions in terms of aggregates are satisfied.

---

[18] The legitimacy of introducing institutional arrangements into the process of aggregation was questioned by Klein (1946a, 1946b) on his end of a controversy appearing in *Econometrica*. The various other participants in this controversy contended that Klein's strict criteria could not be satisfied "in any practical sense."

[19] In fact, all that is required is that the $W(i)$ be stable functions of W.

2. All individuals aggregate in the same way.
3. The wealth of each individual household is a stable function of total wealth.

These conditions are unbelievably restrictive. They imply, for instance, that all households will consume all goods in identical proportions, and supply all kinds of labor services in identical proportions. However, they are not half so preposterous as the restrictions under which there exists an aggregate supply function.

THE OTHER SIDE OF THE MARKET

Consider now the circumstances under which an individual firm (the ith) can rationally plan in terms of aggregates. For the sake of simplicity, assume that it has no capital inputs, and that its production function is written in implicit form as

$$(41) \qquad \phi^i(C_1(i), \ldots, C_u(i), L_1(i), \ldots, L_v(i)) = 0 \qquad (41)$$

where the C's are outputs of consumer goods and the L's are inputs of various kinds of labor.[20] This function is strictly concave and has positive first derivatives with respect to the C's and negative with respect to the L's.

The firm's problem is to maximize its profit, $\Sigma pC - \Sigma wL$, subject to its production function. The appropriate marginal conditions are

$$(42) \qquad \frac{\partial \phi^i / \partial C_j}{\partial \phi^i / \partial C_k} = \frac{p_j}{p_k}; \quad \frac{\partial \phi^i / \partial L_j}{\partial \phi^i / \partial L_k} = \frac{w_j}{w_k}; \quad \frac{\partial \phi^i / \partial C_j}{\partial \phi^i / \partial L_k} = -\frac{p_j}{w_k}$$

Suppose that ϕ^i could be written in the form

$$(43) \qquad \phi^i = \psi^i(C(i), L(i)) = 0$$

where $C(i) = f^{C,i}(C_1(i), \ldots, C_u(i))$ and

$$L(i) = f^{L,i}(L_1(i), \ldots, L_v(i))$$

are linearly homogeneous functions with positive first derivatives. If this were so, then it would also be possible to define price and wage indices

$$p = \frac{\sum_{j=1}^{u} p_j C_j}{C}$$

$$(44) \qquad w = \frac{\sum_{j=1}^{v} w_j L_j}{L}$$

[20] For the sake of what follows, all goods and labor services are listed in the ith firm's production function, although in principle all but one of each might have zero coefficients.

The profit maximization problem could then be written as the maximization of $pC - wL$, subject to (43). The appropriate marginal condition would be

$$(45) \qquad \frac{\psi_C^i}{\psi_L^i} = -\frac{p}{w}$$

This would determine C and L. The firm could then determine its detailed outputs and inputs by

1. maximizing ΣpC subject to $f^C = C$
2. minimizing ΣwL subject to $f^L = L$

This would yield marginal conditions

$$(46) \qquad p_j = \lambda f_j^C \quad \text{and} \quad w_k = \mu f_k^L$$

where λ and μ are Lagrange multipliers. If the left-hand equality in (46) is multiplied by C_j and summed over j, and the right-hand one multiplied by L_k and summed over k, it is apparent that $\lambda = p$ and $\mu = w$.[21] Making these substitutions, (45) and (46) may be combined to reproduce the conditions stated in (42). Therefore, profit maximizing in terms of aggregates is optimal, and each firm has a commodity supply and a labor demand function of the form

$$C(i) = F^{C,i}(w(i), p(i))$$
$$(47) \qquad L(i) = F^{L,i}(w(i), p(i))$$

Since these must be homogeneous of zero degree, they may also be written as

$$C(i) = C^{s,i}\left(\frac{w(i)}{p(i)}\right)$$
$$(48) \qquad L(i) = L^{d,i}\left(\frac{w(i)}{p(i)}\right)$$

The obvious next step is to inquire whether it is possible to write corresponding aggregate functions for a collection of g firms. Following the line of argument pursued with respect to the aggregation of households, this could only be done in a consistent way if all firms formed the same price and wage indices from a given set of detailed prices and wages. This would in turn require that each firm's production function have embedded in it the same homogeneous functions as every other firm. Then aggregate functions could be written as

$$C = \sum_{i=1}^{g} \sum_{j=1}^{u} \frac{p_j}{p} C_j(i) = \sum_{i=1}^{g} C^{s,i}\left(\frac{w}{p}\right) = C^s\left(\frac{w}{p}\right)$$
$$(49) \qquad L = \sum_{i=1}^{g} \sum_{j=1}^{v} \frac{w_j}{w} L_j(i) = \sum_{i=1}^{g} L^{d,i}\left(\frac{w}{p}\right) = L^d\left(\frac{w}{p}\right)$$

---

[21] Recall that the f's are linearly homogeneous and that Euler's theorem applies.

Notice how extraordinarily restrictive is the condition that makes this aggregation possible. If it were in fact satisfied, then all firms would produce all goods in the same proportions and hire all factors in the same proportions. This represents the ultimate in product diversification. However, the most bizarre requirement for consistent aggregation only becomes apparent when the two sides of the market are put together. If the aggregates of consumption goods demanded and supplied are to be meaningful characteristics of the market, it ought to be true that whenever all individual markets are in equilibrium, aggregate demand should be equal to aggregate supply. Equilibrium in all markets implies

$$(50) \qquad \sum_{j=1}^{u} p_j \sum_{i=1}^{h} C_j(i) = \sum_{j=1}^{u} p_j \sum_{i=1}^{g} C_j(i)$$

That is, the sum across goods of the planned amounts spent by all consumers equals the sum across goods of the expected amounts received by all producers. Equality between aggregate demand and aggregate supply implies

$$(51) \qquad C^d \equiv \sum_{i=1}^{h} \sum_{j=1}^{u} \frac{p_j}{p^d} C_j(i) = \sum_{i=1}^{g} \sum_{j=1}^{u} \frac{p_j}{p^s} C_j(i) \equiv C^s$$

where p^d and p^s are the price indices common to demanders and suppliers respectively. A comparison of (50) and (51) shows that if both are to hold, p^d and p^s must be equal. A similar condition holds for the labor market. But if the price and wage indices of households are to equal the corresponding indices of firms, then the homogeneous parts of the utility functions must be the same as the homogeneous parts of the production functions! This, of course, is ridiculously restrictive; it is hardly conceivable that such a condition could hold.

ERRORS OF AGGREGATION

The upshot of all the preceding discussion is that consistent, exact aggregation is not possible under any but the most restrictive circumstances. The relationships of macroeconomics cannot be derived in any straightforward way from the relationships of microeconomics. Stable functions relating detailed variables do not imply corresponding stable functions relating aggregates.

It might seem that this fact would prove deeply disturbing to those practitioners of macroeconomics who seek to justify their procedures by appeal to microeconomics. Such is not the case, however. In much of the literature the aggregation problem is ignored. At one time this was justifiable because the problem was not very thoroughly understood. Given the current state of knowledge, however, it amounts to little more than endemic hypocrisy, the sort of conspiracy of silence that is the theme of the tale of the emperor's new clothes.

There is a perfectly sensible and constructive reaction to the problem, which is to recognize that because of aggregation problems, macro relationships would be inexact even if the underlying micro relationships were exact. Aggregation error is merged with measurement and specification error as well as error attributable to randomness of individual behavior. Such errors complicate the problem of measuring the systematic part of the relationships among aggregates but do not in any way make it senseless to study the properties of the systematic parts.

To get an understanding of the relationship between the parameters of macroeconomic and microeconomic relationships and to appreciate some of the sources of error, consider a very simple demand system. There are h households consuming u goods. Each of the hu demands depends on the u prices and on the wealth of the household doing the demanding; that is,

$$(52) \qquad C_{ij} = C^{ij}(p_1, \ldots, p_u, W(j)) \quad \text{for } i = 1, \ldots, u; j = 1, \ldots, h$$

The utility functions from which these demand functions stem do not, in general, satisfy the peculiar conditions discussed above, so exact aggregation is not possible. The total wealth of all households is denoted by

$$(53) \qquad W = \sum_{j=1}^{h} W(j)$$

and the total consumption of each good by

$$(54) \qquad C_i = \sum_{j=1}^{h} C_{ij}$$

Define a fixed-weight (Laspeyres) price index by

$$(55) \qquad p = \frac{\sum_{i=1}^{u} p_i C_i^o}{\sum_{i=1}^{u} p_i^o C_i^o}$$

where the quantities superscripted by o denote those pertaining at some "base" state of the system. If the system is in the base state, the index has the value one. Finally, define total deflated consumption by

$$(56) \qquad C = \frac{\sum_{i=1}^{u} p_i C_i}{p}$$

By definition, the product of the price index and aggregate consumption is equal to total expenditure.

Suppose that the system is initially in the base state, and that prices and individual amounts of wealth are changed by small amounts. How will aggregate consumption, as defined by (56), change? How will this change be linked to changes in the price index (55) and total wealth (53)?

To answer these questions, it is necessary to calculate some differentials from the base state. That in p is given by

$$(57) \qquad dp = \frac{\sum_i C_i^o \, dp_i}{\sum_i C_i^o p_i^o}$$

Differentiating (56), substituting (57), and remembering that $p^o = 1$, gives

$$dC = \frac{p^o \left(\sum_i p_i^o dC_i + \sum_i C_i^o dp_i \right) - \left(\sum_i p_i^o C_i^o \right) dp}{(p^o)^2}$$

$$(58) \qquad = \sum_i p_i^o \, dC_i$$

Substituting the differentials of the demand functions, this becomes

$$(59) \qquad dC = \sum_{i=1}^{u} p_i^o \sum_{j=1}^{h} \left(\sum_{k=1}^{u} C_k^{ij} \, dp_k + C_W^{ij} \, dW(j) \right)$$

where $C_k^{ij} \equiv \dfrac{\partial C^{ij}}{\partial p_k}$ and

$$C_W^{ij} = \frac{\partial C^{ij}}{\partial W(j)}$$

evaluated in the base state.

Now define two kinds of auxiliary relationships[22] tying together changes in aggregate and individual variables

$$dW(j) = \frac{W^o(j)}{W^o} dW + \epsilon_j; \quad j = 1, \ldots, h$$

$$(60) \qquad dp_k = \frac{p_k^o}{p^o} dp + \mu_k; \qquad k = 1, \ldots, u$$

In effect, these relationships define errors (ϵ's and μ's) that would all be zero if individual quantities all changed in the same proportions as the corresponding aggregates. It can readily be verified that

$$(61) \qquad \sum_{j=1}^{h} \epsilon_j = 0 \quad \text{and} \quad \sum_{k=1}^{u} C_k \mu_k = 0$$

---

[22] The use of auxiliary equations in aggregation is due to Theil (1954).

If the auxiliary relations are substituted in (59), the result is

$$dC = \left[\sum_i p_i^o \sum_j \sum_k C_k^{ij} \frac{p_k^o}{p^o} \right] dp$$

$$+ \left[\sum_i p_i^o \sum_j C_W^{ij} \frac{W^o(j)}{W^o} \right] dW$$

$$+ \left[\sum_i p_i^o \sum_j \sum_k C_k^{ij} \mu_k \right]$$

(62)
$$+ \left[\sum_i p_i^o \sum_j C_W^{ij} \epsilon_j \right]$$

The change in aggregate consumption is a function of changes in the price index and wealth and of the error terms in the auxiliary equations.

There are a number of things to notice about (62):

1. The coefficients of dp and dW are weighted sums of the corresponding partial derivatives of the micro behavior functions.
2. The weights embedded in these sums involve the structure of relative prices and the distribution of wealth, properties of the whole system of which the demand system is only a part.
3. Although there exist weighted sums of the errors that are zero (see 61), the aggregate error terms in (62) will not in general be zero.
4. Because of the error terms, C may move in a way different from that predicted by the systematic part of the relationship.
5. The more it is true that a change in the price index or a change in total wealth is reflected proportionately in all the corresponding micro variables, the more accurate will be the macro relationship.

Notice that these observations do not add up to a cry of despair. The systematic parts of macroeconomic relationships are closely related to and largely derived from corresponding aspects of individual behavior. The aggregation error terms simply introduce an additional element of inexactitude into a set of relationships that few responsible economists ever believed to be exact in the first place. More error is obviously worse than less error, but not in itself a justification for giving up. Moreover, aggregation problems only produce serious misunderstanding when their presence is unsuspected. To the extent that systematic correlation between, say, the ϵ's and the C_W's is well known and understood, its existence may be taken account of in inferring the relationship between dC/dW and the C_W's.

GENERAL EQUILIBRIUM

The analysis of equilibrium, if not the use of the word, is a tradition as old as formal economics. Indeed, for many writers the analysis of static and dynamic equilibria is the extent of economics. So strong is this historical tradition that Keynes thought he had to look to the "underworld" to find precursors of his own theory of deficient demand.[1] Recently, the term *general equilibrium analysis* has come to denote a particular subset of equilibrium economics quite narrow in its range of interests; it confines its attention to questions of the existence, uniqueness, and stability of equilibrium in systems that are avowedly hypothetical.

This chapter is more in keeping with the older tradition of equilibrium theory that uses equilibrium models as an analytical tool of political economy. It attempts to carry out four principal tasks. The first two of these are the strictly analytical chores of describing the structure of interrelated markets and stating the conditions under which the plans of all participants will be consistent. The third is the use of this structure to examine the influence of the size of the money supply and by implication to define constructive monetary policy. The fourth is the analysis of a complex of issues surrounding the relationship between capital accumulation and the functional distribution of income. Examination of these last two issues carries the discussion beyond the narrow bounds of analysis to a consideration of public policy and class interest. It seems productive to do this explicitly, since the social lessons of equilibrium analysis are buried in its theorems, whether one is aware of them or not. Therefore some effort

---

[1] The shady characters whom he cited were Karl Marx, Silvio Gesell, and Major Douglas. See Keynes (1936, p. 32). Of these only Marx was at all prominent, or rather, infamous.

is devoted to discussing the place of equilibrium analysis in economics, to question its relevance, and by implication to question the usefulness of its theorems.

Because of the length and complexity of the chapter, it is divided into three major subsections. The first deals with the structure of the equilibrium system, the second with the role of money, and the third with distribution. There is a brief summary at the end of the chapter.

I. THE STRUCTURE OF EQUILIBRIUM

This section pieces together the behavioral relations developed in earlier chapters. Households and firms are combined with one another in a system of interrelated markets, tied together by a structure of prices which affect them all. Market exchanges are made by means of money, a creature of the banking system. Before analyzing the structure of equilibrium, it is necessary to look briefly at the activities of the banking system and its interrelations with the other parts of the economy, since the banking system is a participant in all the economy's markets.

The Banking System

Modern capitalist economies have extraordinarily complicated financial structures that not only settle transactions among firms and households but also serve such diverse functions as risk bearing and monetary control. Since the whole matter of risk is ignored in this volume, it will be sufficient to consider a greatly simplified financial sector whose only role is to provide the means of payment. Furthermore, little is lost by collapsing into one set of institutions both the mechanics of providing the money supply and the power to decide how much will be provided.

Consider, therefore, a set of institutions to be called simply *banks*. Banks own buildings and employ labor, just as industrial firms do. In addition, they own securities (either stocks or bonds) issued by industrial firms, on which they receive income, to be called profit. Whenever a bank buys an industrial security, it pays for it by creating a deposit. Thus the banks create money. The industrial firms and households pass claim to these deposits back and forth from one to another, and the deposits therefore provide the convenience and productive services that make them desirable assets even though they bear no interest.[2] Since the banks do not pay interest on deposits, they make a profit even though they have to pay workers and replace buildings. This profit is paid to the owners of the banks' securities.

For analytical purposes, it is useful to subdivide the activities of banks into asset transactions and current-account transactions. In the first category are included purchases and sales of business securities and the attendant increases and reductions in the

---

[2] National accounting systems usually recognize these services by imputing to them a money value equal to the interest foregone on deposits. Such an imputation will be made in the analytical portion of this chapter.

money supply. In the second category are included the receipt of returns on the securities owned and outpayments of wages and profits. In addition, the second category includes purchases of capital goods and receipts from the sale of bank securities. All activities in this second category are associated with the provision of current banking services, and as such are properly pooled with the activities of industrial firms.[3] The asset transactions involved in altering the money supply must remain separate, however, since it is these transactions that distinguish banking activity from the activities of other firms. Throughout the subsequent discussion, the asset transactions of the banks will be treated as though they were autonomous and controlling rather than responsive to market forces. However, it will always be assumed that when the banks expand their holdings of industrial securities and therefore the money supply, they must also add more branches, computers, and personnel, so that their profit rate stays on a par with that of industrial firms.[4]

This brief sketch of the functions of the banking system will be supplemented with detail in the sections that follow.

The System of Interrelated Markets

At the level of abstraction and aggregation most appropriate to macroeconomics,[5] households, firms,[6] and banks may be thought to interact in three markets, one for commodities, one for labor services, and one for securities. In each of the three markets, payment is made by means of money. Thus there are four goods changing hands.

The labor market is the simplest. Households exchange a flow of labor services for a flow of money payments made by firms. Since the households and firms are simultaneously participating in other markets, this flow of money is only one component of the change in the distribution of money holdings.

[3] The details of this pooling are presented on pages 96–97.

[4] Implicit in this discussion of money and the banking system are two crucial assumptions: 1) there is no government fiat money, and 2) banks do not make monopoly rents. Under these assumptions, money is not wealth, but merely a form in which people hold title to wealth. For a lucid discussion of the relationship between wealth and the nature of money, see Patinkin (1969). See also Modigliani (1963, pp. 83–88).

[5] There is, of course, room for disagreement about the appropriate groupings of goods into aggregates. In the present chapter bonds and shares are grouped together into "securities"; consumer goods and capital goods are a single aggregate "good." Leijonhufoud (1968, pp. 130–57) recommends that consumer goods be kept separate from capital goods, and that the latter be grouped with bonds. This seems an unhappy choice. Individuals in an advanced capitalist country own title to capital goods mainly through the medium of shares, whose marginal yield may differ from that on capital goods. Furthermore, capital goods require resources for their production; bonds do not. Finally, although there may be some merit in separating capital and consumer goods because of a changing rate of substitution between the two, as Leijonhufoud avers, the same can be said for capital goods and bonds. All in all, capital goods and bonds make strange bedfellows. Nonetheless, Leijonhufoud's discussion is well worth reading. So is another work to which it owes a great deal, that of Tobin (1961).

[6] Throughout this discussion, activities of "firms" are to be understood to subsume the second category of banking activities.

The commodity market is next in order of complexity. Firms exchange one commodity for money payments by two distinct types of demanders. The first type is the household, which consumes the commodity in the act of purchase. The other is the firm, which accumulates the commodity as capital.[7] Its purchases constitute additions to its stock of productive resources. To assume that there is only one commodity is implicitly to assume that the transformation rate between consumption goods and investment goods is minus one in production. An appealing alternative would be to consider two distinct commodities, consumption goods and investment goods, produced in separate industries between which productive resources do not instantly move. However, it is doubtful that the insights provided would compensate for the complexity, both genuine and notational, introduced by bringing in an extra market and an extra commodity.

The third market, that for securities, is complicated by the existence of a stock of "seasoned" issues that are perfectly substitutable for new issues. The suppliers of new issues are firms or banks that provide a flow of securities in exchange for a flow of money payments by demanders, which are households or banks. However, if households, for example, are not content with the distribution of their wealth holdings, they may decide to offer some of their stock of seasoned issues in exchange for a stock of money, or vice versa.[8] This resale market for securities necessitates careful treatment. In equilibrium the stock of securities in existence must equal the stock desired. Furthermore, the flow of net new issues must equal the flow of desired additions. If there were a resale market in used commodities, the same conditions would apply to it as well.

The goods flows through these markets to and from the three sectors may be visualized by examining Figure 5-1. The arrows indicate in each case a direction of flow of the good in question. The pattern of flow of securities is only illustrative, since any of the three sectors could be a net demander or a net supplier. Corresponding to each goods flow is a contrary money flow. In addition, there are money flows that do not show up on the diagram. These comprise the payment of property income (dividends and interest, henceforward to be called simply profit) to holders of securities. Since such payments have no counterpart in current goods flows, they do not pass through any of the markets.

Two kinds of identity conditions must be satisfied by any actual set of flows through the markets, whether equilibrium or not. The first of these states that the value of the goods sold in any of the three markets must equal the value purchased. The second states that the value of goods sold or profits received by any of the three sectors less the value of goods purchased or profits paid must equal the net change in

---

[7] In all subsequent discussion, it will be assumed that capital goods are attached for their entire useful lives to the firms that originally purchased them. Thus there is no secondhand market in capital goods. Ownership of the capital stock may change hands through changes in the ownership of shares, which are part of the stock of securities belonging to households and banks.

[8] Any transaction is seasoned stocks constitutes a redistribution of the ownership of the capital stock.

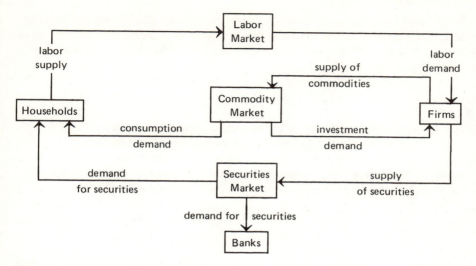

Figure 5-1 Goods flows in three markets.

that sector's ownership of money. In the case of the banking system, this "change in ownership" is the negative of the change of the money supply.

In order to express these conditions compactly, it is necessary to use symbolic notation. Much of it has been presented in earlier chapters, but the symbols are presented here to make it easier to follow the subsequent discussion.

p	the price of consumption and capital goods
q	the price of a security
r	the earnings-price ratio on securities, the rate of return on securities, the interest rate
w	the money wage of labor
C	real consumption
I	real investment
Y	real output
L	employment
K	physical capital
B	the number of securities (whether industrial or bank) in existence
D	depreciation allowances (in money terms)
P	money income paid to the owners of securities—profit
W	household wealth (in money terms)
M	the money value of bank deposits
R	the real value of rents
d, s	superscripts denoting demand and supply, used only when necessary
h, b, β	subscripts denoting households, industrial firms, and banks, used only when necessary

This notation is kept more compact than it would otherwise be through the use of subscripts, particularly in identifying issuers and holders of securities. The meaning of these subscripts is best illustrated by example, so consider the following relationships

$$B_b = B_{b\beta} + B_{bh}$$
$$B_h = B_{bh} + B_\beta$$

(1)

The first states that the number of outstanding securities[9] issued by industrial firms is equal to the number owned by banks plus the number owned by households. The second states that the total number of securities owned by households equals their holdings of those issued by industrial firms plus those issued by banks. A similar notation covers the distribution of profit to the owners of securities; that is

$$P_b = P_{b\beta} + P_{bh}$$
$$P_h = P_{bh} + P_\beta$$

(2)

The other uses of the subscript notation are explained in context.

The identity relationships stating the equality of receipts and expenditures in the three markets may be written as follows

(3) $$pY - rM_h = pC + pI$$

(4) $$wL_h = w(L_b + L_\beta)$$

(5) $$q(\dot{B}_b + \dot{B}_\beta) = q\dot{B}_h + q\dot{B}_{b\beta}$$

The first of these states that the total value of production of goods and services, less the imputed value of banking services,[10] equals the value of expenditures on consumption and investment goods. The second says that the value of labor services sold by households equals the value of labor services purchased by all firms, including banks. The third says that the value of securities sold by businesses, including banks, equals the value purchased by households and banks.

The second set of identity conditions, that expressing the equality of receipts and expenditures for each of the three sectors, is not quite so easy to work out because of the complexity of splitting the activities of the banking system. The receipts and expenditures of industrial firms are given by

(6) $$[p(C + I) + q\dot{B}_b] - [wL_b + pI_b + (P_{bh} + P_{b\beta})] = \dot{M}_b$$

This states that the receipts from the sales of goods and securities less payments for wages and capital goods and payments to security holders equals the change in busi-

---

[9] This chapter follows the common practice of measuring the stock of securities in units equivalent to commitment to pay one currency unit per time period in perpetuity.

[10] These services are not sold on a market, but are provided free in lieu of interest on bank deposits. They are equal in value to the interest foregone. Services provided by banks to other businesses are intermediate goods and are not included in total production.

ness bank accounts. A similar statement for banks is

(7) $$[P_{b\beta} + q\dot{B}_\beta] - [wL_\beta + pI_\beta + P_\beta + q\dot{B}_{b\beta}] = -\dot{M}$$

That is, the receipts from earning assets plus those from the sale of new bank securities less payments for wages and capital goods, payments to security holders, and the value of purchase of new earning assets equals the decline in the liability of the banking system to the rest of the economy.

Some of the activities summarized in (7) are asset transactions which alter the money supply. In fact the rate of change in the money supply equals the rate at which banks are acquiring securities; that is,

(8) $$q\dot{B}_{b\beta} = \dot{M}$$

If (8) is added to (7), what remains after canceling equal quantities is the account of the business activity of banks. This in turn may be added to (6) and simplified to give the receipts and expenditures statement of the consolidated business sector

(9) $$[p(C + I) + q(\dot{B}_b + \dot{B}_\beta)] - [w(L_b + L_\beta) + p(I_b + I_\beta) + (P_{bh} + P_\beta)] = \dot{M}_b$$

In order to simplify this further, it is necessary to make some statement about the financing of investment. As Chapter 3 demonstrated,[11] the particular form of financing is not a matter of much importance. It seems most convenient to assume that firms retain sufficient gross income to cover depreciation, but pay out the rest to the owners of their securities. This assumption implies that firms need raise outside funds only to finance the sum of net investment and (in the case of industrial firms) the accumulation of money; that is,

(10) $$q(\dot{B}_b + \dot{B}_\beta) = p(I_b + I_\beta) - (D_b + D_\beta) + \dot{M}_b$$

where D denotes an amount provided to cover depreciation on capital assets. If (10) is then substituted in (9), the result, after simplification, can be written

(11) $$p(C + I) = wL + P + D$$

This states that the receipts from the sale of goods to consumers and to businesses on capital account must equal wages and profits paid to households plus allowances retained to cover depreciation.[12]

The receipts and expenditures accounting for households is straightforward

(12) $$[wL + P] - [pC + q\dot{B}_h] = \dot{M}_h$$

That is, the sum of receipts from wages and profits less the sum of expenditures on consumption and securities equals the change in households' bank balances.

In effect, the process of accounting for the flows of commodities and money through the three markets has created a little set of national accounts for a closed

---

[11] See Chapter 3, pages 39–41.
[12] If some alternative assumption were made about the financing of investment, the right-hand side of (11) would require an additional term representing retained profit.

private economy.[13] The following relationships are derived with little alteration from (3), (11), and (12)

$$pY = pC + rM_h + pI$$

(13)
$$= wL + P + rM_h + D$$

$$= pC + rM_h + (q\dot{B}_h + \dot{M}_h) + D$$

They state in turn the three ways of resolving the value of gross national product. The first line expresses it as the sum of the values of consumption goods, banking services, and investment goods produced. The second expresses it as the sum of wage, profit, and imputed interest incomes earned in its production, plus depreciation. The third expresses it as the disposition of these incomes to consumption (both market and imputed) and saving (both household and business).

It must be stressed that these relationships hold true whether or not the magnitudes that are traded are satisfactory to anyone. They are statements of consistency, much like the old laws of conservation of energy and matter. Satisfaction of the accounting identities is necessary for equilibrium, but not sufficient. The sufficiency conditions comprise the subject of the next section.

Equilibrium in the Markets for Commodities and Labor

The literature on general equilibrium has two distinct though related lines of development. That most closely following the conception of Walras is the microanalysis of multiple interrelated markets.[14] It tends to be heavily mathematical and abstract and to examine the properties of processes that bear little resemblance to actual economies. The macroanalysis, by contrast, tends to be rough and pragmatic,[15] and to make generalizations believed to apply to real economies.[16] The remainder of the present chapter proceeds along this latter line of development, outlining a macro model of general equilibrium and studying its properties.

[13]For a complete and readable discussion of national accounting, see Abraham (1969). A more cursory treatment may be found in any undergraduate macroeconomics text.

[14]Some of the landmark volumes in this literature are Walras (1877), Hicks (1939), Samuelson (1947), and Debreu (1959). Arrow and Hahn (1971) provide an original and up-to-date synthesis of the whole literature with historical notes. Much of their book is quite demanding, but the first chapter and the notes following each of the other chapters are accessible and interesting.

[15]For example, macro theorists seem to ply their trade with good cheer and self-confidence despite the problems raised by aggregation. This earns them the contempt of more than a few micro theorists.

[16]Major strands in the development of this literature are Clark (1899), Wicksell (1913), Hicks (1932), and Pigou (1935). The greatest modern work on the subject is Patinkin (1965), a piece of extraordinary scholarship and brilliance. For an early mathematical model, see Evans (1934). Special-purpose aggregate models of equilibrium abound in the contemporary literature. One of the most interesting is Modigliani (1963), the subject of Chapter 1. As the Great Depression recedes from memory, general equilibrium theory has come to occupy a larger place in intermediate macro textbooks. See, for example, Miller and Upton (1974), which devotes seven full chapters to neoclassical equilibrium analysis and only parts of two chapters to Keynesian economics.

The accounting discussion of the previous section was cast in terms of realized magnitudes, with no distinctions drawn between quantities demanded and quantities supplied. The time has now come to introduce the conclusions of earlier chapters into the present framework and to focus on the interaction between demanders and suppliers.

Chapter 2 concluded that if a competitive system operated sufficiently well that all rationing was done through prices, household demands for money and consumption goods and their supplies of labor could be written as functions of the real wage rate, the rate of return on securities, and real household wealth.[17] The implied aggregate relationships are

$$(14) \qquad C = C\left[\frac{w}{p}, r, \frac{W}{p}\right]$$

$$(15) \qquad L^s = L^s\left[\frac{w}{p}, r, \frac{W}{p}\right]$$

$$(16) \qquad \frac{M}{p}h = \phi_h\left[\frac{w}{p}, r, \frac{W}{p}\right]$$

Chapter 3 concluded that firms operating within a smoothly functioning competitive system would supply output, demand investment goods, demand labor, and wear out capital in quantities that depended on the real wage, the rate of return on securities, and the existing stock of physical capital. That is, in the aggregate

$$(17) \qquad Y^s = Y^s\left[\frac{w}{p}, r, K\right]$$

$$(18) \qquad I = I\left[\frac{w}{p}, r, K\right]$$

$$(19) \qquad L^d = L^d\left[\frac{w}{p}, r, K\right]$$

$$(20) \qquad \frac{D}{p} = \delta K$$

In order to convert the accounting identities (3), (4), and (5) into necessary conditions of general equilibrium, it suffices to replace each ex post magnitude with a desired magnitude based on one of the behavioral relationships (14)–(20). In the case of the goods market, the appropriate condition is

$$(21) \qquad Y^s\left[\frac{w}{p}, r, K\right] = C\left[\frac{w}{p}, r, \frac{W}{p}\right] + I\left[\frac{w}{p}, r, K\right] + r\,\phi_h\left[\frac{w}{p}, r, \frac{W}{p}\right]$$

---

[17]Recall that this statement rests on an assumption that current prices and expected future prices move together. In comparisons of equilibria, such as those with which this chapter is mainly concerned, this is not a difficult assumption to accept.

That for the labor market is

$$(22) \qquad L^s\left[\frac{w}{p}, r, \frac{W}{p}\right] = L^d\left[\frac{w}{p}, r, K\right]$$

A similar condition could be constructed to express the condition of balance in the security market. However, this is not the most convenient way to close the system made up of (21) and (22), which imposes but two restrictions on the four variables w/p, r, W/p, and K.

At any moment, the stock of capital is given by the history of past accumulation. In the analysis of so-called "momentary" or "short-run" equilibria, it is therefore a parameter. The rate of net investment in momentary equilibrium is not necessarily zero, so that the position of equilibrium evolves over time. It is useful to conceive of a "long-run" equilibrium in which this element of evolution is absent. A condition of long-run equilibrium is then that gross investment exactly match depreciation. That is

$$(23) \qquad I\left(\frac{w}{p}, r, K\right) = \delta K$$

In discussing long-run equilibrium, this relationship will be presumed to hold in addition to (21) and (22). For purposes of short-run analysis, K will be taken as given.

The value of household wealth must be determined in order to complete the system. Wealth is held in two forms, money balances and securities. The amount of real money held is, of course, the nominal amount divided by the price level. Likewise, the real value of security holdings is their nominal market value divided by the price level. Market valuations of securities reflect the value of expected future returns discounted at the interest rates expected to pertain in the meanwhile. Under conditions of changing profits and interest rates, this is complicated business. Suppose for present purposes, however, that the current flow of profit income is expected to persist forever, and the current rate of return is also expected to remain constant. Then the market value of the existing stock of securities owned by households is given by the flow of current profit divided by the current rate of interest, and total real wealth is given by

$$(24) \qquad \frac{W}{p} = \frac{M_h}{p} + \frac{P}{rp}$$

Using the second equation of (13), this may be rewritten as

$$(25) \qquad \frac{W}{p} = \frac{M_h}{p} + \frac{Y - (w/p)L - r(M_h/p) - D/p}{r}$$

Canceling out money holdings and replacing the ex post notation of (25) by the functions describing firm behavior, this in turn may be rewritten

$$(26) \qquad \frac{W}{p} = \frac{Y^s - (w/p)L^d - \delta K}{r}$$

Real wealth equals the capitalized value of output net of the wages and depreciation costs incurred in its production.

It might seem that some sleight of hand has made the value of real balances disappear in going from (24) to (26). Actually, they are still there, embedded in Y^s in the form of production of banking services, whose capitalized value equals the value of households' holdings of real balances.

As an alternative to (26), it may be recognized that the value of production can be resolved into wages, capital costs, and rents; that is,

$$(27) \qquad Y^s = \frac{w}{p} L^d + (r + \delta) K + R$$

If this is substituted in (26) the resulting expression is

$$(28) \qquad \frac{W}{p} = K + \frac{R}{r}$$

That is, real wealth is equal to the stock of capital plus the capitalized value of rents. In a competitive system, such rents arise only when the stock of capital is unequal to its long-run equilibrium value.[18] It will be assumed that whenever there is no incentive for net investment [that is, whenever (23) is satisfied], the value of rent is zero. Under such conditions total wealth is identical to the stock of capital.

Implicit in the foregoing discussion are two systems of general equilibrium. The first is the short-run system made up of (21), (22), and (26); that is,

$$
\begin{aligned}
& Y^s = C^d + I^d + r\phi_h \\
(29) \qquad & L^s = L^d \\
& \frac{W}{p} = \frac{1}{r} \left[Y^s - \frac{w}{p} L^d - \delta K \right]
\end{aligned}
$$

Its simultaneously determined variables are the real wage, the rate of interest, and real wealth. The capital stock is a parameter. The second is the long-run system made up of (21), (22), and (23), that is

$$
\begin{aligned}
& Y^s = C^d + I^d + r\phi_h \\
& L^s = L^d \\
(30) \qquad & I^d = \delta K \\
& \frac{W}{p} = K
\end{aligned}
$$

[18] In effect, this statement assumes that efficiency rents can be eliminated by imitation. Monopoly rents in industry and banking are excluded by the assumption of general competition.

Its simultaneously determined variables are the real wage, the rate of interest, and the stock of capital. Rents are assumed to be zero, and real wealth equal to the stock of capital. The second of these systems is, of course, merely a special case of the first, in which a particular constellation of the variables precludes subsequent change.

Most of the rest of this chapter concerns properties of these systems. Unless something specific is said to the contrary, it is to be understood that these equilibrium equations remain unchanged throughout the discussion. Neither technology nor behavior is subject to evolution, and both the size and the age structure of the population are constant. The method of analysis is that of comparative statics; that is, "How would some things be different if other things were different?" rather than, "How can things be expected to change?" Given the complexity of the subject matter, even this seemingly modest agenda is a full one.

Existence, Uniqueness, and Stability

Each of the systems (29) and (30) is a triplet of equations in three variables that are to be simultaneously determined. One could think of each system as consisting of three surfaces in a space of three dimensions. It is not at all obvious that the three surfaces must have a single point in common. They may have none, a few, or even an indefinitely large number. This raises the possibility that there may be no equilibrium, that there may be several at a distance from one another, or that there may be an infinity of equilibria within a small neighborhood.

The questions of existence and uniqueness of equilibrium are genuine questions.[19] If it were possible to show that no system such as (29) or (30) could have an equilibrium, the method of comparative macro statics would be put in an embarrassing position, to say the least. If it could be shown that any such system must have multiple equilibria, then asking how a given equilibrium might change when parameters change would seem trivial compared with asking how the economy came to be at that equilibrium in the first place. Obviously, one's whole attitude toward the methodology of equilibrium theory depends crucially on whether equilibria exist and are unique.

What is really at issue is whether a real economic system has at any moment a unique equilibrium. The best that can be done, however, is to examine the properties of models through which one hopes to capture the essential elements of the system which they summarize. Unfortunately, the models represented by (29) and (30) bear about as much likeness to a real economy as a one-paragraph précis might to the whole of *War and Peace*. It seems therefore idle to dwell at length on the existence and uniqueness of their equilibria. They will simply be assumed.

A related issue is that of stability.[20] Under what circumstances might a system such as (29) or (30) converge back to equilibrium once disturbed from it? Under what

---

[19] About 70 percent of the text of Arrow and Hahn (1971) is devoted to these questions.

[20] It is interesting to note from Arrow and Hahn (1971, chaps. 11–13), how restricted are the conditions under which general equilibrium theorists of the n-sector type can say anything about stability.

circumstances might it instead move cumulatively away or remain hung up at some point of disequilibrium? Evidently the degree of interest that centers on an equilibrium depends both on its stability and the rapidity of convergence. A system that is either outright unstable or in disequilibrium much of the time cannot be fruitfully studied by equilibrium methods.

Unfortunately, the stability of an equilibrium system cannot be studied merely by examination of the conditions of equilibrium. The study of stability requires the specification of three kinds of reactions missing from the equations of equilibrium exchange:

1. The reactions of households and firms to the frustrations caused by excess supply or demand in the markets in which they participate.
2. The reactions of households and firms to the fact of change.
3. The reactions of prices to the failures of markets to clear.

These may be briefly designated as the problems of disequilibrium transactions,[21] expectations formation,[22] and rates of adjustment.[23]

The problem of disequilibrium transactions is squarely faced by the Keynesians. It has been touched on in earlier chapters and will be dealt with again in the next chapter. The problem of expectation formation will also be discussed in an informal way, although it is not easy to incorporate it into the formal apparatus of Keynesian thought. The problem of rates of adjustment cannot be analyzed in a strictly competitive framework,[24] and is given scant consideration throughout this book. Thus no complete or even systematic treatment of the stability of equilibrium will be attempted. The issue will simply be bypassed.

A person might, then, ask why general equilibria whose stability (not to mention existence) is not guaranteed are nonetheless fit subjects for an entire chapter. That is a fair question. The answer lies in the commanding position occupied by equilibrium analysis in the body of economic thought. For more than a century it has been a major tool with which economists have formulated their world views and analyzed economic

---

[21] The formal literature on disequilibrium transactions has developed rapidly since the stimulating contribution of Clower (1965). Disequilibrium is the major theme of Leijonhufoud (1968), who argues that Keynes's *General Theory* ought to be interpreted as a disequilibrium analysis. A formal model incorporating disequilibrium transactions is given by Barro and Grossman (1971).

[22] It seems fair to say that economists have no well-developed theory of expectations. They have some terminology, due mainly to Hicks (1939, p. 205) and Muth (1961), and some statements about the role of expectations, such as Hart (1940) or almost any of the works of G. L. S. Shackle [see, for instance, Shackle (1949)]. The most pertinent literature is Bayesian decision theory. See Raiffa (1968), for example.

[23] A number of the most important papers on rates of adjustment may be found in Phelps (1970). See particularly the papers by Phelps, Mortensen, and Phelps and Winter. These works appear to have been substantially influenced by the earlier paper of Arrow (1959).

[24] It is hard to imagine what the mechanism for changing prices might be in an unregulated competitive market, since no individual firm in such a market could have any incentive to change its price. See Arrow (1959).

events. Its theorems, although of dubious applicability to economies that are characteristically in disequilibrium, have exercised a powerful influence over the advice that economists have given to people of affairs. It is important to understand the logical origins and limitations of these theorems, for they tend in the main to have decidedly laissez faire, conservative, and antiegalitarian implications.[25] The discussions of the next two major sections are to a considerable extent descriptions of equilibrium theory rather than of the economy itself.

II. THE ROLE OF THE NOMINAL SUPPLY OF MONEY

In the real-world economy, money serves several functions for each of its holders. In the simplified world of the theory of economic behavior under certainty, it serves only one. If the holder is a household, its getting and spending can be accomplished more conveniently with larger average money holdings than with smaller. If the holder is a firm, it can achieve more output with a given bundle of capital and labor if it holds larger average balances. In the one case, the money provides utility; in the other, it enhances productivity.

The capacity of a given money holding to serve these functions depends on how large it is relative to the prices of things bought and sold. Clearly, an economy with a large real money stock would be different in many respects from one with a small real stock. However, what the creator of the money stock controls directly is not the real stock of money but the nominal stock. A long-standing analytical question in economic thought is the extent to which this control over the nominal stock of money gives the banking system control over other variables as well. A related question of social policy concerns the desirability of alternative money stocks that the banks might supply.

This section considers these questions in a context of equilibrium markets. It has three parts. The first outlines the conditions of monetary equilibrium. The second works out the effects of changes in the level of the nominal money supply. The third explores the effects of differences in the money supply's rate of growth.

The Conditions of Monetary Equilibrium

In the section above entitled "Equilibrium in the Markets for Commodities and Labor," the nominal money supply was deliberately merged with security holdings in the transition from Equation (25) to Equation (26). It does not appear as a parameter in either the short- or long-run equilibrium system. Although the real wage, the rate of interest, and real wealth can be determined without reference to this parameter, the general level of prices, for example, cannot. In order to study the implications of changes in

---

[25] For a charming exposition of the conservatism of neoclassical economics, see Stigler (1959).

the money supply, it is necessary to examine explicitly the factors governing the composition of household assets. This requires a close look at the securities market.

The market on which securities and money change hands requires a more careful treatment than do the commodity and labor markets because of the stock-flow relations involved.[26] It is possible for the stock of money, for example, to be smaller than the stock that firms and households wish to hold. It is also possible for banks to try to create money at a rate different from that at which firms and households wish to accumulate it. The failure to distinguish one of these situations from the other can cause considerable analytical mischief.

According to the analysis of Chapter 2, households have a demand for real money that is a function of the variables that determine their consumption demand and labor supply. This has already been introduced to this chapter as Equation (16). They have a demand for real securities that is a function of the same variables. These two demands must add up to total household real wealth. If we use the symbol Δ to denote momentary excess demand (or desired change) the excess demand for nominal money is

$$(31) \qquad \Delta M_h = p\phi_h \left[\frac{w}{p}, r, \frac{W}{p} \right] - M_h$$

The households' excess demand for securities is given by

$$(32) \qquad \Delta q B_h = W - p\phi_h \left[\frac{w}{p}, r, \frac{W}{p} \right] - q B_h = -\Delta M_h$$

The first two terms in the middle express desired security holdings (in value terms); the third expresses actual holdings.

According to the analysis of Chapter 3, business firms demand money in amounts determined by the real wage, the rate of interest, and the stock of capital. Their excess demand function is written

$$(33) \qquad \Delta M_b = p\phi_b \left(\frac{w}{p}, r, K \right) - M_b$$

If firms observe the necessity of financing this money acquisition, they have a simultaneous excess supply of securities, given by

$$(34) \qquad \Delta q B_b = p\phi_b - M_b = \Delta M_b$$

Similarly, if banks have an excess demand for industrial securities,[27] they must simultaneously offer an excess supply of bank balances; that is,

$$(35) \qquad \Delta q B_{b\beta} = \Delta M$$

---

[26] Actually, whenever there exists a secondhand market for commodities, or when there exist inventories, such stock-flow complications exist in the commodity market as well. Although commodity stocks (except for productive capital) will be ignored in this book, they could be treated in a manner analogous to that used to handle money and security stocks.

[27] For the sake of simplicity, securities issued by the banks themselves are omitted from consideration here. They could be introduced in an obvious way.

Suppose it were true that the sum of the excess demands for securities on the part of households and banks just balanced the excess supply offered by firms. It would follow from (32), (34), and (35) that the sum of the excess demands for money on the part of households and firms would equal the excess supplied by banks. All excess demands could be eliminated by an exchange of pieces of paper, leaving all parties satisfied.

Notice carefully that the preceding argument says something about stocks, not about flows. It says that if households and firms are satisfied to hold the balances that banks are satisfied to supply, it must be that banks and households are satisfied to own the securities that firms are satisfied to have outstanding. It does not, for example, say that if firms like the rate at which they are issuing new securities, they are necessarily happy with the rate at which they are accumulating bank balances. A firm that is quite content with its current debt and money holdings, and quite pleased with the rate at which its outstanding debt is growing, may nonetheless view with alarm the rate at which it is losing bank balances because of a failure to sell its output.

The key to keeping things straight is to see that stocks can only be exchanged for stocks, and flows for flows.[28] The model under consideration has four goods: commodities, labor, securities, and money. The first two exist only as flows. The latter two exist as stocks. Flows of securities and money are only the rates of change of stocks.[29] If one of the two stocks has an equilbrium distribution, the other must also. This is "Walras's law" as applied to stocks.[30] There is also a Walras's law for flows, which says that if three of the four flows are in equilibrium, the fourth must be as well. That is, if the markets for goods and labor are in equilibrium, and if firms, households, and banks are content with the rates of growth of security holdings, all must be content with rates of growth of money balances.

This equality may be demonstrated with the following relationships, which are merely equations (9), (12), and (8), the conditions of consistency in the money flows of firms, households, and banks. Where appropriate, however, superscripts s or d have been added to indicate that the quantities appearing are supplies and demands rather than simply realized magnitudes.

$$(36) \qquad [p(C^s + I^s) + q(\dot{B}^s_b + \dot{B}^s_\beta)] - [wL^d + pI^d + P] = \dot{M}^d_b$$

$$(37) \qquad [wL^s + P] - [pC^d + q\dot{B}^d_h] = \dot{M}^d_h$$

$$(38) \qquad q\dot{B}^d_{b\beta} = \dot{M}^s$$

Equations (36) and (37) express each net money flow as the difference between a gross inflow of receipts and a gross outflow of expenditures. If (36) and (37) are added and (38) subtracted, the result, suitably regrouped, is

$$p[(C^s + I^s) - (C^d + I^d)] + w[L^s - L^d] + q[\dot{B}^s_b + \dot{B}^s_c - \dot{B}^d_h - \dot{B}^d_{b\beta}]$$

$$(39) \qquad\qquad\qquad\qquad = [\dot{M}^d_b + \dot{M}^d_h - \dot{M}^s]$$

---

[28] See Klein (1965) for further discussion of the importance of drawing a sharp distinction between stocks and flows. See also Appendix 11 of Patinkin (1965).

[29] Notice, however, the distinction between gross and net flows on the next page.

[30] The reference is, of course, to Walras (1877).

Each of the three expressions in a square bracket on the left is an excess supply of a flow.[31] If each of these is zero, the excess flow demand for money must also be zero. Thus equilibrium in the markets for commodities, labor, and securities implies equilibrium in the flow of money.

The Static Neutrality of Money

Now that the relationship between the demand for money and the demand for securities has been established, it is possible to examine the role of the nominal money stock in general equilibrium. The equation of balance between stock demands and the supply of real money is

$$(40) \qquad \phi_h\left(\frac{w}{p}, r, \frac{W}{p}\right) + \phi_b\left(\frac{w}{p}, r, K\right) = \frac{M}{p}$$

That is, the sum of the real amounts demanded by households and firms equals the real supply.

The demands depend on variables which are determined in system (29) or (30), and may therefore be calculated without reference to the equality of money demand and supply. The left-hand side of (40) therefore determines the right-hand side. The banking system, although it controls the nominal money supply, does not control the real supply. In effect, it controls the price level. But because of the assumed zero-degree homogeneity of demand and supplies in the markets for commodities and labor,[32] this control over the price level provides no lever on the real magnitudes of the system.

How can this be? Consider the following story, which is only illustrative and not intended to be a serious account of a dynamic process. Suppose that the banks were to increase the nominal money supply by buying industrial securities. This would raise their prices, lowering yields. At a lower rate of interest, there would be excess demand for commodities, and prices would rise. The resulting decline in real wages would spread the inflationary pressure to the labor market. Market equilibrium could only be restored by an all-around rise in the price level, the wage rate, and the value of securities sufficient to restore their initial ratio to the nominal money supply.

This proposition, which is usually called the "neutrality of money," is merely a statement about alternative states of a given equilibrium.[33] As such, it sheds little light on the consequences of monetary changes in a functioning economy. It might more properly be called the "static neutrality of money." Nonetheless, it has had an important impact on the development of economic thought. If it were in fact applicable to real economies, it would justify a divorce between monetary theory and value theory. It seems possible that widespread and uncritical belief in the neutrality of money has

---

[31] Compare them with equations (3), (4), and (5) above.

[32] Since each nominal magnitude in either (29) or (30) appears only in ratio to some other nominal magnitude (i.e., w, p, and W appear only as w/p and W/p), then if each is multiplied by a common positive magnitude, the equalities in which they appear are unaffected.

[33] The neutrality proposition is an old one. Patinkin (1965, Note I) traces it back as far as McCulloch (1849).

in part been responsible for the split of economics into macro and micro compartments.[34] If so, it is a pernicious theorem indeed.

There is a companion theorem, valid in the same context as is neutrality, that states that wealth holders themselves may control the real stock of money, even though they have no control over the nominal stock. Suppose, for example, that households were to decide to hold smaller real balances at given values of the real wage, the rate of interest, and real wealth. Suppose further that they were to expand their demand for consumption goods so as to spend the increased interest implied by the switch from money into securities. Resources would have to be shifted from banking to commodity production, but the overall balance of demand and supply in the goods market would not be affected. Neither, therefore, would the equilibrium values of the wage, the interest rate, and wealth. Only the balance of demand for and supply of money and securities would be affected. In effect, consumers would be acting like the banks in the previous anecdote, spontaneously offering money in exchange for securities. Balance in all markets could only be restored by an all-around rise in the price level and the wage rate, with an even greater rise in the nominal value of securities held by households. The latter could be achieved if, for example, the banking system were to hold fixed-value debt of businesses, whose value would shrink along with the real money supply as the price level rose. This would imply a greater than proportionate rise in the value of the shares of those firms whose debt was held by the banks, in effect shifting security ownership from banks to households.[35] The expansion of their real security holdings would just match the reduction in their real balances brought about by the inflation and the inflation-induced shift in nominal balances from households to firms. Thus households would reduce the real money supply despite the banking system's preservation of the nominal supply.

This proposition, together with the neutrality proposition, paints an attractive picture of a monetary system that responds to people's wants but exercises no active control over their real well-being. It contrasts sharply with the Keynesian view, in which under some circumstances the banking system has great power to influence the course of events through its acts of commission and omission. It contrasts even more sharply with the so-called monetarist position that, in the short run at least, monetary shifts are a major source of instability in income and employment.[36]

Inflation and the Neutrality of Money[37]

Thus far the discussion of money and equilibrium has concerned alternative stocks of money at points in time. However, equilibrium analysis has a time dimension. The

---

[34] So strong is the tradition of the "dichotomy" between money and real economics that Joan Robinson (1933), writing in the middle of the Great Depression, called Keynes to task for failing to draw a clear distinction between the theory of money and the theory of output.

[35] There is also an implied redistribution of real wealth from bank shareholders to holders of other securities.

[36] The monetarist school centers around the doctrines of Milton Friedman. See Friedman and Schwartz (1963), Friedman and Meiselman (1963), and Friedman (1968a).

[37] Much of this section reflects Friedman (1968a).

system of short-run equilibrium described by (29) implicitly evolves as a consequence of capital accumulation. As this accumulation nibbles away the rents that induce it, the short-run system comes to rest at a position described by (30). Such is the logical upshot of the model.

It is possible to imagine any of a number of monetary histories accompanying this evolution. It is interesting to inquire whether the monetary history exercises any influence over the real history. Since this inquiry parallels so closely that regarding the static relationship between money and real variables, it seems natural to call it the question of the dynamic neutrality of money.

Picture a system that is always subject to the conditions of short-run equilibrium. Over time the stock of capital changes, and along with it the wage, the interest rate, and wealth. The demand for real money also changes. Let ϕ denote the sum of household and business demands for money. That is,

$$(41) \qquad \phi \equiv \phi_h\left(\frac{w}{p}, r, \frac{W}{p}\right) + \phi_b\left(\frac{w}{p}, r, K\right)$$

Throughout, equality is maintained between the demand for and supply of real balances. This implies that the rate of growth of real money demanded just equals the rate of growth of the nominal money supply less the rate of growth of the price level.

The rate of growth of the money supply is controlled by the banking system. The rate of growth of real demand is governed by the evolution of the real variables. Together they govern an implied rate of inflation that will maintain an equilibrium distribution of assets. It is given by

$$(42) \qquad \rho \equiv \frac{\dot{p}}{p} = \frac{\dot{M}}{M} - \frac{\dot{\phi}}{\phi}$$

Evidently there is some monetary history that will keep ρ always equal to zero. If the system is always in long-run equilibrium, a constant money supply is required, but if the system is evolving, the money supply must evolve with it. Equally evidently, for any given value of ρ, there is a monetary history that will make it possible. Put the other way around, there is a family of monetary histories each of which corresponds to a constant value for ρ. The question of dynamic neutrality is this: does the choice of ρ affect any feature of the system other than the rate of inflation itself?

The immediate answer would be no. Since all real demands and supplies depend only upon ratios of nominal magnitudes, it would not matter whether the numerators and denominators were growing rapidly or slowly, just so long as they were growing at the same rate.

This conclusion, although logically sound, contains an implicit piece of foolishness. It is hard to imagine that the participants in an economic system can perceive steady inflation over an extended period without coming to expect it to continue.[38] If the perceived rate is zero, no problems are created. If it is different from zero, how-

---

[38]Miller and Upton (1974) refer to this as "Lincoln's Law," after Abraham Lincoln, who is believed to have said that "you can't fool all of the people all of the time."

ever, there are really two rates of interest, the real rate and the nominal, or money, rate. The real rate constitutes the terms of trade between present and future goods, the nominal rate between present and future money. The relationship between the two is simple. If securities yield a nominal rate of, say, 10 percent and the rate of inflation is 4 percent, then the real yield on securities is only 6 percent.

The relevant rate of interest for saving and investment decisions is the real rate, but the relevant rate for portfolio decisions is the money rate. A decision to shift a unit of wealth from securities to money implies not only giving up a real yield of 6 percent, but also accepting an erosion of real capital value at the rate of 4 percent. Hence the opportunity cost of holding money is the money rate.

Similarly, the money rate is relevant for figuring the cost of money as an agent of production. If a firm sells new securities, it issues a claim against the income of its present shareholders. This claim has a yield equal to the real rate. If it uses the proceeds in money form, it subjects them to a rate of capital loss equal to the rate of inflation. Physical capital shares in the inflation; its cost is the real rate. Money does not, so its cost is the money rate.

Given the potential dependence of each sector's demands and supplies on the entire set of prices tying them together, it is hard to escape the conclusion that ρ ought to be an argument in each of the demand and supply functions appearing in (29) or (30). Through its control over the rate of inflation, the banking system exercises an influence on the entire set of real variables. In a dynamic sense, therefore, money is not neutral.

In seeming paradox, it remains neutral in the static sense. What influences the real variables is the rate of growth of the money supply, not its level. If two otherwise identical economies have equal rates of monetary growth but different levels of the money supply, the one with the bigger money supply will have a higher price level, but both will have the same real variables and the same rate of inflation.

Even this restricted version requires qualification. Implicit in the structure of the general equilibrium model under consideration is a structure of financial obligations in which every claim to property income is an obligation of some person or firm in the system. Because the structure of claims is closed, changes in the price level cannot create or destroy wealth; they can only redistribute it.[39] However, if members of a system have assets or liabilities denominated in terms of nominal money and representing claims on or obligations to agents outside the system, then even the static neutrality of money is invalidated.[40] Changes in the price level, because they change the real value of "outside" wealth or debt, must affect all the real variables of the system. The wealth effects of price changes will be discussed at greater length in Chapter 9, which analyzes, among other matters, the significance of government debt.

Finally, it must be recalled that neutrality is only an equilibrium property at best.

In its strict sense, therefore, the doctrine of the neutrality of money is so limited

---

[39]For reasons akin to those causing the aggregation problem, even these redistributions interfere to some extent with neutrality. However, they are usually dismissed as being of second order of magnitude.

[40]See Modigliani (1963, pp. 83–88).

in application as to be mainly an analytical curiosity and a relic from the history of thought. In a weakened version, however, it is one doctrine of the monetarist school of contemporary thinking on business fluctuations. This school holds that unanticipated changes in the money supply are a major source of disequilibrium fluctuations in output and employment. Such fluctuations arise in large part from ill-timed attempts on the part of the monetary authority to control real variables. If the monetary authority would only maintain a "stable monetary environment," then disequilibria that stem from real disturbances would be reversed by the inherent stability mechanisms of the system rather than aggravated by clumsy attempts at monetary control.[41] A stable environment could be achieved by steady monetary expansion, such as might be consistent with a ready rate of inflation, fully anticipated by all. In such an environment money would be neutral save for the "distortion" introduced by an inappropriate rate of increase in the price level.[42] Even this nonneutrality could be eliminated by choosing a rate of growth of the money supply whose implied rate of inflation kept the rate of substitution between money and other goods in consumption equal to the rate of transformation in production.[43] In the context of the production assumptions made in this chapter, such equality could only be achieved by price stability.

Thus the extent to which neutrality is a live doctrine comes from its association with monetarism. As such, it is part of a body of thought that emphasizes the ability of the market system to evolve and to adjust to disturbances if only it is left to its own devices. Neutrality in monetarist doctrine is prescriptive rather than descriptive. Whether it is a useful prescription depends in large measure on the same factors that determine the usefulness of equilibrium analysis. This is a topic that will be discussed further in the next chapter.

III. THE DISTRIBUTION OF INCOME

The remainder of this chapter is devoted to a discussion of income distribution in short- and long-run equilibrium, one of the most value-laden portions of general equilibrium theory. It is organized around a discussion of three questions. First, what are the effects on wages and the return to capital of the accumulation that takes place during temporary equilibrium? Second, what sort of distribution characterizes long-period equilibrium? Third, if long-period equilibrium is disturbed by changes in the productivity of capital or the willingness of households to save, what will be the immediate and long-run impacts on distribution? To anyone who believes in the usefulness of equilibrium analysis, the answers to these questions provide an assessment of the harmony or conflict of interest between capitalists and people who depend mainly on wages for their livelihood.

---

[41] See Friedman (1959a, 1968a).

[42] The monetarists seem in the main to believe that the government debt is not outside wealth because of the tax obligation necessary to service it.

[43] See Friedman (1969).

The Effects of Accumulation[44]

Turn now to the first question. What are the effects on wages and the return to capital of the accumulation of capital by firms or its alter ego, the saving of households?

The answer to this question can be obtained by studying the comparative static properties of system (29), which states conditions for equilibria in the markets for goods and labor and in the valuation of wealth. Since this is a system with three dependent variables (the real wage, the rate of interest, and real wealth) and one independent variable (the capital stock), it cannot conveniently be studied by graphical methods. Instead, it is necessary to develop at some length the properties of the total differentials of the relations of (29).

To do so it is most convenient to rewrite them as excess demand functions for commodities, labor, and income from property, that is

$$(43) \quad X^c = I\left(\frac{w}{p}, r, K\right) + C\left(\frac{w}{p}, r, \frac{W}{p}\right) + r\phi_h\left(\frac{w}{p}, r, \frac{W}{p}\right) - Y^s\left(\frac{w}{p}, r, K\right) = 0$$

$$(44) \quad X^L = L^d\left(\frac{w}{p}, r, K\right) - L^s\left(\frac{w}{p}, r, \frac{W}{p}\right) = 0$$

$$(45) \quad X^P = r\frac{W}{p} - \left[Y^s\left(\frac{w}{p}, r, K\right) - \frac{w}{p}L^d\left(\frac{w}{p}, r, K\right) - \delta K\right] = 0$$

An alternative version of (45) making its meaning somewhat clearer is

$$(46) \quad \frac{X^P}{r} = \left(\frac{W}{p} - \phi_h\right) - \frac{1}{r}\left(Y^s - r\phi_h - \frac{w}{p}L^d - \delta K\right)$$

That is, the capitalized excess demand for property income equals the difference between the demand for securities and the supply of capitalized profits.

To calculate total derivatives of wages, interest, and wealth with respect to capital, all partial derivatives of (43), (44), and (45) must be examined.[45]

The derivatives of (43) are

$$(47) \quad \frac{\partial X^c}{\partial w/p} = \frac{\partial I}{\partial w/p} + \frac{\partial C}{\partial w/p} + r\frac{\partial \phi_h}{\partial w/p} - \frac{\partial Y^s}{\partial w/p}$$

$$(48) \quad \frac{\partial X^c}{\partial r} = \frac{\partial I}{\partial r} + \frac{\partial C}{\partial r} + r\frac{\partial \phi_h}{\partial r} + \phi_h - \frac{\partial Y^s}{\partial r}$$

$$(49) \quad \frac{\partial X^c}{\partial W/p} = \frac{\partial C}{\partial W/p} + r\frac{\partial \phi_h}{\partial W/p}$$

---

[44]This section owes much in spirit, if not in detail, to the work of Clark (1899) and Wicksell (1913, esp. vol. I, parts II and III).

[45]The ensuing discussion will be easier to follow if the reader reviews the conclusions at the ends of Chapters 2 and 3.

$$(50) \qquad \frac{\partial X^c}{\partial K} = \frac{\partial I}{\partial K} - \frac{\partial Y^s}{\partial K}$$

The first of these, (47), is surely positive; a rise in wages raises demand and reduces supply. The second, (48), is more complicated. The first term is negative, the last term negligible. The middle three terms measure the effects of interest changes on the total demand for consumption goods and banking services. Since the atemporal substitutions cancel out, what remains are the conflicting income and intertemporal substitution effects. It seems plausible to assume that the positive income effect does not outweigh the negative substitution effect enough to cancel the effect of interest on investment. This amounts to assuming that the whole of (48) is negative. Finally, (49) is clearly positive and (50) negative.

Turn now to the derivatives of (44)

$$(51) \qquad \frac{\partial X^L}{\partial w/p} = \frac{\partial L^d}{\partial w/p} - \frac{\partial L^s}{\partial w/p}$$

$$(52) \qquad \frac{\partial X^L}{\partial r} = \frac{\partial L^d}{\partial r} - \frac{\partial L^s}{\partial r}$$

$$(53) \qquad \frac{\partial X^L}{\partial W/p} = - \frac{\partial L^s}{\partial W/p}$$

$$(54) \qquad \frac{\partial X^L}{\partial K} = \frac{\partial L^d}{\partial K}$$

Because of the income effects on labor supply, there is some ambiguity about (51). However, if the whole expression were positive, the labor market would be unstable.[46] Therefore the assumption of stability reinforces the natural presumption that a rise in wages reduces excess demand. The signs of both terms in (52) are ambiguous. In any case, the direct influence of interest on the labor market is surely negligible. There is no ambiguity in (53) and (54), which are both positive.

The derivatives of (45) are

$$(55) \qquad \frac{\partial X^P}{\partial w/p} = - \frac{\partial Y^s}{\partial w/p} + \frac{w}{p} \frac{\partial L^d}{\partial w/p} + L^d$$

$$(56) \qquad \frac{\partial X^P}{\partial r} = \frac{W}{p} - \frac{\partial Y^s}{\partial r} + \frac{w}{p} \frac{\partial L^d}{\partial r}$$

$$(57) \qquad \frac{\partial X^P}{\partial W/p} = r$$

[46]The proposition that an assumption of stability may be used to deduce comparative results is known as the "correspondence principle" and is due to Samuelson (1947, part II).

$$(58) \qquad \frac{\partial X^p}{\partial K} = -\frac{\partial Y^s}{\partial K} + \frac{w}{p}\frac{\partial L^d}{\partial K} + \delta$$

The first of these, (55), is surely positive. A rise in wages, capital held constant, must reduce profit or increase its negative. Since all the terms in (56) are positive (although the last two are small), it is unambiguous. Likewise (57) is clearly positive. At first glance (58) seems ambiguous, but it is not. Surely accumulation would not take place unless it raised profit at constant real factor prices. Therefore (58) must be negative under the circumstances being studied here.

This analysis provides the raw material for studying the properties of the system (43)–(45), which in differential form is written

$$(59) \qquad \begin{bmatrix} \dfrac{\partial X^c}{\partial w/p} & \dfrac{\partial X^c}{\partial r} & \dfrac{\partial X^c}{\partial W/p} \\[2mm] \dfrac{\partial X^L}{\partial w/p} & \dfrac{\partial X^L}{\partial r} & \dfrac{\partial X^L}{\partial W/p} \\[2mm] \dfrac{\partial X^p}{\partial w/p} & \dfrac{\partial X^p}{\partial r} & \dfrac{\partial X^p}{\partial W/p} \end{bmatrix} \begin{bmatrix} d\dfrac{w}{p} \\[2mm] dr \\[2mm] d\dfrac{W}{p} \end{bmatrix} = \begin{bmatrix} -\dfrac{\partial X^c}{\partial K} \\[2mm] -\dfrac{\partial X^L}{\partial K} \\[2mm] -\dfrac{\partial X^p}{\partial K} \end{bmatrix} dK$$

If we refer to the previous paragraphs, the signs of the coefficients are given by[47]

$$(60) \qquad \begin{bmatrix} + & - & + \\ - & 0 & + \\ + & + & + \end{bmatrix} \begin{bmatrix} d\dfrac{w}{p} \\[2mm] dr \\[2mm] d\dfrac{W}{p} \end{bmatrix} = \begin{bmatrix} + \\ - \\ + \end{bmatrix} dK$$

From the pattern of signs alone, it can be verified that the derivative of the wage with respect to the capital stock is necessarily positive. However, the other two derivatives are ambiguous as to sign unless the magnitudes of the various partial derivatives are known.[48]

When a complicated model produces puzzling results, it is often best to track down their source by looking at a simpler model. Consider therefore an economy without money, which uses commodities as its unit of account (so that $p = 1$). All wealth is held in the form of claims to future commodities. The conditions of equilibrium are

$$(61) \qquad Y^s(w, K) = C(w, r, W) + I(r, K)$$

$$(62) \qquad L^s(w) = L^d(w, K)$$

$$(63) \qquad W = \frac{Y^s(w, K) - wL^d(w, K) - \delta K}{r}$$

[47]In this context, the symbol "0" means "negligible," not literally zero.
[48]These conclusions are most easily reached by applying Cramer's rule to the solution of (60).

Owing to the assumed simplicity of the labor market, the real wage is uniquely determined by the capital stock. Together these two variables determine the numerator on
the right side of (63). However, there are many combinations of r and W consistent
with a given profit flow. These are indicated by the curve PP′ in Figure 5-2. Given K
and w, the combinations of r and W consistent with commodity market equilibrium
are given by the curve CC′. General equilibrium is at α.

The structure of forces determining this equilibrium is best grasped by noting
what might happen if the equilibrium conditions were not satisfied. Again, the tale is
only illustrative and is not intended as a serious dynamic analysis.

Suppose that the interest rate were as high as that indicated at point β. What
mechanism could cause it to fall? To see the answer, notice that the region above CC′
is the region in which the supply of commodities exceeds the demand. If supply exceeds demand, the sum of incomes received in producing the supply exceeds the sum
of consumption and investment. This implies that saving exceeds investment, and that
the demand for additional claims to future commodities (saving) exceeds the supply of
such claims (investment). If this is the case, then the price of future commodities in
terms of present commodities must rise; that is, the interest rate must fall until demand
and production are equal.

A rise in the capital stock raises the demand for labor, if we assume that labor and
capital are cooperating factors. This must result in a rise in the real wage if the labor
market is to clear. The combined influences of the increases in w and K produce an
ambiguous influence on property income, the numerator of the right-hand side of
(63). Capital accumulation presumably takes place when it seems likely to benefit
capitalists. However, an unforeseen effect of this accumulation is a rise in wages. Thus
property income may rise or fall as a consequence of accumulation that is designed to
raise it. This being the case, PP′ may shift either to the right or the left as a consequence of an increase in K.

As if this were not ambiguity enough, the effect of accumulation on CC′ is also
indeterminate. The direct impact of accumulation is to create excess supply. The indirect effect through wages is to create excess demand. The direction of shift depends
on the balance of these influences.

The impact of accumulation on wages is clear-cut. However, no conclusion regarding the impact on wealth or the rate of interest can be reached on the basis of qualitative information alone.

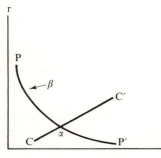

Figure 5-2 The determination of the rate of interest.

The simple system described by (61)-(63) differs from the more complicated system described by (29) in only one essential respect: the implied mechanisms of adjustment to disequilbrium. In the simple system, there is only one form in which households can hold wealth. There cannot therefore be any excess supplies of or demands for assets of the sort described on pages 105-106. The interest rate must be determined solely by the interaction between intended saving and intended investment. However, the process is much more complex in an economy with a monetary alternative to securities as a way in which to hold wealth.

Picture a system much like that just discussed, except that households hold a portion of their wealth in the form of money, which also provides the unit of account. Firms hold no money, so that the entire supply is owned by households. The equations of general equilibrium for this system may be written

$$(64) \qquad X^C\left(\frac{w}{p}, r, \frac{W}{p}, K\right) = 0$$

$$(65) \qquad X^L\left(\frac{w}{p}, K\right) = 0$$

$$(66) \qquad \psi\left(r, \frac{W}{p}\right) = \frac{Y^s(w/p, K) - rM/p - (w/p)L^d(w/p, K) - \delta K}{r}$$

$$(67) \qquad \phi\left(r, \frac{W}{p}\right) = \frac{M}{p}$$

$$(68) \qquad \frac{W}{p} = \frac{Y^s - (w/p)L^d - \delta K}{r}$$

As before, the capital stock together with the condition of labor market equilibrium determines the real wage. The wage and capital stock again determine the combinations of real wealth and the interest rate consistent with (68). Other combinations are consistent with (64), and Figure 5-2 may again be used to locate the general equilibrium. Equations (66) and (67) are superfluous with respect to the determination of the real wage, the rate of interest, and wealth.

They are crucial for understanding the process of adjustment, however. Suppose that the system were in equilibrium so the (64)-(68) were all satisfied. Suppose further that households' preferences changed so that the demand for securities (ψ) increased and the demand for money (ϕ) diminished. At unchanged values of the arguments of (66) and (67) and an unchanged real money supply, there would be an excess demand for a stock of securities and an excess supply of a stock of money. At unchanged profit income, the price of securities would rise, and the interest rate would fall. At unchanged commodity prices, real wealth would increase. The fall in interest and the rise in wealth would have to proceed to the point at which the demands for and supplies of the two assets matched one another.

The implied rise in wealth and drop in the interest rate would produce an excess demand for commodities. However, this excess demand could not exert any direct influence on the interest rate, which in a monetary economy is ruled by the conditions of stock equilibrium. If (66) and (67) were not satisfied, the implied stock disequilibria would translate into enormous flows per time period, utterly swamping any discrepancy between saving and investment. In a general equilibrium system incorporating money, the balance of supply and demand for commodities must act on the price of commodities in terms of money. In the case at hand, the excess demand would drive up prices. Higher prices would create excess demand for labor and higher money wages. The resulting destruction of real money would feed back on the securities market, requiring further adjustments. Ultimately the wage, the interest rate, and wealth would have to be restored to their original values, but enough real money would have to be destroyed through inflation to accommodate the change in preferences.

With this sort of adjustment mechanism in mind, turn now to the impact of an increase in the stock of capital. As before, the direct impact on the labor market would raise the money and real wages. The change in property income would influence security values and disturb the balance of supply and demand in the asset market. At an unchanged level of commodity prices, equilibrium in the asset market would require a definite adjustment in the interest rate and a definite change in wealth. However, the new interest rate and wealth would not in all likelihood be consistent with commodity market equilibrium at the new wage and capital stock. The resulting change in commodity prices would feed back onto the asset market through a change in the real money stock necessitating further changes in wealth and the interest rate. The only firm conclusion regarding the upshot of this process is that the real wage must rise as the consequence of accumulation. All else is ambiguous. Accumulation may raise or lower the interest rate. It might even lower wealth if it has too adverse an impact on rents.

The positive relationship between the capital stock and the real wage stems, ultimately, from the assumption that capital and labor are cooperating factors. If the sign of the derivative of excess labor demand with respect to capital is reversed in (60), the derivative of the wage with respect to capital becomes ambiguous. In the simpler systems made up of (61)-(63) or (64)-(68), in which wealth effects on the labor supply are absent, an increase in the capital stock clearly lowers wages. In all three systems a higher capital stock implies higher real wealth. Evidently the assumption that capital and labor are cooperating factors is a very powerful one.

It is hard to know whether the widespread belief that cross partial derivatives of production functions are positive[49] stems from careful analysis or merely excessive preoccupation with two-factor, constant-returns production functions. Consider a two-factor function, with both factors expressed as positive multiples of a single positive parameter λ. That is, let

(69) $$Q = F(K, L) = F(\alpha\lambda, \beta\lambda)$$

If this function is twice differentiated with respect to λ, the result is

(70) $$\frac{d^2Q}{d\lambda^2} = \alpha^2 F_{11} + 2\alpha\beta F_{12} + \beta^2 F_{22}$$

---

[49] Rader (1972, p. 99) refers to the positivity of the cross partial as "Wicksell's Law." Wicksell himself (1913) seems to enunciate his law on page 157 of vol. 1, but clearly recognizes on page 183 the special circumstances under which it holds.

The value zero for this derivative marks the dividing line between increasing and decreasing returns to scale. If the returns are increasing or constant (corresponding to a nonnegative value of $d^2Q/d\lambda^2$, the fact that α and β are necessarily positive and F_{11} and F_{22} negative implies that F_{12} must be positive. If, however, returns to scale are diminishing, then F_{12} may be negative. Furthermore, if there are more than two factors, it is not necessary that every cross partial be positive in the case of nondiminishing returns, only that at least one be.

Whatever the source of the belief that capital and labor are cooperating factors, it is clear that it implies a substantial harmony of interest between wage earners and the owners of capital. Savers and investors who attempt to enrich themselves by accumulating capital are the benefactors of wage workers, although they may lower both their own wealth and its yield in the process. This is one of the major conservative lessons of equilibrium economics. It argues against efforts to equalize the distribution of wealth and income on the ground that such efforts are shortsighted.

The Rate of Interest in the Stationary State

The previous discussion took place against a backdrop whose features—population, technology, and behavior—were assumed to be stationary. This was done in order to focus on the forces of motion inherent in the system rather than those imposed upon it by a changing environment. The only agent of change was the accumulation of capital. This section focuses on the properties that the equilibrium system has when even this source of change is absent.

The long-run equilibrium system is characterized by equilibrium in the goods and labor markets and by a zero rate of net investment. In addition, rents are assumed to be zero when net investment is zero. The system (30), which is reproduced here, summarizes these conditions

$$
\begin{aligned}
Y^s &= C^d + I^d + r\phi_h \\
L^s &= L^d \\
I^d &= \delta K \\
\frac{W}{p} &= K
\end{aligned}
$$

(30)

For the purpose at hand, the first equation is not particularly convenient to work with. Rather, it must be reorganized into an equivalent but more tractable condition. The first change is to lump the consumption of banking services in with the consumption of goods, using the symbol C to denote their total. The second change is to multiply the condition of labor market equilibrium by the real wage and add it to the first equation. The third is to use the third equation to eliminate I from the first, replacing it by δK. The result of these operations is

(71)
$$
\left[Y^s - \frac{w}{p} L^d - \delta K \right] + \frac{w}{p} L^s - C^d = 0
$$

The fourth step is to notice that the bracketed portion in (71) is simply profit, which equals rK when rents are zero. The final step is to notice that the whole left side of (71) is household income less consumption; that is, household saving. The conditions of equilibrium in the goods and labor markets, zero net investment, and zero rents imply that household saving must be zero.[50]

The entire system may then be rewritten as

$$(72) \qquad S \equiv rK + \frac{w}{p} L^s\left(\frac{w}{p}, r, K\right) - C\left(\frac{w}{p}, r, K\right) = 0$$

$$(73) \qquad X^L \equiv L^d\left(\frac{w}{p}, r, K\right) - L^s\left(\frac{w}{p}, r, K\right) = 0$$

$$(74) \qquad I^N \equiv I\left(\frac{w}{p}, r, K\right) - \delta K = 0$$

which is in a convenient form for analysis.

Long-run equilibrium, or the stationary state, is mainly used as a methodological device, although from time to time major figures in the development of thought have viewed the stationary state as an asymptotic state of a real economic system.[51] As a device, it is mainly used to separate the general features of an economy from the special features that are products of change. A traditional question of this kind is whether the rate of interest is necessarily zero in the absence of growth.[52] Interest has often been thought of as the reward for saving, or "abstention." It is at least superficially plausible that accumulation might continue so long as this reward is positive.

In order to determine whether interest is a feature peculiar to growth, it is necessary to examine the properties of combination of geometrical and analytical means. Equation (72) is the least familiar of the three, and its properties require the most careful analysis to uncover. The partial derivatives, written in an artful way, are

$$(75) \qquad \frac{\partial S}{\partial w/p} = L^s - \left[\frac{\partial C}{\partial w/p} - \frac{w}{p} \frac{\partial L^s}{\partial w/p}\right]$$

[50]Recall the assumption that firms retain exactly enough income to balance depreciation. If some other assumption had been made, the equilibrium condition for household saving would be that it must just match the borrowing necessary to cover the excess of depreciation over retained income. If this borrowing were positive, households would sustain a steady capital loss on seasoned securities just matching the flow of new issues, leaving their real wealth intact. The saving out of distributed income would necessarily equal the implicit dissaving through a decline in capital values.

[51]The most famous such view is that of Ricardo (1821, Chap. VI), but there are numerous more modern instances.

[52]The work on which much of the rest of this section is based is that of Pigou (1935, 1943). See also Cassel (1903).

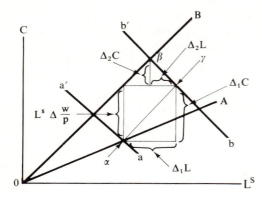

Figure 5-3 Effects of a wage change on saving.

(76)
$$\frac{\partial S}{\partial r} = K - \left[\frac{\partial C}{\partial r} - \frac{w}{p}\frac{\partial L^s}{\partial r}\right]$$

(77)
$$\frac{\partial S}{\partial K} = r - \left[\frac{\partial C}{\partial K} - \frac{w}{p}\frac{\partial L^s}{\partial K}\right]$$

The first term of each of these measures a lump-sum addition to saving arising out of a change in the variable with respect to which differentiation has taken place. The two terms in brackets measure the influence of the variable of differentiation on the excess of consumption over wage income.

The bracketed derivates in Equation (75) contain both substitution and income effects. They are most easily examined with the aid of a diagram, Figure 5-3.[53] Consider the typical household in the stationary state, which is doing no saving and is therefore located at a point α on budget line OA and expansion path a'a. The Slutsky substitution effects of a rise in the real wage lead it to move to point γ on the higher-wage budget line passing through α, increasing its consumption by $\Delta_1 C$ and its labor supply by $\Delta_1 L$. To this must be added the income effects, which will involve moving out on expansion path b'b passing through γ. The ultimate position might be β, on a new budget line OB passing through the origin and maintaining zero saving, so that

$$L^s\Delta\frac{w}{p} - \left\{(\Delta_1 C + \Delta_2 C) - \frac{w}{p}(\Delta_1 L + \Delta_2 L)\right\} = 0$$

The combined income and substitution effects in the bracketed portion of (75) could just cancel out the first term, leaving saving unaffected by the wage change.

Nothing in this argument hinges on the initial position's being one of zero saving. The entire bird's nest of lines in Figure 5-3 could be given a constant vertical displacement relative to the axes without disturbing its consistency with consumption theory.

[53]The reader who needs to refresh his or her memory about this sort of a diagram should refer to Chapter 2, pp. 18-19.

It is therefore possible that no one in the age distribution of households, whether a saver or a dissaver, should change its saving in response to a rise in wages. Moreover, it is also possible that in every period following a wage change, each household's saving should be exactly what it would have been if wages had not changed. This would be consistent with the lifetime budget constraint and, at least to a first approximation, would maintain intertemporal optimality.

There is, of course, no necessity that things work out this way.[54] Two major influences,[55] retirement and bequests, militate in favor of a positive relationship between wages and saving. The marginal conditions of intertemporal optimality call for some portion of the benefits of a wage increase to be carried over to retirement consumption and a bequest, if any is planned. Because of these influences, it seems best to conclude that (75) should be positive.

Turn now to (76). By an argument similar to that just completed, it is possible to establish that the income and static substitution effects in the parenthetical expression might just counterbalance the rise in profit income coming from a rise in the rate of return, K held constant. However, there still exist intertemporal substitutions to contend with. These reduce consumption and increase work effort. Therefore (76) is positive.

Equation (77) expresses the dependence of saving on a lump-sum wealth transfer. The expression in brackets is positive, since an increase in wealth must raise consumption and lower labor supply. Moreover, it must be larger than r over a dominant portion of the life cycle unless the wealth elasticity of bequests is extraordinarily high.[56] This being the case, it must be larger than r over a dominant portion of the age distribution of a stationary population and (77) must therefore be negative.[57]

[54] The substitution effects must always balance out, since

$$\lim_{\Delta \frac{w}{p} \to 0} \frac{\Delta_1 C}{\Delta_1 L} = \frac{w}{p}$$

[55] There can also be minor influences stemming from peculiarities in the prevalent pattern of time preference.

[56] To see what is involved here, consider a middle-aged household with no retirement plans, expecting a steady wage income over the remaining 25 years of its life. Suppose its wages comprise 75 percent of its income and property income the remaining 25 percent. Thus its property comprises only a little more than 25 percent of its total resources (the figure would be exactly 25 if the working life were not finite). If its property were suddenly to double, the resources at its disposal would therefore increase by about 25 percent. Assuming that its initial saving was close to zero, about a 14 percent increase in consumption and a 14 percent reduction in work effort would keep saving unchanged. If it continued this kind of reaction over the rest of its life span, just maintaining the saving it had initially planned, then the whole of the windfall would be carried over as a bequest. This would imply a wealth elasticity of bequests of about four, as compared with the assumed elasticities of consumption and labor supply of only a little over a half.

[57] In any case, it must be negative for sufficiently small r, regardless of the wealth elasticity of bequests.

The derivatives of (73) are all more or less familiar from the previous section of this chapter. They are

$$(78) \qquad \frac{\partial X^L}{\partial w/p} = \frac{\partial L^d}{\partial w/p} - \frac{\partial L^s}{\partial w/p}$$

$$(79) \qquad \frac{\partial X^L}{\partial r} = \frac{\partial L^d}{\partial r} - \frac{\partial L^s}{\partial r}$$

$$(80) \qquad \frac{\partial X^L}{\partial K} = \frac{\partial L^d}{\partial K} - \frac{\partial L^s}{\partial K}$$

and are respectively negative, negligible, and positive. The derivatives of (74) are

$$(81) \qquad \frac{\partial I^N}{\partial w/p} = \frac{\partial I}{\partial w/p}$$

$$(82) \qquad \frac{\partial I^N}{\partial r} = \frac{\partial I}{\partial r}$$

$$(83) \qquad \frac{\partial I^N}{\partial K} = \frac{\partial I}{\partial K} - \delta$$

If we appeal again to previous results, they are respectively small (but negative if capital and labor are cooperating factors), negative, and negative.

The fact that the rate of interest is not very important to the labor market expedites the remaining analysis. From the signs of (78) and (80), wages and the capital stock must move in the same direction to maintain labor market equilibrium.[58] This result may be used to eliminate wage variations from the conditions of zero saving and investment, (72) and (74), leading to the relationships

$$(84) \qquad \frac{\partial S}{\partial r}dr + \left[\frac{\partial S}{\partial K} + \frac{\partial S}{\partial w/p} \cdot \frac{dw/p}{dK} \right] dK = 0$$

$$(85) \qquad \frac{\partial I^N}{\partial r}dr + \left[\frac{\partial I^N}{\partial K} + \frac{\partial I^N}{\partial w/p} \cdot \frac{dw/p}{dK} \right] dK = 0$$

If $d(w/p)/dK$ were zero, the locus of K, r combinations producing a zero saving rate would slope upward and that producing a zero investment rate would slope downward. The effect of the capital-wage relationship is to flatten the saving locus and make the investment locus steeper. The possibility that they might cross the wrong way will be ignored.

The factor rewards in long-period equilibrium may now be studied with the aid of a diagram. In Figure 5–4 the top panel shows the combinations of K and r at which (84) and (85) are satisfied. The bottom panel gives the combinations of K and w/p

---

[58]Recall that in the current context, there is no possibility that wealth and the capital stock might move in opposite directions.

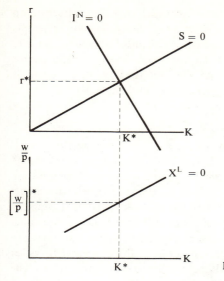

Figure 5-4 Factor returns in long-run equilibrium.

that clear the labor market. At the indicated general equilibrium, the interest rate is positive.

Two tacit assumptions ensure this result:

1. Capital will produce a positive return if there is a sufficiently small stock of it.
2. At a zero rate of interest, households will not want to hold any substantial wealth.

The first of these is plausible enough. The second requires some discussion.

Suppose that all households expected a constant lifetime wage, had zero time preference, and planned neither to retire nor to leave a bequest. Then each would exactly consume its wages at a zero interest rate, and none would ever hold any wealth. At a positive interest rate the young would save and the old dissave, leading the representative household to hold some wealth. Thus there are some circumstances under which the $S = 0$ line might emanate from the origin. It is, of course, by no means necessary. Predominantly positive time preference tends to increase the r intercept. Both planned retirement and intentions to bequeath more than one inherits tend to lower it. If the latter two forces were stronger than the former one, the aggregate of households would be willing to hold some wealth even at a negative rate of interest. Unless capital were so productive that its marginal productivity could never sink below its depreciation rate, an economy with such households could have a negative equilibrium interest rate.[59]

---

[59] An economy with a negative real rate of interest could only be viable with a rate of monetary expansion sufficiently high to make its money rate of interest positive. At a negative money rate, money would have a higher real yield than securities, and no one would want to own either industrial firms or banks.

Whether or not a positive rate could exist in a stationary state depends, then, on the relative strengths of the net productivity of capital and the willingness of people to own it. To call the interest rate the reward for saving is to miss the mark; it is really the reward for owning. A zero rate of saving can sustain any level of wealth. If people want to hold a lot of wealth at a low interest rate, they will get a low interest rate. If they want to hold only a little at a low rate, they will get a high rate.

Saving, Investment, and Distribution

The concern with the ultimate determinants of the rate of interest is part of a long-standing concern for the determinants of the "functional" distribution of income.[60] The answer that general equilibrium theory provides to the question of distribution goes something like this. In the short run, the stock of capital is given. If markets clear, labor will receive its marginal product times the amount of labor it supplies. The owners of capital receive the balance of total product. In the long run, the stock of capital is not a given, but expands or contracts in response to disequilibrium rents. Ultimately it must come to rest at a level that saturates both the desires of firms for capital and the desires of households for wealth at a common rate of interest. The owners of capital receive that rate of interest times their equilibrium stock of capital. Labor again receives its marginal product times the amount of labor it supplies. The value of output is entirely distributed in this way owing to the absence of rents in long-run equilibrium.

The two preceding sections of this chapter have detailed some aspects of this process. The first described the changes in distribution implied by the transition from short- to long-run equilibrium. The second discussed the determinants of the long-run position. The present section analyzes the short- and long-run effects of changes in these determinants. In order to keep the discussion within bounds, it focuses on only two patterns of shift in the behavior functions:

1. A shift on the part of households from consumption to saving, with no change in other household behavior functions
2. An upward shift in both the goods supply and investment demand functions resulting in net excess supply, with no shift in the demand function for labor

The first of these would result from a general reduction in time preference, the second from a capital-using technical change.[61] The method to be used to analyze these shifts

---

[60]The most famous statement of this concern is found in the Preface to Ricardo (1821): "To determine the laws which regulate . . . distribution is the principal problem in Political Economy." The major early statement of neoclassical theory is Clark (1899). For a survey of neoclassical thought on the matter, see Stigler (1941).

[61]"Capital using seems a more descriptive term than Hicks's "labor saving." (Hicks [1932]) It denotes a change that raises both output and the marginal product of capital at given inputs, leaving the marginal product of labor unchanged. A capital-using technical change was selected for analysis rather than a labor-using change since its implications for wages are more subtle than those of the latter.

could, of course, be used to study the impact of changes in other behavior functions as well.

The long-run effects of these shifts are readily seen from Figure 5-4. A downward shift in the consumption function is, in effect, a decision by households to hold more wealth at a given rate of interest. An upward shift in the investment function is a decision by firms to use more capital at a given rate of interest. The first shifts the $S = 0$ schedule and the second the $I = 0$ schedule to the right. Both shifts raise the equilibrium real wage because both raise the equilibrium stock of capital. However, the increased desire to save, technology constant, can only be saturated at a lowered rate of return. By contrast, the increased desire to use capital can only get financing from savers at a higher rate of return.

The short-run effects of these shifts are also readily seen. The effects of the consumption-function shift may be examined by replacing the right-hand side of (59) with the vector $[\Delta S, 0, 0]$, where ΔS is the negative of the shift in the consumption function. From the pattern of signs on the left-hand side of (60), it is evident that an increased willingness to save raises the real wage, lowers the interest rate, and raises real wealth.

In order to show why things work out this way, it is again necessary to sketch out some of the disequilibrium forces created by changes in the parameters of equilibrium. The proximate effect of higher saving is excess supply in the commodity market, necessitating a lower price. At a lower price and a consequently higher real wage, there is excess supply in the labor market. This necessitates a lower money wage. If prices and wages drop in the same proportion, real profits are unchanged, but money profits are lower. The money value of securities must drop to reflect their real value. However, real money holdings are now higher, and there is therefore an excess demand for securities. Their real price rises, and the interest rate drops. The supply side counterpart to this increase in wealth is the appearance of rents owing to the fall in capital costs. The increased wealth lowers the supply of labor, necessitating a higher real wage to restore equilibrium in the labor market.

The effects of the shift in the investment and supply functions may be examined by replacing the right-hand side of (59) by the vector $[\Delta Y^s - \Delta I, 0, \Delta Y^s]$. Since the first and third elements in this vector are both positive,[62] it is clear from the left-hand side of (60) that these changes must raise wages and wealth. Their effect on the interest rate is ambiguous. Why? The assumed pattern of change affects the goods market in much the same way as a rise in saving, since it constitutes net excess supply. However, the shift in the supply function also has a direct impact on the asset market. Given the assumption of an unchanged labor demand function, the increase in supply is exactly mirrored as an increase in profit. The implied wealth increase reinforces the goods-market impacts on wages and wealth. However, it creates a portfolio imbalance opposite in sign to that created by the excess supply of goods. The result is an ambiguity in the change in the interest rate.

---

[62] If it had been assumed that the proximate effect of the technical change was to create excess demand for goods, what follows would not be true.

To summarize, both the savings change and the particular technical change examined here raise the real wage in short and long run. The saving shift lowers the interest rate in both the short and long run. The production-investment shift has no clear impact on the interest rate in the short run but raises it in the long run. It should be noticed that both changes raise rents in the short run.[63] The first operates through a drop in the interest rate, the second through an increase in productivity. Thus both increase not only the equilibrium stock of capital, but also the incentives to accumulate.

The social message of this analysis is that savers and investors are the benefactors of wage earners, in the long run as well as the short. Again, this argues against income and wealth equalization or any other public policy that might impair accumulation. The harmony of markets in equilibrium is echoed in the harmony of interest of the classes that participate in them.

Summary

The material in this chapter by no means exhausts the range of questions that may be examined with the aid of general equilibrium models. The topics covered have been picked with an eye for the possibilities of contrasting general equilibrium results with the results of Keynesian analysis applied to the same questions. The principal results are the following:

1. It is possible to conceive of a system of households, firms, and banks dealing with one another in goods, labor, and security markets that harmonize their desires.
2. Such a system has two quite distinct states of equilibrium, a short-run state in which capital accumulation is taking place, and a stationary state in which it is not.
3. The level of the nominal stock of money has no implications for the real magnitudes of the system; it affects only the general level of prices.
4. The capital accumulation that advances the system from short-run equilibrium to long raises wages, although it may lower wealth and the rate of return thereon.
5. Providing that capital is sufficiently productive and willingness to own it sufficiently scarce, there will be a positive return on wealth even in the rent-free stationary state.
6. An increase in the desire to save raises wages and lowers the rate of return both in the short run and the long.
7. A capital-using technical change will raise the wage in the long run and may also in the short. It also raises the rate of return in the long run, although it may lower it in the short.

---

[63] This is easily verified by noticing that wealth increases at an unchanged capital stock.

These propositions all pertain to a system of simultaneous equations. Whether or not they pertain also to an economic system depends on the answers to several questions.

1. Do the equations, although highly abstract, somehow capture the essential elements of the complex market system that they purport to describe?
2. If so, do they have a unique equilibrium?
3. If so, does the system of disequilibrium transaction, changing expectations, and rates of adjustment that governs the economy out of equilibrium produce not only stability but also speedy convergence?

Only if these questions, taken in turn, have affirmative answers is there any justification for using equilibrium analysis as a basis for a world view or a guide to policy. Since the very first is unanswerable, one can only marvel at the extent to which Walras's vision has beguiled economists for more than a century. The mere fact that it survived the Great Depression is a tribute to its intellectual and ideological attractiveness.

The next chapter presents the body of Keynesian thought that was developed and took root during the Depression. It has provided the world view for most policy makers in recent decades, but it has by no means supplanted equilibrium analysis as the dominant orthodoxy. The latter continues to be a powerful argument heard on behalf of conservative, laissez faire policy.

KEYNESIAN ANALYSIS

General equilibrium analysis is occupied with the properties of hypothetical economic systems in which there always exists a special sort of harmony. Prices are always right for the tastes, technology, and capital stock of the community that they regulate, so that the demands and supplies they call forth match one another. No one ever has to adjust to an unsatisfied demand or an unsold supply. By contrast, analysis which follows the tradition of the Keynesians accepts disequilibrium as a matter of course. Full employment is not the natural state of affairs, but rather a landmark that an economy might pass on its way from excess demand for labor to excess supply. Disequilibria are not short-run affairs, but continuing features of an economic system that, by the standard of harmony, functions quite badly.

Although all Keynesians[1] agree on the pervasiveness of disequilibrium, not all agree on its source. There are at least four schools of thought. The first is that of the extreme income-expenditure theorists.[2] Their analysis assigns such a minor role to prices, wages, and the interest rate that they can hardly be said to admit the conceptual usefulness of equilibrium in the neoclassical sense. The second recognizes the concept of equilibrium, but argues that in some historical circumstances there exist

---

[1] There seems to be some difference of opinion about how many bona fide Keynesians there are. Friedman (1968b, p. 15) opines that "in one sense we are all Keynesians now; in another, no one is a Keynesian any longer."

[2] This group includes those econometricians whose models assign little or no role to wages and prices, such as Klein and Goldberger (1955) and Suits (1962). It also includes the business cycle theorists whose models are built around the multiplier-accelerator interaction, such as Samuelson (1939a, b), Metzler (1941, 1947), Goodwin (1950, 1951), and Hicks (1950). It also seems fair to include in this group Duesenberry (1958), even though his model takes into account a much broader range of considerations.

no equilibrating values of prices, wages, and interest rates.[3] The third accepts the existence of equilibrium, but argues that wage and/or price rigidities interfere with the equilibrating mechanism.[4] The fourth admits both the existence and the efficacy of price, wage, and interest rate flexibility, but argues that change itself is so time-consuming and destabilizing that the system is normally out of equilibrium despite the functioning of the equilibration process.[5] There is evidence in the *General Theory* linking Keynes to all the last three groups. In this respect he is reminiscent of the servant woman who was scolded by her mistress for cracking a bowl she had borrowed. In her defense, the servant argued that in fact she had never borrowed it, that it had already been cracked when she took it home, and that it had been whole when she returned it.

In addition to the various groups of Keynesians, there is a school which has been styled the "post Keynesians," centering around Joan Robinson, Pasinetti, Sraffa, and Kaldor.[6] They explicitly reject much of the marginalist apparatus that Keynesian and neoclassical economics have in common, especially the production function. However, they attach great importance to wages, prices, and the interest rate, since the distribution of income is in their system a major determinant of effective demand.

This chapter will set forth the four major strands of Keynesian thought. It is divided into four major sections. The first of these expounds the theory of aggregate demand and discusses the income-expenditure model. The second section completes the Keynesian model and discusses the other three accounts of the persistence of disequilibrium. The third concentrates on the role of money in Keynesian economics and draws contrasts with the conclusions of the corresponding part of Chapter 5. Similarly, the fourth section focuses on distribution and makes comparisons with the results of the previous chapter. There is a brief summary at the end of the chapter.

I. THE THEORY OF EFFECTIVE DEMAND

The term "effective demand" was coined by Keynes to denote that level of demand which is consistent with multiplier, monetary, and goods-market equilibrium.[7] In

---

[3] This group and the next are so large and overlapping that it would require a bibliographical article to list them. A prominent statement is that of Klein (1947, esp. chap. 3), which argues that no equilibrium exists and that wage rigidity prevents a perpetual deflationary spiral that would occur if wages were flexible. This view is also to be found more or less explicitly in Keynes (1936, chap. 19).

[4] The landmark article stressing the importance of wage rigidity in Keynes's thought is Modigliani (1944). See also Haberler's article in Harris (1948). Most of the essays in that volume are worth reading.

[5] The position that Keynesianism is the economics of disequilibrium is the thesis of Leijonhufoud (1968). This is also the contention of Patinkin (1965, esp. chap. 14), although he points out that there is little practical difference between this position and the belief that equilibrium does not exist.

[6] Because Joan Robinson's contributions are so scattered, it is not possible to give a short bibliography for this group. For an extensive set of references, see Eichner and Kregel (1975) and Kregel (1973).

[7] See Keynes (1936, chap. 3).

Humpty-Dumpty fashion, economists of the past decade or so have altered the meaning of the word, making it more general in one respect and more specific in another. The person most responsible for this alteration is Clower, whose paper entitled "The Keynesian Counterrevolution"[8] has contributed enormously to clarifying Keynesian demand theory.

Imagine a person whose economic life is very simple. He works for wages and buys carrots with the entire proceeds. He has a supply curve for labor and a demand curve for carrots.[9] Each is a function of the ratio of his money wage rate to the price of carrots. At a given carrot wage, the corresponding demand for carrots is called by Clower his "notional demand." His actual demand will equal the notional demand *provided he is able to sell his "notional supply" of labor*, that is, the amount that is indicated by his supply curve. Suppose, however, he cannot sell all the labor that he wishes. Because of the implied income restriction, his "effective demand" for carrots will be smaller than his notional demand. By contrast, suppose that he is unable to buy his notional demand for carrots. Since he has no alternative use for income, he will restrict his offering of labor. His "effective supply" of labor will be smaller than his notional supply.

Expanding upon the above illustration, it is apparent that effective demand or supply in any one market may be influenced by disequilibrium conditions in any other market. Providing that transactions take place at disequilibrium prices,[10] demand and supply functions cannot be written solely in terms of prices and wealth. Markets are tied together by the "spillover effects" of unsatisfied demands and supplies[11] as well as by prices.

Keynes's own theory of demand recognized one of these spillovers. By stressing the dependence of consumption on realized income, Keynes was in effect arguing that the demand for goods is influenced by the extent of disequilibrium in the market for labor. However, he did not see spillovers as a more general phenomenon, and his analysis of the labor market suffered as a consequence.[12] Moreover, he seemed to regard the consumption function as a replacement for traditional demand theory rather than as a refinement, thus encouraging the breach between income theory and the theory of choice.

---

[8] See Clower (1965).

[9] Because he spends his entire income on carrots, the two curves are not functionally independent.

[10] Trading at disequilibrium prices is sometimes called "false trading," and the prices "false prices." This terminology, which is due to Hicks (1939), is particularly unfortunate and will not be used here.

[11] These spillovers of disequilibrium from one market to another were first clearly recognized by Patinkin (1956, p. 217), who called them "dynamic intermarket pressures." Patinkin did not do a particularly successful job of integrating them into his theory. [See Davidson (1967) for a criticism of Patinkin's handling of the labor market.] Indeed, there is some justice to Hicks's claim [Hicks (1957)] that Patinkin's work is "modernized classical economics." More recent papers by Grossman (1971) and Tucker (1972) have explicitly incorporated spillovers into demand and supply models with a distinctly Keynesian flavor.

[12] Grossman (1972) argues convincingly that Keynes's treatment of the labor market shows that he did not appreciate the significance of disequilibrium transactions.

The aggregate demand theory that is developed in this section has its roots in the neoclassical theory of choice. However, since it explicitly recognizes the dependence of households' choices on the demand for their labor and of firms' choices on the demand for their output, it incorporates the income-expenditure feedback loop which is the hallmark of Keynesian analysis.

Effective Demand and the Multiplier

As a starting point for the discussion of Keynesian theory, consider an economic system that is in a state of general deficient demand. Households are unable to sell all the labor and firms all the output that they would like at the ruling configuration of prices, wages, and interest rates. Such a situation might be the product of a sudden collapse of expectations or it might be the product of more chronic difficulties. For the moment, ignore the source of the demand deficiency and concentrate instead on the properties of the system in depression, whatever its cause.

Both employment and output are governed by effective demands. For purposes of this chapter fiscal activities of government are ignored,[13] so all the demands are private. The effective demand for consumption goods, including banking services,[14] is given by

$$(1) \qquad C = C\left(\frac{w}{p}, r, \frac{W}{p}, L\right)$$

It differs from the notional or equilibrium demand function by its inclusion of the level of employment as one of its independent variables. Whenever conditions in the labor market constrain employment to a level below that given by the notional labor supply function, households will respond by reducing their consumption below the level given by the notional demand function. Hence the derivative of C with respect to L is positive. The size of this derivative depends crucially on the relationship between the current level of employment and expected future availability of employment. If a drop in employment is expected to be long-lasting, its effect on consumption demand will be much more marked than if it is expected to be temporary.[15]

The effective demand function for investment goods is given by

$$(2) \qquad I = I\left(\frac{w}{p}, r, K, Y\right)$$

It differs from the notional demand function by the inclusion of the level of production as one of its independent variables. In the face of deficient demand in the goods

[13] They comprise the main substance of Chapter 7.

[14] In this chapter there is no particular reason to separate the consumption of banking services from the consumption of other goods and services, so they are lumped together in the discussion of demand and production. However, it is necessary to address explicitly the household demand for money in the discussion of the securities market.

[15] For a fuller discussion of this matter, see Chapter 2, pages 26–28.

market, this level of production is regulated by the available demand; that is

$$(3) \qquad\qquad Y = C + I$$

If firms did not tailor the supply of goods to demand, they would pile up supplies of unsold goods in time of slack demand. Variations in the level of demand must also lead to investment changes if firms are to avoid grossly incorrect factor proportions in recessions. Again, the expectational element is important. A slump that is expected to last for quite a while will have a much greater impact on the optimum path of capital accumulation than will one that is expected to be short-lived.[16]

The levels of production and employment are linked by the effective demand for labor, which is given by

$$(4) \qquad\qquad L = L\left(\frac{w}{p}, r, K, Y\right)$$

Like the investment function, the labor demand function includes the level of production as an argument. Since labor is a current input, there is no expectational element involved in this case; employment simply moves up and down with current production, regardless of expectations.[17]

The presence of the real wage and the rate of interest in the effective demand function for labor needs some explanation. Since the level of output is demand-determined, the response of labor demand to changes in the wage and interest rates is limited to substitution effects. There are no scale effects. The real wage affects labor demand in two ways. First, a rise in the real wage encourages the substitution of real balances for labor. Second, it may also lower investment, lowering the amounts of both labor and money needed to produce a given output.[18] Both these effects go in the same direction. A rise in the rate of interest encourages the substitution of labor for real balances, but because of its depressing effect on investment, it lowers the demand for both variable factors. These two effects of the interest rate are offsetting. For the sake of simplicity, the the interest rate will therefore be ignored in future discussions of labor demand, although the real wage will not.

Equations (1)-(4) comprise the familiar income-expenditure relationships of multiplier theory. However, they must be supplemented by an additional relationship, since wealth fluctuates with the level of income owing to variations in rents. In the previous chapter, it was appropriate to write wealth in a simple form, the stream of profit divided by the rate of interest. However, in the analysis of disequilibrium it is dubious to assume that the elasticities of wealth with respect to profits and the interest rate are as big as one in magnitude. If fluctuations are expected to be reversed in time, the elasticities may be much smaller than they would be under static expecta-

[16] For a fuller discussion, see Chapter 3, pages 68–71.

[17] There is a substantial literature that treats labor as a "quasi-fixed factor" that is underutilized in periods of slack demand. See Oi (1962). A discussion of this literature would lead too far afield.

[18] To recall why this might or might not be so, see Chapter 3, page 63.

tions. Therefore wealth will be written as a function θ of the interest rate and the flow of real profit. It decreases with respect to the interest rate and increases with respect to the profit flow. In full, steady equilibrium it is equal to capitalized profits.

The complete income-expenditure subsystem, here collected for convenience in future reference, may therefore be written

$$Y = C\left(\frac{w}{p}, r, \frac{W}{p}, L\right) + I\left(\frac{w}{p}, r, K, Y\right)$$

(5)
$$L = L\left(\frac{w}{p}, K, Y\right)$$

$$\frac{W}{p} = \theta\left(r, Y - \frac{w}{p}L - \delta K\right)$$

This subsystem can only operate when both the following inequalities are satisfied

$$C\left(\frac{w}{p}, r, \frac{W}{p}, L\right) + I\left(\frac{w}{p}, r, K, Y\right) \leqslant Y^s\left(\frac{w}{p}, r, K\right)$$

(6)
$$L\left(\frac{w}{p}, K, Y\right) \leqslant L^s\left(\frac{w}{p}, r, \frac{W}{p}\right)$$

That is, whenever the effective demands for goods and labor are less than or equal to the corresponding notional supplies.[19] This is the realm in which the Keynesian multiplier holds sway, unconstrained by shortages of goods or labor.

The multiplier may be derived by substituting the second two relations of (5) into the first, thus expressing Y as a function of itself, the rate of interest, the real wage, and the capital stock. For the sake of subsequent notation, it is convenient to write the results of this substitution as follows

(7)
$$Y = Z\left(Y, r, \frac{w}{p}, K\right)$$

The multiplier equation, in condensed notation, is written

(8)
$$dY = \frac{1}{1 - \partial Z/\partial Y}\left[\frac{\partial Z}{\partial r}dr + \frac{\partial Z}{\partial w/p} \cdot dw/p + \frac{\partial Z}{\partial K} \cdot dK\right]$$

If it is viewed as a relationship between Y and r that is shifted by changes in the real wage and the capital stock, it is also the equation of the IS curve.[20]

---

[19]The effective demand and supply functions cannot be written independently of their notional counterparts, since both sets of functions represent the optimizing behavior of the same firms and households. The relationship between the two sets is the following: general equilibrium values that are solutions to a system of notional demands and supplies also satisfy (5) and, with equality, (6).

[20]This is essentially an augmented version of the standard textbook model. However, the partial derivatives of Z are the summation of many influences, as subsequent paragraphs will show.

The derivatives of Z with respect to its arguments are given by[21]

(9)
$$\frac{\partial Z}{\partial Y} = \frac{\partial C}{\partial W/p} \cdot \frac{\partial W/p}{\partial Y} + \frac{\partial C}{\partial L} \cdot \frac{\partial L}{\partial Y} + \frac{\partial I}{\partial Y}$$

where $\dfrac{\partial W/p}{\partial Y} = \dfrac{\partial \theta}{\partial P/p} \left(1 - \dfrac{w}{p} \dfrac{\partial L}{\partial Y} \right)$

(10)
$$\frac{\partial Z}{\partial r} = \frac{\partial C}{\partial r} + \frac{\partial C}{\partial W/p} \cdot \frac{\partial W/p}{\partial r} + \frac{\partial I}{\partial r}$$

where $\dfrac{\partial W/p}{\partial r} = \dfrac{\partial \theta}{\partial r}$

(11)
$$\frac{\partial Z}{\partial w/p} = \frac{\partial C}{\partial w/p} + \frac{\partial C}{\partial L} \cdot \frac{\partial L}{\partial w/p} + \frac{\partial C}{\partial W/p} \cdot \frac{\partial W/p}{\partial w/p} + \frac{\partial I}{\partial w/p}$$

where $\dfrac{\partial W/p}{\partial w/p} = - \dfrac{\partial \theta}{\partial P/p} \cdot \left(L + \dfrac{w}{p} \dfrac{\partial L}{\partial w/p} \right)$

(12)
$$\frac{\partial Z}{\partial K} = \frac{\partial C}{\partial W/p} \cdot \frac{\partial W/p}{\partial K} + \frac{\partial C}{\partial L} \cdot \frac{\partial L}{\partial K} + \frac{\partial I}{\partial K}$$

where $\dfrac{\partial W/p}{\partial K} = - \dfrac{\partial \theta}{\partial P/p} \left(\dfrac{w}{p} \dfrac{\partial L}{\partial K} + \delta \right)$

Although these expressions are not very tidy, considerable sense can be made of them.

Equation (9) expresses the direct feedback from production to demand, which comprises half of the multiplier loop.[22] With the wage and interest rates given, increases in production affect consumption through increases in wealth and employment.[23] In addition, increases in production that reflect increased demand raise the profitability of capital accumulation. All the terms in (9) are therefore positive.

Equation (10) expresses the influence of r on total demand as the sum of three influences. The first is the mishmash of partial influences of r on consumption, holding wealth constant. It is indeterminate as to sign. The second term represents the indirect effects of changes in r on consumption by way of the influence of r on capitalized profits. Holding output, wages, employment, and depreciation constant, a rise in the rate of interest must lower the capitalized value of rents, and with it, wealth. This fall in wealth will inhibit consumer demand. The third term in (10) is also clearly negative. Whatever the sign of the first term, it will be assumed to be dominated by the last two, so that the overall influence of interest on demand is negative.

---

[21] The derivatives are calculated by differentiating the first equation of (5), taking due account of the second and third.

[22] The other is, of course, the impact of demand on production.

[23] If production is effectively limited by demand, it must be that the real wage is smaller than the marginal product of labor. Otherwise firms would restrict supply below the level of demand. Since this is the case, the product of w/p and $\partial L/\partial Y$ (which is the reciprocal of the marginal product of labor) must be less than one, and $\dfrac{\partial W/p}{\partial Y}$ must be positive.

The first three terms on the right-hand side of (11) represent the effects on consumption of a rise in the real wage, holding output constant. As the wage rate goes up, so does labor income,[24] and with it consumption. However, the rise in labor income reduces profits and therefore wealth, lowering consumption. The weight of tradition argues that a redistribution from profits to wages raises consumption, although there is little in the life-cycle theory of consumption to support this view.[25] Moreover, any positive influence that a wage increase might have on consumption is likely to be offset by a contrary movement in investment. Since there is no convincing case to be made one way or the other about the sign of (11), the influence of the wage on demand will not be systematically pursued in what follows.

The first two terms on the right-hand side of (12) also reflect redistributive influences. A rise in the capital stock reduces wage costs by more than it increases depreciation.[26] It therefore raises profits and wealth. With output held constant, however, a rise in the capital stock reduces employment. The two influences on consumption work in opposite directions, with uncertain outcome. However, the third term in (12) measures the negative influence of capital on further investment. It will be assumed to dominate the whole expression.

This analysis of the derivatives of demand with respect to income, the interest rate, and real wage, and the capital stock points up several properties of Equation (8). They are most conveniently stated if it is written in integral form[27]

$$(13) \qquad Y = Y(r, K)$$

The most striking feature of (13), which may be regarded as the solution to the equation system (5), is that neither of its derivatives is determinate as to sign. Even though demand decreases with respect to both r and K, the multiplier equilibrium may go up or down with respect to either variable, and the IS curve may slope in either direction. Everything depends on the magnitude of $\partial Z/\partial Y$, which appears in the denominator of (8). If it is smaller than one, the equilibrium value of Y moves in the same direction as Z, but if greater, then equilibrium production is reduced by a fall in the interest rate, even though the proximate effect of such a fall is to raise demand! What is going on?

The answer may be approached by looking at Figure 6-1, which must be familiar to anyone who has recently looked at a principles book. The line labeled Z_0 gives Z as a function of Y, holding r, w/p, and K constant. It comes from Equation (7). The line labeled Z_1 corresponds to a lower level of the interest rate, and to a higher level of demand at any given level of production. Because the slope of the Z function is greater than one, its intersection with the line $Z = Y$ shifts to the left when the Z function shifts upward.

[24] To say otherwise would assume extraordinary substitutability between labor and money.
[25] If bequests are luxuries, then a redistribution away from well-to-do recipients of property income will lower saving. However, such a redistribution also transfers resources from retired people to those of working age, raising saving. One cannot deduce from theory alone which effect will dominate.
[26] If this were not so, the investment would hardly be undertaken.
[27] The real wage is omitted because of the inconclusiveness of the direction of its influence.

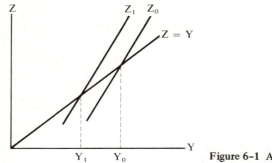

Figure 6-1 An unstable multiplier.

Whenever $\partial Z/\partial Y$ is greater than one, the sum of consumption and investment demand rises with respect to income by more than the sum of consumption and saving. That is, an increase in income raises intended investment by more than intended saving. Under these circumstances, production response to a demand increase cannot restore multiplier equilibrium. Increases in production only raise the excess of planned investment over planned saving, or its alter ego, the excess of demand over production. The multiplier viewed as a dynamic process is unstable. Only if increases in demand somehow led firms perversely to cut their output could a shift from Z_0 to Z_1 lower production from Y_0 to Y_1.

By contrast, when $\partial Z/\partial Y$ is less than one, increases in production reduce the excess of demand over production, restoring equality between the two. In this circumstance, the Z curve is flatter than the $Z = Y$ line. When it shifts up, its point of equality with Y moves to the right. The multiplier is positive, and the process is stable.

The significance of the stability or instability of the multiplier can only be evaluated in context. Multipler processes are parts of larger systems of relationships that determine not only the level of production consistent with a given rate of interest, but also the rate of interest itself. Even if the income-expenditure loop were not self-stabilizing, its effects on the rate of interest might feed back with sufficient strength to curtail a cumulative movement. Thus the system of relationships summarized by the IS and LM curves might be well-behaved even though it contained a volatile multiplier process. This issue will be dealt with in due course, after the determinants of equilibrium in the securities market have been dealt with.

Money and Securities

Because of the static neutrality of money, it was possible in the last chapter to express the conditions of general equilibrium without reference to the supply of money.[28] In Keynesian analysis of disequilibrium, money is not neutral, and it is necessary to bring it directly into focus. Thus when faced with the choice between analyzing the demand for and supply of securities or of money, it seems best to choose money, remembering

---

[28] See Chapter 5, page 104.

always an excess supply of one of these assets is mirrored in an excess demand for the other.[29]

In Keynesian models it is usually assumed that the market for securities is an island of equilibrium in a system of markets that is otherwise characterized by excess demands and supplies.[30] Nonetheless, the securities market is affected by disequilibrium in other markets. To the extent that firms' production is curtailed by deficient demand, their demand for money and supply of securities will be similarly curtailed. To the extent that households' labor income and consumption are restricted by unemployment, their demand for money balances will also be restricted, and their demand for securities will be increased at a given total wealth. These considerations lead to effective money demand functions of the form

(14)
$$\phi^h = \phi^h \left(\frac{w}{p}, r, \frac{W}{p}, L \right)$$

$$\phi^b = \phi^b \left(\frac{w}{p}, r, K, Y \right)$$

These relationships may be combined with the definition of wealth, the effective demand function for labor (4), and the supply of real balances to give the following condition of monetary equilibrium

(15)
$$\phi^b + \phi^h = \phi \left(\frac{w}{p}, r, K, Y \right) = \frac{M}{p}$$

This condition implicitly defines the LM curve.

The properties of the LM curve must be uncovered by differentiating the demand for money with respect to its determinants. The derivatives are

(16)
$$\frac{\partial \phi}{\partial w/p} = \frac{\partial \phi^h}{\partial w/p} + \frac{\partial \phi^h}{\partial L} \cdot \frac{\partial L}{\partial w/p} + \frac{\partial \phi^h}{\partial W/p} \cdot \frac{\partial W/p}{\partial w/p} + \frac{\partial \phi^b}{\partial w/p}$$

(17)
$$\frac{\partial \phi}{\partial r} = \frac{\partial \phi^h}{\partial r} + \frac{\partial \phi^h}{\partial W/p} \cdot \frac{\partial W/p}{\partial r} + \frac{\partial \phi^b}{\partial r}$$

(18)
$$\frac{\partial \phi}{\partial K} = \frac{\partial \phi^h}{\partial W/p} \cdot \frac{\partial W/p}{\partial K} + \frac{\partial \phi^h}{\partial L} \cdot \frac{\partial L}{\partial K} + \frac{\partial \phi^b}{\partial K}$$

(19)
$$\frac{\partial \phi}{\partial Y} = \frac{\partial \phi^h}{\partial W/p} \cdot \frac{\partial W/p}{\partial Y} + \frac{\partial \phi^h}{\partial L} \cdot \frac{\partial L}{\partial Y} + \frac{\partial \phi^b}{\partial Y}$$

[29] See the discussion of Walras's Law in Chapter 5, pages 104–107.

[30] Barro and Grossman (1971) is seemingly an exception, since it admits of excess demand for or supply of money. However, they curiously omit any reference to securities or the interest rate, so there is no alternative asset whose yield can change so as to equilibrate money demand and supply. Their model is a lot less general than the title of the paper would suggest. A genuine exception is Rose (1966).

The derivatives of wealth and employment that are buried in Equations (16)–(19) are spelled out in the discussion of the IS curve on pages 132–135.

The first three terms in (16) represent redistributive influences. A rise in the wage, holding wealth and the interest rate constant, increases the flow of income and expenditure. Assuming complementarity between consumption and money holding, this increase will make households want to hold a greater share of their wealth in money form. However, at a given level of production, a higher wage reduces wealth. Thus the first three terms involve conflicting influences. The fourth term does as well. A rise in the wage rate encourages firms to substitute money for labor. However, it also reduces investment and therefore the quantities of both variable factors needed to produce a given output. In view of all the ambiguities involved in the sign of (16), it seems foolish to waste further time considering the implications of a change in the real wage. They will simply be ignored.

The first two terms in (18) also represent redistributive influences. An increase in the capital stock raises wealth and lowers labor income, with conflicting effects on the demand for money. Because of this ambiguity, the implications of a change in the capital stock will also be ignored, despite the fact that the third term in (18) is negative barring strong complementarity between capital and money.

There is no ambiguity about the other two derivatives. All the terms in (17) are negative and all those in (19) are positive. For a given money stock, therefore, the level of production and the rate of interest move in the same direction. The LM curve is upward sloping. It shifts to the right or left as the real money stock rises and falls.

The Interaction of the Demands for Money and Goods

The forces summarized by the IS and LM curves determine simultaneously the levels of production, consumption, investment, and the interest rate that are consistent with both monetary and multiplier equilibrium. The independent variables that govern the positions of the IS and LM curves are the real money supply and the stock of capital. Changes in these variables shift the curves, changing the dependent variables in the process.

Changes in government spending and taxes also affect the IS and LM curves. Discussion of these effects is largely deferred until the next chapter, which focuses on the government. The nominal money stock is controlled by the banks, which are assumed in turn to be under the control of the government.[31] However, the real money stock is a joint creation of the banks and the entire system of price determination. It is necessary to discuss it in this chapter, since it is partly endogenous.

Most macroeconomic texts bring out in some detail the importance of the relative slopes of the IS and LM curves in determining what happens when one of the inde-

---

[31] In a banking system such as that of the United States, there is a lot of institutional and economic slippage in the execution of monetary policy. Part of this stems from the independence of the Federal Reserve Board, part from the incompleteness of its information, and part from the indirectness of its instruments of control. For an insider's view of this fascinating process, see Maisel (1973).

pendent variables or underlying relationships shifts. A recognition that the slope of (13), the IS curve, may plausibly be either positive or negative enriches the range of possible responses. A positively sloped IS curve corresponds to a multiplier process, which, taken alone, is unstable. Stability is imparted, if at all, by forces outside the income-expenditure interaction.

To see the possibilities of stability and instability, consider three cases. In the first case, the derivative of demand with respect to production ($\partial Z / \partial Y$) is larger than one, but not by much. Although the IS curve slopes upward, it is not so steep as LM. This is depicted in panel (a) of Figure 6-2. Panel (b) depicts the case in which $\partial Z / \partial Y$ is enough greater than one that the IS curve is steeper than LM. The bottom panel (c) shows the pattern in which $\partial Z / \partial Y$ is less than one and IS is downward sloping.

Because the derivative of demand with respect to the interest rate is negative, the region above the IS curve is the region in which production exceeds demand; in the region below, demand exceeds production. In panels (a) and (c), the left-hand half of the LM curve lies in the region below IS, but in (b) this left-hand portion lies above. Panels (a) and (c) have therefore quite different implicit dynamic properties than those of (b).

To see why, suppose that production always changes in the direction of the excess of demand over production. Suppose further that the demand and supply for money are always kept in balance by rapid adjustment in the price of securities. This means that the system depicted in Figure 6-2 must always be on the LM curve, moving in a direction whose right-left component has the same sign as $Z - Y$. In panels (a) and (c), whenever demand is excessive relative to production, the interest rate rises rapidly enough to choke off the excess. However, in panel (b), the interest rate cannot rise fast enough to get the system out of the region of excess demand once it gets in it. The monetary feedback is not strong enough to stabilize a very powerful multiplier.

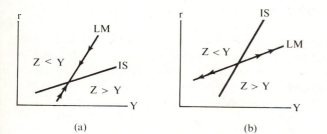

(a)   (b)

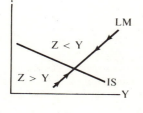

(c)

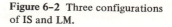

Figure 6-2 Three configurations of IS and LM.

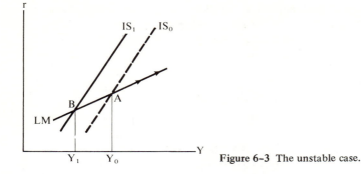

Figure 6-3 The unstable case.

A clearer appreciation of this instability may be gained by examining Figure 6-3. Suppose that an economy were initially at a position such as point A, with income level Y_0. An autonomous increase in demand would shift the IS curve upward; that is, if demand rose autonomously, an increase in the interest rate would be required to restore multiplier equilibrium. Such a shift would move the intersection of IS and LM to the left, say to B. However, the system would initially be at A, which is in the region of excess demand relative to IS_1, the new IS curve. The only possible consequence of the autonomous demand increase would be a cumulative movement away from equilibrium. The interest rate would rise, but not precipitously enough to check the cumulative expansion.

The dynamic assumptions of this example are not very general, and it is not intended to be more than an elementary exercise in dynamic analysis.[32] Its main thrust is to show that an odd static result can be ruled out by the instability that it implies.[33] In future static analysis, it will always be assumed that whatever its slope, the IS curve cuts LM from above, as in panels (*a*) and (*c*) of Figure 6-2. In both of these cases, an autonomous increase in demand raises the equilibrium income rather than lowering it.

Ruling out the wrong-way cross reduces the variety of static results, but the number of interesting matters is still quite large. In order to explore them thoroughly without an endless array of diagrams, it seems productive to examine the differentials of the IS and LM curves. After dropping the capital stock from the LM curve and the real wage from both curves,[34] these differentials may be written

(20)
$$\left(1 - \frac{\partial Z}{\partial Y}\right) dY - \frac{\partial Z}{\partial r}\, dr = \frac{\partial Z}{\partial K}\, dK$$

$$\frac{\partial \phi}{\partial Y}\, dY + \frac{\partial \phi}{\partial r}\, dr = d\,\frac{M}{p}$$

---

[32] It can, however, be shown that permitting the securities market to be in disequilibrium reduces the range of stable configurations rather than increasing it.

[33] This is an application of Samuelson's (1947) correspondence principle. See also Chapter 5, footnote 46.

[34] Recall the discussion above on pages 135 and 138.

To say that the LM curve is more positively sloped than the IS curve is to say that

$$(21) \qquad \frac{-\partial\phi/\partial Y}{\partial\phi/\partial r} > \frac{(1 - \partial Z/\partial Y)}{\partial Z/\partial r}$$

It can readily be verified that this is equivalent to saying that the determinant of the coefficients of dY and dr in (20) is negative; that is, that

$$(22) \qquad D \equiv \left(1 - \frac{\partial Z}{\partial Y}\right)\frac{\partial\phi}{\partial r} + \frac{\partial Z}{\partial r}\cdot\frac{\partial\phi}{\partial Y} < 0$$

The equivalence of these two conditions points up the importance of the restriction on the slope of IS. Unless the sign of D is determinate, no comparative statics may be deduced.

The effects on Y of shifts in the capital stock and the money supply are given by

$$(23) \qquad \frac{dY}{dK} = \frac{1}{D}\cdot\frac{\partial Z}{\partial K}\cdot\frac{\partial\phi}{\partial r}$$

$$(24) \qquad \frac{dY}{dM/p} = \frac{1}{D}\cdot\frac{\partial Z}{\partial r}$$

where D is given by (22). Since all the factors on the right sides of (23) and (24) are negative, the left sides are respectively negative and positive. The larger the capital stock, the smaller is the IS-LM equilibrium; the larger the real money supply, the larger the equilibrium.

The response of income to a change in capital is typical of its response to any autonomous change that reduces aggregate demand. Hence all the income responses of the IS-LM system to an increase in the capital stock can be expected as well to follow a downward shift in either the investment or consumption function.[35] Similarly, the responses to a downward shift in the money demand function would be the same as those to an increase in supply.

A number of factors influence the magnitudes of these responses.[36] The most convenient way to organize them is to look sequentially at the implications of the income and interest sensitivities of Z and ϕ. In exploring these implications, it is helpful to see (23) and (24) written in alternative ways

$$(23a) \qquad \frac{dY}{dK} = \frac{\dfrac{\partial Z}{\partial K}\cdot\dfrac{\partial\phi}{\partial r}\bigg/\dfrac{\partial Z}{\partial r}}{\left(1 - \dfrac{\partial Z}{\partial Y}\right)\left(\dfrac{\partial\phi}{\partial r}\bigg/\dfrac{\partial Z}{\partial r}\right) + \dfrac{\partial\phi}{\partial Y}}$$

[35] The composition of equilibrium demand would depend, of course, on whether it was the investment or the consumption function that shifted.

[36] To see the basis for some of these conclusions, it might help in some cases to sketch the corresponding diagrams on scratch paper.

(23b)
$$\frac{dY}{dK} = \frac{\dfrac{\partial Z}{\partial K}}{1 - \dfrac{\partial Z}{\partial Y} + \dfrac{\partial Z}{\partial r}\left(\dfrac{\partial \phi}{\partial Y} \middle/ \dfrac{\partial \phi}{\partial r}\right)}$$

(24a)
$$\frac{dY}{dM/p} = \frac{1}{\left(1 - \dfrac{\partial Z}{\partial Y}\right)\left(\dfrac{\partial \phi}{\partial r} \middle/ \dfrac{\partial Z}{\partial r}\right) + \dfrac{\partial \phi}{\partial Y}}$$

(24b)
$$\frac{dY}{dM/p} = \frac{\dfrac{\partial Z}{\partial r}\ \dfrac{\partial \phi}{\partial r}}{1 - \dfrac{\partial Z}{\partial Y} + \dfrac{\partial Z}{\partial r}\left(\dfrac{\partial \phi}{\partial Y} \middle/ \dfrac{\partial \phi}{\partial r}\right)}$$

1. From (23b) and (24b) it is seen that, within the bounds set by stability, the higher is the impact of production on demand ($\partial Z/\partial Y$), the greater in magnitude is the impact on production of a change in capital or the money supply.
2. As $\partial Z/\partial r$ gets large, dY/dK approaches zero (from 23a) and $dY/dM/p$ approaches the reciprocal of $\partial \phi/\partial Y$ (from 24a). Since this reciprocal is the marginal velocity of money, this result is essentially the quantity theory.
3. As $\partial Z/\partial r$ approaches zero, the money supply becomes completely ineffective (see 24b) and dY/dK approaches the full multiplier, untrammeled by monetary feedback (see 23b).
4. A low value of $\partial \phi/\partial Y$ acts much like a high value of $\partial Z/\partial Y$, and a high $\partial \phi/\partial Y$ like a low of $\partial Z/\partial Y$. From (23a) and (24b), the lower is the income sensitivity of the demand for money, the further a cumulative multiplier movement will carry before it is limited by the monetary feedback.
5. From (23a), as $\partial \phi/\partial r$ goes to zero, changes in the capital stock lose their effect. A small decline in income will lower the interest rate enough to offset the impact of a higher capital stock. Under the same circumstances, however, the quantity theory again holds (see 24a).
6. Finally, if money demand is highly interest sensitive, changes in the money supply are ineffective (from 24b) and changes in the capital stock have the full multiplier effect (from 23b).

Four polar cases are worthy of particular comment. In one case, the IS curve is virtually horizontal, either because $\partial Z/\partial Y$ is close to one or because $\partial Z/\partial r$ is very large. Changes in the supply of or demand for money are extremely powerful, and changes in the capital stock (or any other parameter of the IS curve) completely unimportant. Real income moves in proportion to the real money stock. The rate of interest is fixed at a "natural rate" that equates intended saving and investment at all levels of income. This case is illustrated in panel (a) of Figure 6-4. A second case is illustrated in panel (b). Because the demand for money has zero interest elasticity, the LM curve is vertical. Again the real money stock is all important. In the third case,

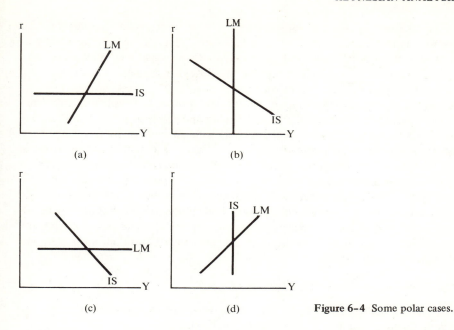

Figure 6-4 Some polar cases.

the LM curve is horizontal because of an extremely high interest elasticity of the demand for money. The real money stock is irrelevant; only disturbances to the IS curve matter. This is shown in panel (*c*). In the final case, which is shown in panel (*d*), the IS curve is vertical because demand is completely insensitive to the interest rate. Again the money stock is irrelevant and only the IS curve matters.

The first two of these cases (particularly the second) are referred to by many textbook writers as "classical." Because income is proportional to the real money stock, the elasticity of equilibrium demand[37] with respect to the price level is minus one. In the third and fourth cases, the price elasticity of demand is zero, since changes in the real money stock have no effect on income. These two pairs of cases set outer limits on the price elasticity of demand.

The third and fourth cases are often referred to by the same writers as "Keynesian." Whether or not the term classical is appropriate for the first two cases, the term Keynesian clearly is for the last two. In Chapter 18 of the *General Theory*, entitled "The General Theory of Employment Re-stated," Keynes put forth a series of propositions which may be translated into the ordinary X-shaped IS-LM diagram. However, in Chapter 22, "Notes on the Trade Cycle," he stated that in at least some phases of the business cycle, the demand for goods might be very interest inelastic and the demand for money very elastic.[38] Under such circumstances the price mechanism and the banking authority are powerless, and the economy is locked in the grip of the

[37]That is, money-multiplier equilibrium demand.
[38]His belief in the high elasticity of the demand for money stemmed from his now-discredited theory of "liquidity preference." See Keynes (1936, chap. 13, esp. p. 172).

income-expenditure cycle. For some writers[39] who disregarded Chapter 18, this became the central message of the *General Theory*. They ignored the possibility of equilibrium in the general sense, and constructed a "new economics" in which prices, wages, and interest rates had little if any role. What Keynes thought of as a special and temporary aberration was taken to be the general case.

A particularly interesting strand of this extreme form of Keynesianism is the literature built around the "interaction of the multiplier and accelerator."[40] This literature combines the Keynesian consumption function with an investment function whose arguments, at least in some formulations, are the level of production and the stock of capital. Because of the delays in capital accumulation and the negative influence of capital on current demand, such models are capable of producing cyclical time paths of production. The thought that a fairly simple and plausible model of demand determination could provide an endogenous explanation of the business cycle delighted a generation of income theorists. Some constructed mechanical, electrical, and even hydraulic analogs of their models. The next section sets forth one such analytical model to give the general flavor of the genus.[41]

Capital Accumulation and the Business Cycle

Suppose that neither the interest rate nor the real wage has an appreciable influence on either component of demand. Then demands can be written

(25)
$$C = C(Y) \quad \text{and}$$
$$I = I(Y, K)$$

where, for present purposes, I denotes net investment. Suppose further that whenever the sum of C and I differs from Y, producers increase their output at a rate equal to the difference.[42] Suppose finally that if production and demand differ, investment plans are realized.[43] If the remaining output is bigger than consumption demand, the excess is thrown away. If it is smaller, consumers are frustrated.

This bundle of assumptions leads to a dynamic model of the form

(26)
$$\dot{Y} = C(Y) + I(Y, K) - Y$$
$$\dot{K} = I(Y, K)$$

This dynamic system has an equilibrium, or singular point, at which both variables are stationary. At this point the equations

(27)
$$0 = C(Y) + I(Y, K) - Y$$
$$0 = I(Y, K)$$

[39] See footnotes 2 and 3 of this chapter.

[40] The phrase is due to Samuelson (1939a). See also the other references in footnote 1 of this chapter.

[41] It does so, however, without benefit of gears, wires, or pipes.

[42] This is a rather special assumption, made only in the name of simplicity.

[43] Again, this is a special assumption. Models of this kind are very sensitive to such assumptions, but since the current model is only illustrative, this sensitivity will not be explored.

implicitly define the equilibrium values Y_0 and K_0. Define deviations from equilibrium by

(28)
$$y \equiv Y - Y_0$$
$$k \equiv K - K_0$$

Equations (26) may be linearly approximated in the neighborhood of equilibrium, and written[44]

(29)
$$\dot{y} = \left(\frac{\partial C}{\partial Y} + \frac{\partial I}{\partial Y} - 1 \right) y + \frac{\partial I}{\partial K} \cdot k$$

$$\dot{k} = \frac{\partial I}{\partial Y} \cdot y + \frac{\partial I}{\partial K} \cdot k$$

These equations describe the motion of the system in that neighborhood.

The ratios of y to k that make $\dot{y}$ and $\dot{k}$ respectively zero are given by

(30)
$$\left. \frac{y}{k} \right]_{\dot{y}=0} = \frac{-\partial I/\partial K}{(\partial C/\partial Y) + (\partial I/\partial Y) - 1}$$

$$\left. \frac{y}{k} \right]_{\dot{k}=0} = \frac{-\partial I/\partial K}{\partial I/\partial Y}$$

The slope of the $\dot{y} = 0$ locus depends on the ambiguous sign of the denominator; it will be assumed positive, and the whole fraction likewise positive. The slope of the $\dot{k} = 0$ locus is also positive. Providing that $\partial C/\partial Y$ is less than one, the $\dot{y} = 0$ line is the steeper of the two. This is assumed.

The motion of the system is illustrated in Figure 6–5. In the region to the right of $\dot{y} = 0$, k is big enough relative to y to make demand fall short of production, and production is falling. Below $\dot{k} = 0$, k is big enough relative to y to make net investment negative, and capital is falling. In the region labeled I, output is falling, but net investment remains positive. In II, output has fallen so far relative to capital that net investment is negative. In III, output has turned around, but investment is still negative. In IV, output has risen far enough relative to capital that net investment is again positive.

This system has two delayed responses. Capital follows output with a lag, and output lags behind demand. Two-lag systems of this sort produce oscillations for a wide variety of parameter values. According to the values of the parameters, the oscillations may be convergent, of constant amplitude, or divergent. Roughly speaking,

---

[44]This linearization is simply a first-order Taylor expansion around the equilibrium. Since Y_0 and K_0 are stationary, their time derivatives do not appear in (29). The method used to analyze these equations is set forth in Andronow and Chaikin (1949).

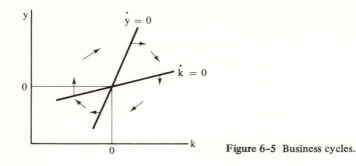

Figure 6-5 Business cycles.

the issue hinges on whether the negative influence of capital on investment is strong enough relative to the multiplier to turn the spiral inward.[45]

The charm of models of this sort is the economy of means by which they explain the cycle. But one person's economy of means is another person's oversimplification. Too much of the traditional economic analysis is omitted from equations such as (26). Serious attempts to integrate prices, wages, and the interest rate into the analysis soon collapse from their own complexity. One of the main problems is the difficulty of analyzing systems with more than two lags, for which diagrams such as Figure 6-5 are not useful.[46] On the whole, economic dynamics has not progressed very far, even on its own terms. Keynesian comparative statics covers a much broader range of issues. The analysis of effective demand is only a part of Keynesian theory. The next major section is devoted to the development of the remainder of the system.

II. THE COMPLETE KEYNESIAN SYSTEM

The theory of effective demand is the heart of all that is distinctively Keynesian in macroeconomic analysis. Yet the realm of effective demand is circumscribed by the willingness of suppliers of goods and labor to meet the demand. Its borders are defined by equality between effective demands and the corresponding notional supplies. The first two parts of this section are devoted to defining these boundaries and thereby completing the outlines of the Keynesian system.

The remaining two parts explore two related issues. The first is to show what must be true if an economy which fits the Keynesian model is to be in general equilibrium. The second is to show why general equilibrium is a special case that is not of great practical significance.

---

[45]Given the other assumptions of the model at hand, a sufficient (and necessary) condition for local convergence is that

$$\left(\frac{\partial C}{\partial Y} + \frac{\partial I}{\partial Y} - 1 - \frac{\partial I}{\partial K} \right)$$

be less than one.

[46]One of the most ambitious attempts is that of Rose (1966). However, he has to resort to some highly questionable assumptions about the relative speeds with which variables adjust.

Limits on the Supply of Goods

The boundary between the territory ruled by effective demand for goods and that regulated by the marginal calculations of suppliers may be defined in various ways. The most straightforward is to say that the level of production must equal the notional supply of goods, that is[47]

$$(31) \qquad\qquad Y = Y^s\left(\frac{w}{p}, K\right)$$

At a given real wage and capital stock, production is confined to the realm of values smaller than Y^s. This limit is indicated in the top panel of Figure 6-6 as a function of the real wage. The limit shifts up or down according to whether the capital stock is higher or lower.[48]

To compare effective demand with supply, it is helpful to add a second panel to the diagram. The vertical line labeled SS in the middle panel of Figure 6-6 is constructed from the top panel. It indicates the most profitable level of output Y_0 at the real wage $(w/p)_0$. It shifts to the right as the real wage decreases or the capital stock increases.

The remainder of the middle panel of Figure 6-6 is an ordinary IS-LM diagram.[49] It has been constructed on the assumption that it is possible for multiplier equilibrium to be achieved at a level of output equal to Y_0, providing only that the interest rate could be brought to the level r_0. It is also assumed that it is possible to achieve the interest rate r_0 if the price level is equal to some value, say p_0, to which there corresponds an LM curve,[50] LM (M_0, p_0), cutting IS at the point r_0, Y_0. Thus the price level p_0, the real wage $(w/p)_0$, the interest rate r_0, and the level of production Y_0 comprise one possible configuration of values at which the effective demand for goods matches the notional supply.

This matching of demand and supply may also be seen in another way. In the bottom panel of Figure 6-6, the line marked SS (w_0, K_0) is derived from the Y^s curve by fixing the money wage at the level

$$w_0 = \left(\frac{w}{p}\right)_0 \cdot p_0$$

and varying the real wage by changing the price level. It is essentially a schedule of the supply prices of various levels of output at a particular level of the money wage. The

[47]This is simply the supply curve developed in Chapter 3 and used extensively in Chapter 5. The rate of interest has been dropped for the sake of convenience. Since its effect on supply is the sum of minor and conflicting influences little is lost by dropping it.

[48]This is another consequence of the assumption that labor and capital are cooperating factors.

[49]The IS curve indicated corresponds to a particular value of the capital stock, K_0. There is no loss in generality in drawing it downward-sloping. Wherever this is the case, it will be drawn that way.

[50]This LM curve corresponds to a particular nominal money supply, M_0, as well as a particular price level.

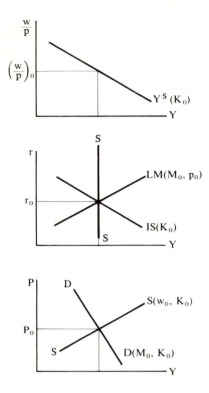

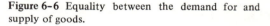

Figure 6-6 Equality between the demand for and supply of goods.

line marked DD (M_0, K_0) is constructed by tracing out the intersections of IS and the LM curves corresponding to different values of the price level. It is therefore a locus of multiplier-monetary equilibria drawn for a particular money supply and capital stock. Its intersection with SS illustrates the same goods-market equilibrium as that appearing in the middle panel.

The various parts of Figure 6-6 will become familiar through use in subsequent sections of this and the next chapter. For the moment, simply notice that equality between the effective demand for goods and the supply is achieved by a money wage, a price level, and a nominal money supply that bear the appropriate ratio one to the other.[51] The real wage governs supply, the real money stock demand. The lower the real wage, and consequently the higher the supply of goods, the larger must the real money supply be if demand is to equal supply.

Limits on the Supply of Labor

The conditions under which the effective demand for labor balances the supply are somewhat more complicated than the conditions of equilibrium in the goods market.

---

[51] This is not an assertion of the neutrality of money, since no assumption is made that the necessary ratios will be achieved.

There will be a balance whenever[52]

(32)
$$X^L \equiv L\left(\frac{w}{p}, K, Y\right) - L^s\left(\frac{w}{p}, \frac{W}{p}\right) = 0$$

where $\dfrac{W}{p} = \theta\left(r, Y - \dfrac{w}{p}L - \delta K\right)$

This relationship must be differentiated to uncover the properties of the locus of full-employment points. Its derivatives are

(33)
$$\frac{\partial X^L}{\partial Y} = \frac{\partial L}{\partial Y} - \frac{\partial L^s}{\partial W/p} \cdot \frac{\partial W/p}{\partial P/p}\left(1 - \frac{w}{p}\frac{\partial L}{\partial Y}\right)$$

(34)
$$\frac{\partial X^L}{\partial r} = -\frac{\partial L^S}{\partial W/p} \cdot \frac{\partial W/p}{\partial r}$$

(35)
$$\frac{\partial X^L}{\partial w/p} = \frac{\partial L}{\partial w/p} - \frac{\partial L^s}{\partial w/p} + \frac{\partial L^s}{\partial W/p} \cdot \frac{\partial W/p}{\partial P/p}\left(L + \frac{w}{p}\frac{\partial L}{\partial w/p}\right)$$

(36)
$$\frac{\partial X^L}{\partial K} = \frac{\partial L}{\partial K} + \frac{\partial L^s}{\partial W/p} \cdot \frac{\partial W/p}{\partial P/p} \cdot \left(\frac{w}{p}\frac{\partial L}{\partial K} + \delta\right)$$

The first two of these derivatives have unproblematic signs. Whenever the binding constraint on employment is either the demand for goods or the supply of labor, the marginal product of labor exceeds the real wage.[53] Since $\partial L/\partial Y$ is the reciprocal of the marginal product of labor, the parenthetical expression on the right side of (33) is positive, and so therefore is the whole derivative. The right side (34) is also clear, in this case negative. The remaining two derivatives are more problematic. If output is fixed, a rise in the wage increases labor income,[54] so the third term in (35), like the first, is negative. However, conflicting income and substitution effects make the second term ambiguous. It will be assumed that if the labor supply curve is backward-bending, this effect does not dominate the other two terms. It will also be assumed that an increase in the capital stock does not reduce the labor supply through its influence on wealth by as much as it reduces demand. Thus (35) and (36) are negative.

The signs of the derivatives of (32) establish the following relationships between Y and the other variables appearing in (32)

(37)
$$\frac{\partial Y}{\partial r} = -\frac{\partial X^L/\partial r}{\partial X^L/\partial Y} > 0$$

$$\frac{\partial Y}{\partial w/p} = -\frac{\partial X^L/\partial w/p}{\partial X^L/\partial Y} > 0$$

$$\frac{\partial Y}{\partial K} = -\frac{\partial X^L/\partial K}{\partial X^L/\partial Y} > 0$$

[52]Since the direct effect of the interest rate on labor supply is the sum of the conflicting income and substitution effects, little is lost by omitting it from the labor supply function.

[53]If this were not so, the notional supply of goods would be the binding constraint.

[54]This implicitly assumes inelastic substitution of labor for money, a plausible assumption.

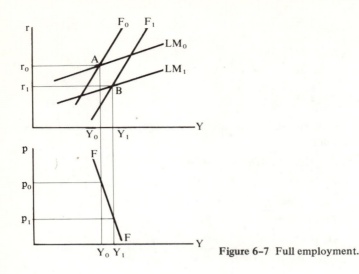

Figure 6-7 Full employment.

It is most convenient to think of this full-employment locus as a positively inclined line in r, Y space, such as the FF lines in the top panel of Figure 6-7. The slope is positive because a rise in the interest rate reduces wealth and increases the notional labor supply. This must be offset by an increase in effective demand.

The interest sensitivity of full-employment output means that the latter cannot be determined without referring to the securities market. If the securities market is always cleared, then the only points on FF which are relevant are those which are also on LM. The intersection marked A in Figure 6-7 represents one such intersection. If the price level were lower than the one corresponding to LM_0, the LM curve would lie further to the right, say at LM_1. However, a lower price level, other things equal, would imply a higher real wage. This would shift FF to the right, since a higher level of output would be needed to restore equality between the effective demand for labor and the supply. In Figure 6-7 the point on the new FF and LM curves, B, lies to the right of the old intersection, and the FF curve in the bottom panel is negatively sloped. However, a different configuration of slopes and shifts could yield a vertical or positively sloped relationship between the price level and the level of output at which the labor market is cleared.[55]

The reason for the ambiguity is a conflict between wage and wealth effects. A cut in the price level implies a higher real wage, increasing labor supply relative to demand. It also implies a lower interest rate and increased wealth, lowering the labor supply. Whether there remains any slack to be taken up by a change in output depends on whether these forces balance out. In order to avoid giving the impression that the matter is conclusive, the lower-panel FF curve will always be drawn as a vertical line

---

[55]Certain configurations of IS, LM, and FF may be ruled out by the correspondence principle. It is possible, for instance, to draw a pattern in which a rise in the price level reduces full-employment output by more than it reduces effective demand.

in subsequent diagrams.[56] In the top panel it will always be drawn so that it cuts LM from below. This ensures that an increase in the money wage or the capital stock raises full-employment output.

This analysis of the factors governing the full-employment level of output completes the development of the pieces of the Keynesian model. It consists of three major subassemblies: the regimens of effective demand, limited supply, and full employment. The next section outlines the conditions that must be satisfied if these components are to fit together in equilibrium.

Full Equilibrium of the Keynesian System

Picture an economy in which the effective demands for goods and labor match the notional supplies. Since goods and labor markets are cleared, the demanders perceive no constraints stemming from unsold supplies in other markets. Their effective demands are therefore coincident with their notional demands, and the economic system as a whole is in general equilibrium.

Such an equilibrium is a conceivable special condition of an economy subject to the forces that are described by Keynesian theory. In order to see what must be true if such an economy is to have an equilibrium, consider the following construction that is carried out in Figure 6–8.[57]

1. Pick an arbitrary nominal money supply and keep it fixed throughout the construction.
2. Draw in the top panel of Figure 6–8 the IS curve corresponding to the economy's demand functions and its historically given stock of capital. This curve will remain fixed throughout the construction.
3. Draw various LM curves corresponding to different price levels and construct the DD curve in the bottom panel. Since the nominal money stock is fixed, the DD curve is also.
4. Pick an arbitrary money wage, w_0, which may subsequently have to be modified, and draw the SS curve in the bottom panel that corresponds to it.

---

[56]The fact that full employment output is invariant with respect to the price level does not mean that it is unaffected by changes in the money wage. At a given price level, an increase in the money wage constitutes an increase in the real wage. This shifts the upper-panel FF curve rightward relative to the LM curve, shifting the lower FF curve as well.

[57]Diagrams like Figure 6–8 occupy a prominent place in the arguments of this chapter and the next. They must be interpreted with care. Since output is constrained to be the smallest of demand, supply, and the full-employment level, only the inner, or leftmost, envelope of DD, SS, and FF in the bottom panel is observable. If, for instance, supply alone constrains output, then demand cannot be read from DD, which presupposes multiplier equilibrium; demand lies somewhere between production and the point on DD corresponding to the ruling price level. Similarly, in such circumstances the level of output that fully employs the ruling notional labor supply cannot be read from FF, which presupposes labor market equilibrium. If output is smaller than the level indicated by FF, then wealth is smaller than is implied in the construction of FF, and the labor supply is larger than that implied in its construction.

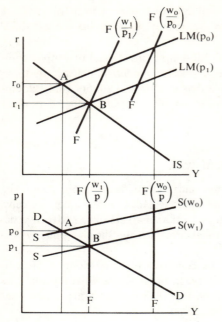

Figure 6-8 The location of general equilibrium.

5. Draw in the top panel the LM curve that corresponds to the intersection of SS and DD in the bottom panel.
6. Draw in the top panel the FF curve corresponding to the real wage implied by the SS-DD intersection in the bottom panel.
7. Draw in the bottom panel the FF curve corresponding to the FF-LM intersection in the top panel.
8. If the FF curve just drawn goes through the intersection of DD and SS, the general equilibrium is located there. If not, alter the money wage by a small amount in the same direction as the implicit excess demand for labor, draw a new SS curve, and go back to step 5.

Figure 6-8 shows two iterations of this process. The first one produces a goods-market equilibrium at Y_0, a level which fails fully to employ the labor force at a real wage equal to w_0/p_0. The second iteration successfully locates the equilibrium values Y_1, w_1, p_1, and r_1. The equilibrium wage is smaller than the initial wage.

The temptation to weave a dynamic story around this mental iteration is irresistible, although risky.[58] Imagine an economy is at point A in both panels. Its goods

---

[58]It is dangerous on two counts. First, changes in prices and wages take time. It is not legitimate to treat the IS curve, for example, as though it remained stationary over this time, since it is shifted by the capital accumulation or decumulation that is implicitly taking place. Second, it is not legitimate to ignore completely the expectational consequences of changes in prices and wages, since changes in expectations about prices and wages influence the demand and supply curves.

market is in equilibrium, but there is excess supply of labor, and the effective demand for goods is smaller than the notional demand. A deflation of wages and a relatively smaller deflation in prices are necessary to close the employment gap. The price deflation successfully reduces the interest rate and raises effective demand.[59] The wage deflation makes the price reduction possible, raises the notional supply of goods, and reduces the full-employment level of output. Equilibrium is achieved at B.

The main usefulness of such a story is that it makes it easier to see why no equilibrium might exist in any reasonable neighborhood of an initial position. Consider two cases:

1. The demand for money is highly sensitive to changes in the rate of interest.
2. The demand for goods is virtually insensitive to the rate of interest and the supply of labor is virtually insensitive to the level of wealth.

In the first of these two "Keynesian" cases,[60] a decline in the price level has negligible impact on the rate of interest, since wealth holders will absorb greater real balances without much increase in security prices. With little change in the rate of interest, there is little interest effect either on effective demand or (through the wealth effect) on the supply of labor. In the second case, even though a cut in prices lowers the interest rate, its impact on effective demand and its wealth effect on labor supply are weak.

Both cases may be illustrated in Figure 6-9. The initial position of the system is at w_0, p_0, Y_0. At that point, there is excess supply of labor. If wages fall, say to w_1, the notional supply schedule for goods shifts down in the same proportion. Because demand is totally unresponsive to price changes, the price level that restores equality between the effective demand for goods and the supply is p_1, which bears the same ratio to p_0 as w_1 does to w_0. Although there are no wealth effects on labor supply, a cut in w cuts the real wage, and shifts FF down in the same proportion. However, the relative positions of SS, FF, and p are unchanged, leaving the gap between employment and the labor supply unaffected by the deflation. The goods market is cleared at an infinity of price-wage levels, none of which will clear the labor market.[61]

To a considerable extent, this analysis clears up one of the issues that were unresolved in the previous chapter, the question of the existence of equilibrium.[62] It does so, however, by stepping outside the general equilibrium framework and analyzing the forces which regulate income and employment when markets are uncleared. Unless changes in the price level can control the interest rate and through it the level

[59] If the IS curve slopes upward, the interest rate at IS-LM equilibrium output is raised by deflation. However, the interest rate at the old level of production is reduced, engendering a cumulative expansion that only terminates when a higher rate is reached.
[60] See pages 143–144
[61] Keynes's own analysis of the inability of wage flexibility to maintain equilibrium in the labor market is considerably more elaborate than this discussion, containing a number of dynamic elements (and a number of inconsistencies). See Keynes (1936, chap. 19). See also Patinkin (1948) for a discussion of the dynamic aspects of deflation.
[62] See Chapter 5, pages 102–104.

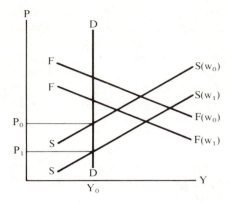

Figure 6-9 A system without equilibrium.

of effective demand, there is no reason to suppose that there exist price and wage levels that clear goods and labor markets simultaneously. If not, rigidity in prices and wages cannot be blamed for underemployment. Rather, it is a source of stability, for it prevents a perpetual deflationary spiral whose expectational effects could have disastrous consequences on the "animal spirits" of investors.[63]

Keynes thought that the situation depicted in Figure 6-9 might be characteristic of deep depression, but he believed that ordinarily there would exist an equilibrium price, wage, and interest rate.[64] Most of his followers, with the exception of the extreme income-expenditure theorists, would agree. But in an economy which has no "auctioneer" to ensure that trades take place only on equilibrium terms, those terms lose much of their interest. Attention centers instead on the day-to-day workings of disequilibrium markets.

Varieties of Disequilibrium

A common method of analyzing macroeconomic models is to begin from a state of general equilibrium, to change one or more parameters, to discuss the nature of the disequilibrium that is created, and to point out the appropriate endogenous changes to restore equilibrium. The ultimate position is then compared with the original one to see if the parameter disturbance affects the equilibrium values of the real variables of the system, or merely the nominal values.

This procedure has dubious methodological merit because it tends to elevate equilibrium to the status of the general case, from which exceptions are only temporary aberrances. In an economic system whose adjustment processes take time, if indeed they operate at all, equilibrium is a special, almost accidental, case. The present is regulated as much by the legacy of past events as it is by the economic forces of the moment. The future will reflect the forces of the present, but their working out may go unrecognized because of the heavy overlay of intervening events.

---

[63] Recall from Chapter 3, page 73, the importance that the Keynesians attach to swings in investor confidence. See also Keynes (1936, chap. 12, esp. page 162).
[64] See Keynes (1936, chap. 19).

It is very difficult to avoid focusing on equilibria, if only because two crossed lines have locally only one point in common, but so many that lie only on one or the other.[65] Nonetheless, to appreciate fully the generality of Keynesian theory, it is necessary to examine a variety of possible states of an economic system, only some of which may be represented by intersections. In addition to the general equilibrium shown in Figure 6-8, there are six distinct alternative states of the system. Three are partial equilibria, but in three neither the goods market nor the labor market is cleared.

The first three situations are illustrated in Figure 6-10.[66] In all three there is unemployed labor. The first, which is depicted in panel (a), is historically the most important, because it corresponds to the "underemployment equilibrium" of that school of Keynesians that attributes persisting unemployment to downward rigidity in the money wage.[67] The position of the system is denoted by the letter "a", both in the IS-LM diagram and in the commodity-market diagram.[68] The commodity market is cleared, but at the ruling real wage, the supply of labor exceeds the notional (and effective) demand. If the money wage were lower and the price level suitably adjusted so as to keep the effective demand for labor in line with notional demand, employment would be higher. But if money wages are rigid in a downward direction, there are no endogenous forces of expansion implicit in the situation shown.[69] Moreover, if wages are flexible, it is possible that general deflation will generate expectations of further deflation, with adverse effects on investor confidence. The net effect might be to worsen the unemployment rather than to eliminate it.

In a decentralized market system with no authority that sets prices at market-clearing levels, there is no reason to suppose that either the goods or the labor market will be cleared at any particular moment.[70] Panels (b) and (c) depict "pure" cases in which the level of production is limited solely by demand and supply respectively. In (b), there is excess supply of goods and labor. A reduction in the price level would increase employment, but a reduction in the wage would have no effect, since the real wage is already below the marginal product of labor. In (c) there is also excess supply of labor, but excess demand for goods as well.[71] Employment would be increased by

[65] For a fascinating account of the power of such "salient" points, see Schelling (1960, esp. chap. 3).

[66] In studying Figures 6-10 and 6-11, recall footnote 57.

[67] See, for example, Modigliani (1944).

[68] In all further panels of this and the next diagram, the state of the system is denoted by the same lower-case letter as the panel itself.

[69] For an account of the assymetries in the process of money wage adjustment, see Keynes (1936, chap. 19) and Tobin (1972). The latter reference is full of insights into Keynesian economics.

[70] Security markets are usually quite organized, with traders whose attempts at profit making keep supply and demand prices in line with one another. It is therefore not farfetched to assume that the security market clears even though the others do not.

[71] Whenever output is constrained by supply or full employment, the level of demand is smaller than that indicated by the DD curve but larger than the level of output. Notice that point c is in the region below the IS curve, which is the region of excess demand.

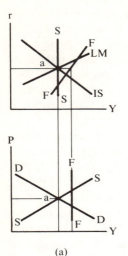

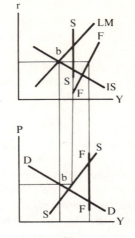

(a)　　　　　　　　　　　(b)

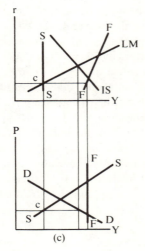

(c)

Figure 6-10 Underemployment disequilibria.

either a cut in the money wage or an increase in the price level, since the level of the
real wage is the effective barrier to a higher level of employment.

In addition to the three types of underemployment disequilibrium, there are
three patterns of disequilibrium at full employment. These are shown in Figure 6-11.
In panel (*d*), there is excess demand in both goods and labor markets. A rise in the
price level would reduce the excess demand for goods, but intensify the excess demand
for labor, which could only be reduced by an increase in the money wage. In (*e*) the
goods market is in partial equilibrium, in the sense that demand matches production.
However, at the ruling real wage, producers would like to employ more labor and supply more goods than the available labor supply permits. A rise in the money wage
would reduce both the excess supply of goods and the excess demand for labor.

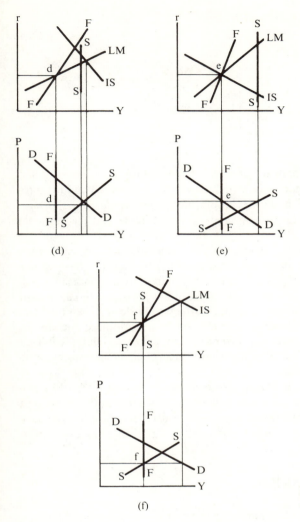

(d)   (e)

(f)

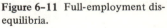

Figure 6-11 Full-employment disequilibria.

Finally, in panel (*f*) the labor market is in equilibrium, but there is excess demand
for goods. A rise in the price level would reduce this excess, but would create excess
demand for labor, which could only be eliminated by a money wage increase proportional to the price increase.

The relationships depicted in Figures 6–10 and 6–11 may be further appreciated
by examining Table 6-1, which depicts for goods and labor markets the relationships
among notional and effective demands (ND and ED), notional supplies (NS), and the
levels of output and employment (Y and L). The first three cases have in common a
shortfall of employment below the notional supply of labor, and therefore a demand
for goods that is constrained by the available employment. Effective demand falls
short of the notional demand as a consequence. In the last three, there is equality

Table 6-1 Demands and supplies in disequilibrium

Diagram	Goods market	Labor market
10a	ND > ED = Y = NS	ND = ED = L < NS
10b	ND > ED = Y < NS	ND > ED = L < NS
10c	ND > ED > Y = NS	ND = ED = L < NS
11d	ND ≠ ED > Y < NS	ND = ED > L = NS
11e	ND ≠ ED = Y < NS	ND > ED = L = NS
11f	ND = ED > Y = NS	ND = ED = L = NS

between employment and the supply of labor, so that in all cases the notional and effective demands for consumer goods are equal. However, in cases (*d*) and (*e*), production is below the level which employers would prefer, owing to labor shortage, and the effective demand for investment goods may differ from the notional demand.[72]

A person who is accustomed to focusing only on general and Keynesian underemployment equilibria might reasonably ask what cases (*b*) through (*f*) have to recommend them. The answer is simply that they depict possible circumstances in which an economy might be observed. Although each may contain pressures for adjustment toward equilibrium, if these pressures produce their effects only slowly, then the "real time" log of the economy will be filled with stretches of disequilibrium of one kind or another. Moreover, if the adjustment is sufficiently slow, parameter shifts will keep the economic system perpetually out of equilibrium. Under such circumstances, equilibrium points lose much of their interest.

The remainder of this chapter is devoted to the study of various kinds of parameter changes: changes in the stocks of money and capital and shifts in the investment and consumption function. It is largely concerned with contrasting the effects of such changes in a disequilibrium system with the effects of similar changes in a system of general equilibrium.

III. MONEY IN DISEQUILIBRIUM

In a theoretical system that assumes that markets always clear and that the participants are free from money illusion, monetary economics is as dull as ditchwater.[73] It begins and ends with the analysis of neutrality. The real stock of money is a determinate of the system, and is independent of the nominal stock, which only determines the general level of prices.[74] In the disequilibrium world of day-to-day economic events,

---

[72] The direction of the difference is unclear because of conflicting scale and substitution effects.

[73] Milton Friedman, the major figure of the monetarist school, has stated, with approbation, that "It is a commonplace of monetary theory that nothing is so unimportant as the quantity of money expressed in terms of the nominal monetary unit. . . ." Friedman (1969, p. 1).

[74] The rate of growth of the nominal stock has a broader influence, however. See Chapter 5, pages 108–111.

money exercises a much more powerful influence.[75] This was recognized by the neoclassical framers of general equilibrium theory, whose monetary theory was much broader in scope than the neutrality doctrine.[76] However, the disequilibrium theory of the neoclassical economists never fitted comfortably into the basic framework of their system of thought. By contrast, since the analysis of disequilibrium is the main focus of Keynesian analysis, monetary theory is an integral part of its analysis of income, employment, and distribution.

The nominal stock of money performs two functions. First, when the money stock is fixed, it is the fulcrum by means of which changes in the price level may exert control over the level of effective demand. Second, when the money stock is varied relative to the price level, it becomes an independent force exerting leverage on effective demand.

The first of these two functions has already been examined at some length in discussing the determinants of effective demand. Changes in the price level change the ratio of the real money supply to the real stock of securities. The reestablishment of equilibrium in the securities market requires that the interest rate move in the same direction as the price level. The change in the interest rate in turn moves effective demand in the opposite direction. This is the mechanism responsible for the negative slope of the DD curve and is one of the major stabilizing feedbacks of the process of income determination. Since this mechanism has already been analyzed in this chapter, the present section will not pursue it but will concentrate instead on the consequences of changes in the nominal money supply.

The Origins and Consequences of Changes in the Money Supply

Variations of domestic origin in the nominal money supply may take place in any of three ways. First, in a fractional-reserve banking system, changes in profit prospects may lead private banks to alter the ratio between their investments and their owned reserves.[77] Second, in times of general economic collapse, there may be widespread bank failures with attendant loss of deposits. Third, the banking authority may expand or contract the money supply in a deliberate attempt to control the course of economic events.

The first kind of monetary change is easily incorporated into the IS-LM apparatus. Rather than being given, the nominal money supply is a function of the rate of interest and the quantity of unborrowed reserves. The latter magnitude is under the control of the monetary authority, but because the interest rate is endogenous, so is the nominal supply of money, which moves in the same direction as the rate of interest. The effect of this dependence is to make the interest rate less sensitive to changes in the level of

[75]Thus the same Milton Friedman who was quoted in footnote 73 could say, in speaking of the Great Depression, "The contraction is in fact a tragic testimonial to the importance of monetary forces." Friedman and Schwartz (1963, p. 300).

[76]For a discussion of neoclassical monetary theory, see Schumpeter (1954, part IV, chap 8).

[77]For a brief introduction to the mechanism by which banks achieve these changes in the American institutional context, see Smith and Teigen (1974, pp. 87–91).

income than it would be if only the demand for money were responsive to changes in the rate of interest. This, in effect, flattens the LM curve and decreases the price sensitivity of effective demand. It also makes effective demand more responsive to changes in the capital stock or shifts in the expenditure functions.[78]

Bank failure is another endogenous source of changes in the money supply. Whether or not it is a major factor depends on institutional arrangements for coping with bank insolvency. In times of general deflation, firms and individuals which have contracts to pay banks specified amounts of nominal money find themselves unable to do so. In a *laissez-faire* banking system, the default of a bank's borrowers implies a consequent inability of the bank to honor its deposit liabilities.[79] One result is a contraction of the nominal money supply.[80] If bank failure is a sufficiently widespread consequence of deflation, a falling price level may actually lower the real money supply rather than raising it. If, however, there exists an institutional arrangement for "bailing out" the banking system, say through governmental refinancing of the banks or guaranteeing of deposits, then this endogenous link between the price level and the nominal money supply is broken.[81]

It is tempting to incorporate the phenomenon of bank failure into the Keynesian system by making the nominal money supply an increasing function of the price level. The effect of this would be to reduce the price sensitivity of effective demand, perhaps making the DD curve slope backwards. It is probably not a good idea to succumb to this temptation, however. Bankruptcy brought on by deflation is so largely a dynamic phenomenon that it is a mistake to analyze it with static tools. What matters is not whether prices are high or low, but whether they are falling so fast that debtors cannot cope with the rate of increase in the real value of their liabilities. Perhaps the best way analytically to envision the consequences of financial collapse is to picture the DD schedule shifting backward at a greater rate than the price level declines. The deflation fails to stimulate effective demand because nominal money is being destroyed through bank failure at a greater rate than real money is being created through deflation. The price, money supply, interest rate nexus simply breaks down. Even though a low price level might depress the interest rate and increase effective demand, a falling price level increases it. This monetary influence on the nominal rate of interest is added to the

---

[78] See the discussion of pages 140–144 regarding the importance of the slope of the LM curve.

[79] Borrower default is by no means the only source of bank failure. A common source of failure of American banks up until recent times was a loss of depositor confidence in the solvency of the banking system. This produced a rash of withdrawals of specie, or, in later years, currency, precipitating the very insolvency which it anticipated. However, it seems reasonable to suppose that if nonfinancial business had not been so deflation-prone, the banking system would not have been so precarious nor runs on the banks so common. For a history of the instability of American banking from the Civil War through the Bank Holiday of 1933, see Friedman and Schwartz [1963, Chs. 2–7].

[80] Another consequence is a destruction of wealth. At first glance, the default of a liability might seem to be merely a transfer of wealth from the creditor to the debtor. If the default puts the debtor in receivership, however, his physical assets pass out of private hands for the time being, in effect reducing private wealth. Moreover, the uncertainty and pessimism surrounding bankruptcy further impairs wealth by dimming expectations of future rents.

[81] The development in the United States of guarantee institutions such as the Federal Deposit Insurance Corporation was a direct outgrowth of the bank failures of the 1930's.

expectational effect of falling prices on the real rate of interest, with depressing consequences for the level of investment. Thus monetary changes through bank failure, where institutions permit, are a dangerous source of downward instability in effective demand.

The final source of changes in the nominal stock of money is the deliberate activity of the authority of monetary control. Because the nominal stock of money is an argument of the LM curve, it is also an argument in the DD schedule that links effective demand to the price level. Providing that the demand for money is less than infinitely elastic with respect to the rate of interest, the banking authority can exercise control over the interest rate through its control of the nominal money supply. Providing that the demand for goods is at all elastic with respect to the interest rate, the monetary authority has indirect control over the level of effective demand. This control provides the banking system with stabilization powers that it may use to compensate for the deficiencies of a poorly functioning price system.

One of the most obvious uses of monetary control is the substitution of monetary expansion for deflation as a means of expanding employment and production. This policy operates most directly when effective demand is the only barrier to full employment. In Figure 6–12, such a condition is indicated by point "b" on the demand curve $D_0 D_0$.[82] A sufficient monetary expansion will shift the effective demand schedule to $D_1 D_1$ and raise the level of production to the full-employment level without any adjustment in prices.[83] In the absence of such monetary expansion, an increase in production will not take place unless the price level is downwardly flexible. Because of expectational effects, creation of real money through deflation may not work, leaving nominal monetary expansion as the only effective means of expanding demand.[84]

The case for monetary expansion is less obvious when unemployment is due to factors other than simple demand deficiency. If the goods market is initially in equilibrium, as depicted at point "a" in Figure 6–12, monetary expansion depends for its effectiveness on the ability of excess demand for goods to depress the real wage through raising the price level. Under such conditions, the influence of monetary control depends not only on interest rate flexibility and the responsiveness of demand to changes in the interest rate, but also on upward flexibility in prices relative to money wages. Although such upward flexibility may be more characteristic of markets than are downward price and wage flexibility, lags in price adjustment place limits on the power of monetary expansion.

The same arguments that can be made on behalf of monetary expansion as a deliberate means of reducing unemployment can be made for monetary contraction as

[82] The various lower case Latin letters indicating initial disequilibria correspond to those used in Figures 6–10 and 6–11. These figures should be consulted for the IS-LM diagrams corresponding to the initial positions.

[83] It may also reduce the level of full-employment output through interest and wealth effects on the labor supply.

[84] All this discussion, of course, ignores the fiscal activities of government, which are treated in the next chapter.

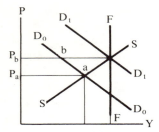

Figure 6–12 Monetary expansion and employment.

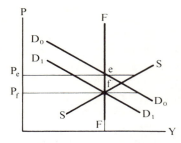

Figure 6–13 Monetary contraction and inflation.

a means of controlling inflation. Whenever there is excess demand for goods, a reduction in the real money supply can eliminate it, providing that the interest rate in fact exerts control over demand. A rise in the price level can achieve the needed reduction. However, rising prices may engender expectations of further increases, lowering the real interest rate even as the nominal rate increases. A reduction in the nominal money supply can achieve the same reduction in the real supply without engendering such expectations.

Again the case for monetary control is most strong when excess demand for goods is the only source of upward pressure on the price level. If an economy is at position "f" in Figure 6–13, a sufficient reduction in the nominal money supply will eliminate excess demand without the need for any increase in prices or wages. If the initial price level is high enough that there is also excess demand for labor, such as at "e", then some increase in prices and wages is required to eliminate all excess demands. Reliance cannot be placed entirely on monetary control, since the feedback mechanisms of the market system must also operate to secure an appropriate adjustment in the real wage.

Arguments such as these establish a presumption on behalf of active control over the nominal money supply as a supplemental means of correcting disequilibria. Whereas general equilibrium theory points to a dichotomy between real and nominal values, disequilibrium analysis recognizes that "money matters." General equilibrium is, of course, a limiting case of the Keynesian system, and the real values of equilibrium are not influenced by changes in the nominal money supply. Not so, however, the real values that actually occur in day-to-day situations of disequilibrium, which are very much under monetary control.

The belief that money matters is not quite synonymous with a belief in the desirability of an active monetary policy, however. There is one school of thought that proclaims the power of money yet argues against deliberate attempts to control output and employment through monetary changes. Before leaving the subject of money in disequilibrium, it is well to give this line of thought some consideration.

Monetary Changes as a Source of Disturbance

The belief that cyclical changes in the money supply are a source of cycles in output and employment is a doctrine that goes back as far as the nineteenth century.

Wicksell[85] argued that booms are produced through a steady expansion of bank credit that pegs the market rate of interest at a level below the prospective return on investment. Because the expansion of credit is limited by the reserves of the banking system, it is self-terminating and is inevitably followed by a period of contraction during which the rate of interest first equals and then exceeds the yield on physical capital. Although Wicksell emphasized the implications of credit cycles for changes in the price level, it is evident that a theory of the employment cycle could be devised along similar lines.

The villains in Wicksell's theory are laissez faire banks that expand and contract the money supply in response to profit incentives. It might seem that a strong central bank could exercise sufficient control over the private banking system not only to prevent it from being a destabilizing influence but also to induce it to act to offset other sources of instability.

Friedman has from time to time[86] expressed a contrary view. He argues that the lags in the response of the real system to changes in the nominal money supply are long and variable. A well-intentioned central bank may institute monetary expansion at a time when effective demand is depressed, only to find that its consequences are so delayed that they ultimately add inflationary pressures to an endogenous recovery. The central bank then reels from ill-timed expansion to ill-timed contraction, perpetually aggravating the instability of the system it is attempting to stabilize. Friedman argues that a policy of steady, moderate,[87] and predictable expansion of the money supply is more likely to promote stability than an attempt to "fine-tune" the economy through deliberate control.

Whether it is possible to stabilize demand through timely monetary control is largely an empirical issue, hinging on the predictability of fluctuations in demand and the reliability of controls. Whatever the facts of the matter are, the theory of disequilibrium suggests that monetary changes exert a major influence on income and employment. Thus one's attitude toward changes in the nominal money supply must be strongly influenced by whether he accepts equilibrium or disequilibrium as the normal state of economic affairs.

The next and final section of the chapter deals with a number of other major issues about which the equilibrium and disequilibrium world views have very different things to say. Particularly, it deals with the relationships between saving-investing process and the distribution of income. This is one of the areas of economic analysis in which theory and ideology are most deeply intertwined.

---

[85] See Wicksell (1898).

[86] These views are expressed in Friedman and Schwartz (1963), Friedman (1968a), and most emphatically in Friedman (1959b, p. 351), in which he says, "Relatively small changes in the stock of money, properly timed and correct in magnitude, may be adequate to offset other changes making for instability. On the other hand, relatively small changes in the stock of money, random in timing and size, may equally be an important source of instability. If the reaction mechanism I have described is in any substantial measure valid, the system may not have a large tolerance for mistakes in monetary management."

[87] For a discussion of the appropriate rate of expansion, see Chapter 5, page 111.

IV. CAPITAL AND DISTRIBUTION

The analysis of equilibrium systems in Chapter 5 arrived at several major conclusions regarding the effects of capital accumulation on distribution.[88] The most important of these were the following:

1. An increase in the capital stock must raise the real wage, although it may raise or lower the return on wealth.
2. An increase in the willingness to save at given values of the wage, the interest rate, and wealth raises the real wage and lowers the return on wealth, both in the short and the long run.
3. A capital-using technical change that raises both the average and marginal products of capital at given input levels raises both the real wage and the return on wealth in the long run. Provided that the immediate impact on production is greater than that on investment demand, it also raises the real wage in the short run.

Although these propositions are the products of abstract analysis, they carry a heavy ideological overlay, since they imply a substantial harmony of interest between the working class and the accumulators of private wealth. In order to explore the extent to which this vision of harmony depends on the assumption that markets are normally in equilibrium, each of the following sections takes up the impact of one of the three changes on an economy subject to persistent disequilibrium.

The Effects of Accumulation

An increase in the capital stock has three direct influences on the variables of the Keynesian system. They may most conveniently be discussed with reference to a diagram of the commodity market such as those used extensively in this chapter. A higher capital stock shifts the curves of such a diagram in the following ways:

1. The DD curve shifts to the left because of the depressing effect of increased capital on further investment demand. This direct impact is, of course, amplified by the multiplier but damped by the monetary feedback.
2. The SS curve shifts downward at a fixed money wage, since an increased capital stock implies both a higher marginal product of labor at a given level of employment[89] and a lower level of employment at a given rate of production.[90]
3. Because a higher capital stock implies lower employment at a given level of production, the FF curve shifts to the right.

[88] See Chapter 5, pages 117–118.
[89] This is implied by the assumption that labor and capital are cooperating factors.
[90] If employment shrinks at a given level of production, so does marginal cost, since lower employment implies a rise in the marginal product of labor additional to that which is the direct consequence of a higher capital stock.

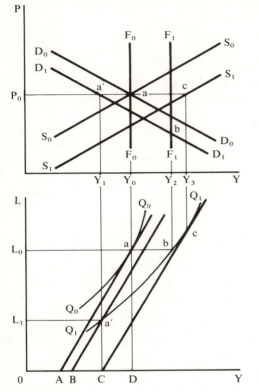

Figure 6-14 The effects of accumulation.

The impact of these shifts depends on the position of the system prior to change. In order best to appreciate the differences between equilibrium and Keynesian conclusions, assume the initial position to be one of general equilibrium, such as point "a", the intersection of $D_0 D_0$, $S_0 S_0$, and $F_0 F_0$ in the top panel of Figure 6-14.

An accumulation of capital shifts the curves of the top panel to $D_1 D_1$, $S_1 S_1$, and $F_1 F_1$. The new general-equilibrium level of production is Y_2, at which the real wage is higher than initially.[91] However, the proximate effect of the accumulation is to leave the system at "a'", at a level of production Y_1. In the absence of immediate price and wage adjustment, the new capital effectively leads to a depression through increasing supply and reducing demand.

The direct effects on distribution may be seen in the bottom panel. The curves $Q_0 Q_0$ and $Q_1 Q_1$ relate employment and production before and after the accumulation. Because the initial position is a general equilibrium, the marginal product of labor at L_0 is equal to the real wage, and the initial wage bill is AD, leaving OA as the total of profit and depreciation. After the accumulation, the new production function is

---

[91] It may be verified that the money wage adjustment necessary to achieve equilibrium is smaller than the price adjustment. Possible wealth effects on the labor supply have been ignored.

Q_1Q_1. The point at which its slope equals the marginal product of labor at the old equilibrium is "c", corresponding to an unchanged real wage in the top panel. Therefore the marginal product of labor at "b", the new general equilibrium,[92] is higher than at the old. However, the immediate move is to "a'", at which the marginal product of labor exceeds the real wage because the effective demand for labor is constrained by a want of demand for goods. The wage bill has shrunk to BC, and the sum of profits and depreciation has risen to OB. Whether profit itself has risen or fallen depends on the amount of new depreciation.[93]

If the initial position had involved excess demand for goods or labor, the direct effect of accumulation would have been to relieve the excess. However, where there is no excess, additional capital produces unemployment and underutilization. The realization of the equilibrium effects of capital accumulation depends entirely on the ability of the price system to cope with excess supply. If it copes badly, the supposed rise in real wages is illusory.[94]

An Increase in the Saving Rate

The consequences of a rise in households' desired rate of saving are fairly easily traced, since the only direct effect of such a shift is to lower effective demand. If households consume less at given values of the wage rate, the interest rate, wealth, and employment, the IS curve is shifted downward. Unless the excess demand for money has zero elasticity with respect to the interest rate, the ultimate effect is to lower effective demand at the existing price level and to produce unemployment.[95] Whatever the supposed equilibrium benefits of such a shift, the direct effect on the labor force is a reduction in its income.

Curiously enough, a rise in the rate of intended saving may not even raise the rate of saving actually realized. With the capital stock and the real wage given, the amount of investment and therefore saving is an increasing function of the level of production and a decreasing function of the rate of interest. A downward shift in the IS curve lowers both production and the interest rate in money-multiplier equilibrium. If the LM curve is flatter than the equal-investment contour through the initial IS-LM intersection, then the production effect will dominate. Thus if the demand generation forces are "Keynesian," with a high interest elasticity of the demand for money and a low interest elasticity of investment demand,[96] an attempt to increase the rate of saving will in fact lower it. This phenomenon is known as the "paradox of thrift."

[92] In Figure 6-14, the level of employment is shown to be unchanged from one equilibrium to the other. Whether or not this would happen depends on the precise characteristics of the labor supply function. It is certainly a possibility.

[93] If the DD curve shifts far enough, the sum of profit and depreciation can fall rather than rise.

[94] The secondary consequence of an increase in the capital stock may be either to raise or to lower the real wage rate. It all depends whether prices or wages fall more rapidly in the face of excess supplies in the goods and labor markets. This is not a matter which can effectively be pursued with tools which are designed for static comparisons.

[95] This assumes, of course, that the initial position is not one of excess demand.

[96] See above, pages 143-144.

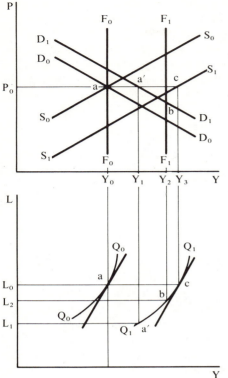

Figure 6–15 The effects of technical change.

Capital-Using Technical Change

The effects of a technical change that raises the incentive to invest are more complicated than those of an increase in the desire to save. Suppose that the change raises both the marginal and average products of capital at unchanged levels of inputs but leaves the marginal product of labor unchanged. Starting from an initial general equilibrium such as point "a" in Figure 6–15, all curves in both panels shift. At the initial level of employment, total output rises to Y_3, but the marginal product at point "c" is the same as at "a". Since the implied rise in wealth reduces the labor supply relative to demand at an unchanged real wage, the general-equilibrium labor supply is lowered from L_0 to L_2, and the full-employment level of production is Y_2, at a real wage higher than the initial level.

What happens to the actual levels of employment and production? This depends on the shift in demand induced by the higher rate of return on investment. Unless the increase in investment together with its induced multiplier effects is sufficiently strong, the immediate impact of the technical improvement will be to produce unemployment, as at the point "a'." Again, the promised real-wage increase depends for its realization on the responsiveness of the price structure.

A sufficiently large demand shift may move the demand for labor directly to the full-employment level or even beyond, leaving it to a combination of price reduction and money wage increase to effect the adjustment in the real wage.[97] Thus a technical change of this sort, unlike capital accumulation or a saving-rate increase, need not redound immediately to the disadvantage of labor.

This demand-creating impact of technical change is likely to be felt fairly quickly, but it contains the seeds of its own destruction. A period of heightened investment demand is simultaneously a period of rapid accumulation, with implications for employment that have been discussed just above.[98] Although the requisite price and wage adjustments for the maintenance of full employment may be postponed by an investment boom, they cannot be postponed forever. As Keynes said:[99]

> Ancient Egypt was doubly fortunate, and doubtless owed to this its fabled wealth, in that it possessed *two* activities, namely, pyramid-building as well as the search for the precious metals, the fruits of which, since they could not serve the needs of man by being consumed, did not stale with abundance. The Middle Ages built cathedrals and sang dirges. Two pyramids, two masses for the dead, are twice as good as one; but not so two railways from London to York.

Summary

This chapter has been devoted to the development of the Keynesian model, the major alternative to general equilibrium analysis as a tool for understanding the market system. Although this development could build on the previous chapter, it was a lengthy task. Disequilibrium models are inherently more complicated than equilibrium models because of the extra set of interrelationships among their markets.

The task of contrasting the differing conclusions of the two systems was only begun here. Because the macroeconomic role of government fiscal activities has yet to be introduced, no complete contrast of the two is possible at this juncture. Instead, this contrast will be deferred to the end of the next chapter.

[97]In order for the increase in the real wage to be forthcoming at all, the demand shift must not carry as far as point "c." See Chapter 5, pages 124–126, especially footnote 62.

[98]The dual capacity- and demand-generating aspects of investment led to the development of a substantial dynamic literature whose early milestones were Harrod (1939) and Domar (1948).

[99]Keynes (1936, p. 131).

SEVEN

THE MACROECONOMIC EFFECTS OF GOVERNMENT POLICY

Questions about the viability of the market system and the extent of class harmony under capitalism are largely the province of cranks, revolutionaries, and social philosophers. They are hardly ever mentioned in the newspapers. But questions about the proper levels of government spending, taxes, and debt issue are perpetually at the center of public debate. Analysis, ideology, and politics intertwine in annual discussions of the budget, frequent reviews of the tax system, and occasional challenges to the institutional structure that conducts fiscal and monetary policies. In all these debates, both the analytical tools and the preconceptions of economists play a major role.

Up to now, this book has mainly focused on the interactions of purely private agents. The only public activity so far discussed has been the creation of deposits by the banking system. Obviously, explicit treatment of the macroeconomic effects of government policy is necessary in order to provide the tools for debating policy issues. This chapter therefore introduces into the previously developed systems of analysis a government that taxes, borrows, and spends, and controls the banking system.

The chapter is divided into three major sections. The first discusses the various ways in which the government influences the supplies and demands that govern the market system. The second traces the effects of policy changes in a system of general equilibrium. The third evaluates the effects of similar policy changes in a Keynesian system of uncleared markets. A final brief section contrasts the conclusions of equilibrium and Keynesian analyses. It is, in effect, a summary not only of the present chapter, but also of the two previous chapters as well.

I. GOVERNMENT IN THE MARKET SYSTEM

Governments differ drastically from one another even within the group of nations whose economies are largely dominated by market capitalism. Among the main sources of variety are differences in the nature and magnitude of public enterprise, in the extent of direct control over private enterprise, and in the mechanisms of indirect control over resource allocation and income distribution.[1] In addition, the institutions of monetary and budgetary decision making differ considerably from country to country.[2] However, nearly all such governments share a common set of instruments by means of which they may influence the aggregate levels of activity of their countries' markets. These instruments fall into three broad groups:

1. Direct participation in the markets through the purchase of commodities and labor services and the sale and purchase of government securities
2. Indirect control through the effects of taxes and transfer payments on private demands and supplies
3. Indirect control through the ability to influence deposit creation and the size of the nominal money supply

Within these broad instrumental categories there is room for considerably institutional variety. In order to limit the scope of the present discussion, attention will be restricted to an abstract government which has the following powers:

1. It buys commodities and labor services on the same competitive terms as those paid by private buyers.
2. It buys and sells its own securities, which are indistinguishable from private issues, on the same terms available to private traders in both private and government securities.
3. It levies taxes at a constant proportional rate on all household income from wages, interest, dividends, and capital gains, whether realized or not; included in taxable income are interest and capital gains on securities issued by the government.[3]
4. It controls by directive the deposit creating activities of the banking system.

Although this highly stylized government would hardly provide the raw material for a treatise either on public finance or money and banking, its activities are sufficiently complicated to raise most of the interesting theoretical issues regarding the macroeconomic impact of government.

---

[1] For comparative studies which cover both capitalist and socialist economies, see Pryor (1968, 1973) and Shepherd et al. (1976).

[2] For a comparative survey of the conduct of monetary policy, see Hodgeman (1974). Musgrave (1969) surveys the conduct of fiscal policy. The multilingual reader may wish to consult Schneider (1968) for a survey of decision-making processes in Western Europe, the United States, and Canada. The paper on the United States, written by the present author, is also published in Smith and Teigen (1974).

[3] Depreciation expense is assumed to be exempt from taxation.

This section is divided into three parts. The first is devoted to the direct and indirect ways in which governments affect the goods and labor markets. The second covers the impact of income taxation on private demands and supplies. The third is devoted to the complicated issues raised by the government's ability to run deficits and thereby become indebted to individuals and private banks. Since the assumed mechanism of monetary control is so simple, there is no need of a fourth section devoted to changes in the money supply, which in any case were discussed in the past two chapters.

Government Demands for Commodities and Labor

Ostensibly, at least, the direct participation of the government in goods and labor markets is a simple matter. The equality between the demand for and production of commodities may be written[4]

$$(1) \qquad\qquad C + I + G = Y$$

where G denotes the real value of government purchases from private firms and Y denotes the level of private production of commodities, whether sold to households, firms, or government. In an equilibrium system, all these symbols denote notional demands. In a Keynesian system, they denote effective demands.[5,6] Thus, (1) may be interpreted as an equation of market or of multiplier equilibrium, depending on the context.

The equality between the demand for and production of labor services may be written

$$(2) \qquad\qquad L^d + L^g = L$$

where L^d and L^g are respectively business and governmental demands. In an equilibrium system, L^d is notional demand and L equals L^s, the notional supply, so that (2) is a statement of labor market equilibrium. In a disequilibrium system, L^d is effective demand, and (2) simply states that total employment is the sum of effective private and governmental demands.

Providing that the government purchases goods and labor services on the same terms as those facing households and firms,[7] one price level will do for all commodities and one wage level for all employment. Thus the participation of the government

---

[4] In order to avoid complicating the discussion in ways that are not essential, the government is treated as though it kept no bank balances of its own. Households' balances are subsumed in C and Y except when the demand for and supply of money are under explicit consideration.

[5] The distinction between notional and effective demands is presented in Chapter 6, pages 129–131.

[6] In this chapter, no distinction will be drawn between notional and effective demands on the part of the government. Implicitly, therefore, tax revenues do not constrain government expenditures.

[7] In order for this to be an acceptable assumption, it must be true that firms' transformation rates between private and government production and households' substitution rates between private and public employment are both minus one.

in the goods and labor markets does not apparently alter the fact that household demands and supplies are governed by the real wage, the interest rate, and (in disequilibrium) the level of employment. Nor does the government's participation obviously alter the dependence of firm decisions on the real wage, the interest rate, the capital stock, and (in disequilibrium) the level of effective demand. It would seem therefore that the government's direct influence in these markets could be taken account of simply by substituting (1) and (2) for their counterparts in the systems analyzed in Chapters 5 and 6.[8]

Although nothing is wrong with this interchange of equations, the impact of government market participation is not so simple a matter as it might seem. Governments ordinarily make use of the goods they buy and the workers they hire, and many of the activities to which the government allocates resources are complementary to or competitive with activities that might be undertaken by private parties. For instance, if the government decides to pay for physicians' care for the aged, individuals need not provide this service for themselves. For people who already are retired at the time the government decides to pay their medical bills, only the distribution of private expenditures among goods is likely to be affected. However, for people who are not yet retired, the appropriate distribution of private expenditure over time will be affected by the expectation of free physicians' care during retirement, and current consumption will rise. If the government decides to provide goods and services that are only usable by the relatively young, private consumption will fall as the young redirect their own spending toward their retirement. Similar examples can be brought forth to show how government spending may alter the factor demand and commodity supply functions of private firms.

Perhaps the best way to view the government's participation in the goods and factor markets is to think of it as a separate production sector that buys its inputs from private industry and the labor market, produces factor and consumer services, and gives them away to firms and households.[9] Since part of the government's purchases represents capital accumulation, there is no rigid link between its current purchases and its current provision of consumer and factor services. Like private output, government output is produced with capital as well as current inputs. However, unlike the productive activities of private firms, neither the government's factor purchases nor its output levels are regulated by factor prices or effective demand. They are instead regulated by political decisions. However they are set, the levels of government production affect households' utilities and firms' production possibilities. What the government does is therefore parametric to private decision making, and enters into the demand and supply functions of private firms. Thus changes in government purchases have indirect as well as direct effects on the market system.

Unfortunately, the formalization of the indirect effects is not an easy matter. It

---

[8]The counterparts to Equation (1) are Equation (21) in Chapter 5 and Equation (3) in Chapter 6. Those to (2) are (22) in Chapter 5 and (4) in Chapter 6.

[9]Even though most government output is financed by taxation, most individual tax liabilities (other than user charges) are unaffected by the individual's use of government services. At the margin, therefore, the use of government services is free.

will not do simply to include the levels of government purchases of goods and labor as arguments in private demand and supply functions. One reason is that investment-capital problem alluded to in the previous paragraph. The main reason is that analysis of the problem requires disaggregation in an intrinsic way. The pattern of complementarity and substitutability between public and private output is essential to the matter. Any formal treatment would require that the composition of government production be explicitly recognized. This is not possible in a general treatment of macroeconomic analysis, and it will not be attempted here. The analysis of government spending will be restricted to the direct effects that are recognized in Equations (1) and (2). However, the indirect effects will be mentioned again toward the end of the chapter.

Taxation and Household Behavior

If taxes are levied even-handedly on all forms of household income, neither the production nor the financing decisions of firms can be influenced by the size of the tax rate.[10] The tax rate can only influence the demands and supplies of households. In order to study the effects of taxation on the private economy, it is therefore necessary to expand the analysis of Chapter 2 to take account of income taxation.

Fortunately, a flat-rate income taxation enters into the decision-making process in a fairly simple way.[11] The rate of increase of a household's wealth is equal to its after-tax income less its consumption expenditure. If the income tax rate is denoted by τ and ρ is defined to be $(1 - \tau)$, then the rate of increase in wealth can be written

$$(3) \qquad \dot{W} = \rho r(W - M^h) + \rho w L - pC$$

In integral form, this amounts to[12]

$$(4) \qquad W(n) = \int_n^d e^{-\rho r(t-n)} [pC + \rho r M^h - \rho w L] \ dt$$

The household planning problem is to maximize the utility of its lifetime consumption, work effort, and money-holding plan, subject to the constraint implied by (4) and by any current and expected unemployment. Notice from (3) and (4) that ρ (and therefore τ) enter as decision parameters only in association with r and w. Thus the higher is the tax rate, the lower, in effect, are the wage rate and the rate of interest. Any variation in the tax rate will have an impact on the household that is a combination of the income and substitution effects of changes in the interest and wage rates.

Consider first the income effects. If (4) is differentiated with respect to τ and the

[10] Two major articles on the effects of alternative tax systems on the financial and production decisions of firms are Modigliani and Miller (1958) and Hall and Jorgenson (1967).

[11] However, the reader is urged to review Chapter 2 before proceeding with this section.

[12] If households plan bequests, the right-hand side includes an additional term equal to the present value of $W(d)$.

derivative is suitably simplified,[13] the result is

$$(5) \qquad \frac{\partial W(n)}{\partial \tau} = \int_n^d e^{-\rho r(t-n)} [r(W - M^h) + wL] \ dt$$

That is, the compensating variation per unit change in the tax rate is equal to the present value of the income subject to tax along the prechange plan.[14] If the compensating variation is not made, a rise in the tax rate has income effects similar to those of a lump-sum loss in wealth. Consumption and money demand will drop, and labor supply will rise.

The substitution effects must be studied with the aid of the relevant marginal conditions. After modification to take account of taxes, they are[15]

$$(6) \qquad -F_L = \rho \frac{w}{p} F_c$$

$$(7) \qquad F_{M/p} = \rho r F_c$$

$$(8) \qquad \frac{dF_c}{dt} = -\rho r F_c$$

Take first the static substitutions. A rise in τ (hence a fall in ρ) will lower the amount of consumption that can be obtained by surrendering leisure. As a consequence, both work effort and consumption will be reduced. If we combine (6) and (7), we see that a change in the tax rate leaves the rate of substitution between work effort and money holding unchanged. Since the marginal disutility of labor is to fall when work effort is decreased, the marginal utility of money should fall as well. This argues for more money holding. However, consumption is to fall, and if there is a complementarity between consumption and money holding, the fall in consumption will lower the marginal utility of money at an unchanged money holding. Apparently, the overall result is ambiguous and depends on the strength of the complementarity.

Since a rise in the tax rate lowers the effective rate of interest, there are intertemporal substitution effects that must also be accounted for. According to (8), the higher is the tax rate (and the lower is ρ), the lower is the rate at which the marginal utility of consumption should decline over the life span. Therefore a higher tax rate implies higher consumption in the present and lower consumption in the future. If we assume that leisure and money holding are normal goods, their current values will also be increased relative to future values owing to the intertemporal substitution effect.

---

[13] To see how this differentiation is done, see Chapter 2, pages 30–32.

[14] Since the tax rate is a proportion, a one-unit change is equal to 100 percentage points, so that if the rate were ever increased by a whole unit, the yield would be equal to the whole of the income subject to tax. The yield of a one percentage point increase in the rate would be one hundredth of the before-tax income.

[15] Recall that $-F_L$, $F_{M/p}$ and F_c are respectively the marginal disutility of labor and the marginal utilities of real balances and consumption.

Table 7-1 Effects of a tax increase

Type of effect	Effects on		
	C	L^S	M^h
Income	–	+	–
Static substitution	–	–	?
Intertemporal substitution	+	–	+

The income and substitution effects are summarized in Table 7-1. Not surprisingly, the analysis is inconclusive because of conflicts between income and substitution effects. For the sake of subsequent analysis, assume that the income effects dominate consumption and money demand, and that the overall impact on labor supply is negligible. This leads to the formulation of an altered set of household behavioral equations, replacing those used in the previous two chapters. They are

$$(9) \qquad C = C\left(\frac{w}{p}, r, \frac{W}{p}, L, \tau\right)$$

$$(10) \qquad L^s = L^s\left(\frac{w}{p}, r, \frac{W}{p}, \tau\right)$$

$$(11) \qquad \frac{M^h}{p} = \phi^h\left(\frac{w}{p}, r, \frac{W}{p}, L, \tau\right)$$

Their derivatives with respect to τ are respectively negative, negligible, and negative. Following the practice of Chapter 5, we will drop the level of employment from the effective demand functions, (9) and (11), when discussing general equilibrium.

The Government Debt and Private Wealth

To appreciate the place of government debt in the process that determines private demands and supplies, it is necessary first to trace the flow of property income through the business and banking systems to households, the ultimate owners of property. For this purpose, some notation is required. Let a government bond be a promise to pay one currency unit in perpetuity. Then the number of government bonds outstanding (B^g) is equal to the flow of interest paid by the government. This interest is divided into direct payments to households (B^{gh}) and payments to banks ($B^{g\beta}$) in proportion to the distribution of immediate ownership of the government debt.[16] Of course

$$(12) \qquad B^g = B^{gh} + B^{g\beta}$$

Industrial firms make profits (P^b) that are divided between direct payments to households (P^{bh}) and payments to banks ($P^{b\beta}$), again in proportion to the distribution of

---

[16] For simplicity, it is assumed that industrial firms do not own government bonds.

immediate ownership of the corresponding securities. Since this distribution is exhaustive

$$(13) \qquad P^b = P^{bh} + P^{b\beta}$$

Banks deduct their expenses from the receipts that they get from the government and from industrial firms, and pay the balance (P^β) to the owners of their securities.[17]

The flow of property income from firms to households may be stated as

$$(14) \qquad P^{bh} = p(C + I + G) - wL^b - pD^b - P^{b\beta}$$

That is, it equals the value of privately produced commodities[18] less wages, depreciation, and payments to banks. The flow of property income from banks to households may be stated as

$$(15) \qquad P^\beta = P^{b\beta} + B^{g\beta} - wL^\beta - pD^\beta$$

Households also receive interest directly from the government and imputed interest on their bank balances, so that their total property income is given by

$$(16) \qquad P^{bh} + P^\beta + B^{gh} + rM^h = (pY - wL - pD) + B^g$$

This result is obtained by adding (14), (15), B^{gh}, and rM^h, substituting (12) and (13), and recalling that[19]

$$(17) \qquad pY = p(C + I + G) + rM^h$$

If real household wealth is defined to be the capitalized value of property income measured in commodity units, then it is given by

$$(18) \qquad \frac{W}{p} = \frac{1}{r} \left[Y - \frac{w}{p} L - D \right] + \frac{B^g}{rp}$$

Since B^g/rp is the real value of the government debt, the debt is apparently private wealth.

It is hard to imagine any matter in economic analysis about which there exists more confusion than the question of the nature of the public debt.[20] Although much of the literature on the subject is not relevant in the current context, the question as to whether the debt is an asset, a liability, or a washout must be dealt with in assessing the impact of government activity on the market system.

---

[17]This chapter continues the practice of previous chapters in assuming that both banks and industrial firms retain just enough earnings to cover depreciation and pay the balance to their security owners.

[18]At the moment, this value is measured exclusive of the value of banking services; so is the value of C. Subsequent to this accounting exercise, C will again be understood to include the value of banking services.

[19]Equation (17) differs from (1) only because of the difference in inclusiveness of the symbol C.

[20]Many of the major papers are included in Ferguson (1964). On the issue most pertinent to the present context, whether the debt is wealth, see Barro (1974).

The easiest place to begin is with something that is not controversial. Suppose that a government that initially has no outstanding debt issues some bonds and gives them away. It finances the interest on its bond issue by levying lump-sum taxes. The market value of the bond issue is equal to the present value of the future interest payments; the future tax liabilities have a present value equal to the value of the bond issue. Apart from distributional effects, the private sector is neither better nor worse off.

It is necessary, however, to treat the debt as an asset in order to account properly for the transaction. The reason is that the amount of any tax must enter as an argument in household demand and supply functions in order to reflect correctly the impact of tax changes that have nothing at all to do with the debt. When a tax increases, it will have an income effect on demands and supplies equivalent to that of a loss in wealth equal to the present value of the tax increase. If the debt-tax package is to register as a washout in the demand and supply functions, the public debt must be included as a part of private wealth.

The argument is much the same if the debt service is financed through income taxation. Because of the possibility of substituting leisure for market goods, the present value of the tax increase measured at initial levels of work effort will have to exceed the market value of the debt, imposing an "excess burden" by comparison with lump-sum taxation.[21] However, providing that the income effects of this tax increase are correctly reflected in the demand and supply equations, the public debt must again be counted as part of private wealth in order correctly to reflect the impact of the debt-taxation package.

Suppose that the government issues debt and does not raise tax rates, intending instead to pay the interest by borrowing further. Ought this to be treated as an increase in wealth, with no corresponding increase in tax liability? If so, will private demands and supplies not react as they would to any other increases in wealth?

To see why this is a controversial matter, it is necessary to appreciate that the present value of taxation necessary to finance a debt is independent of whether the taxation is levied as soon as the debt is incurred or deferred to a later date and then raised to a level sufficient to cover the then larger debt. Suppose that a debt equal in value to one currency unit is incurred at date n. At date t_0, subsequent to n, the value of the debt together with accumulated interest is equal to $e^{r(t_0-n)}$, and the interest thereupon is $re^{r(t_0-n)}$. If the government begins at t_0 to pay this interest by taxing, the value as of date n of the subsequent stream of taxation is given by

$$(19) \qquad X(n) = \int_{t_0}^{\infty} e^{-r(t-n)} \left(re^{r(t_0-n)} \right) dt$$

It is easy to verify that this value is one, irrespective of t_0, provided only that t_0 is finite. That is to say, the value of the taxation implied by a given debt is independent of the extent to which interest is temporarily financed through further borrowing.

Another example may help to bring out the practical import of this fact. In order

---

[21] For a general discussion of excess burdens, see Musgrave and Musgrave (1976, pp. 461–81).

to cover a deficit, the government must issue securities equal in value to that deficit.[22] That is

$$(20) \qquad \frac{\dot{B}^g}{r} = pG + B^g - T$$

The value of current bond sales equals current purchases plus interest payments minus tax revenues.[23] Providing that the debt in the long run grows at a rate smaller than the rate of interest, (20) may be integrated to give

$$(21) \qquad \int_n^\infty e^{-r(t-n)} T(t)\, dt = \int_n^\infty e^{-r(t-n)} pG(t)\, dt + \frac{B(n)}{r}$$

That is, the present value of future tax liabilities always equals the present value of future expenditures plus the current debt. This in turn implies that the present value of taxes is independent of the current rate of taxation. Any change in the debt is exactly matched by a change in tax liabilities, leaving the net worth of the household sector unchanged.

Whether or not the public debt constitutes private wealth depends on whether households correctly perceive this fact. If they do, changes in the debt cannot affect private demands and supplies.[24] If, however, households hold static expectations about tax rates, an increase in the debt with no change in the current tax rate will have effects just like those of any other wealth increase. It will increase consumption and the demand for money and reduce labor supply.

Throughout the next two major sections of this chapter, the public debt will be treated as part of private wealth and the tax rate that enters into the behavior functions of households will be the current rate. This is consistent with the practice followed throughout most of the book of assuming static expectations. However, the issue of the debt will be brought up again toward the end of the third section.

The modifications of earlier analysis that have been introduced in this section have the effect of substituting Equations (1), (2), (9), (10), (11), and (18) for their counterparts in the two previous chapters. These changes alter the conditions of equality between demand and supply in the goods and labor markets to account for the government's direct participation, the household behavior equations to take account of taxation, and the definition of wealth to account for the public debt. The next two sections are devoted to showing what difference these changes make.

---

[22] This assumes that the government does not create "fiat money" and that all money creation is done by the banking system.

[23] If the government pays wages, they should, of course, be added to pG.

[24] This statement must be qualified to take account of the fact that an increase in the debt may go to households whose behavior differs from that of the representative taxpayer. It also must be recognized that expected changes in tax rates will have substitution effects.

II. GOVERNMENT AND GENERAL EQUILIBRIUM

Since each of the government activities—buying goods, hiring labor, taxing income, and selling bonds—impinges on the market, changes in the levels of these activities have the potential for altering the characteristics of general equilibrium. It is the purpose of this section to trace the equilibrium impacts of changes in G, L^g, τ, and B^g, assuming that all other variables adjust so as to clear goods, labor, and securities markets. In addition, the presence of a government debt requires a reevaluation of the impact of changes in the nominal supply of money.

The section is divided into three parts. The first is devoted to the influence of government activities on short-run equilibrium, in which the stock of capital is given. In this part the effects of price-related changes in the real value of the debt are suppressed. These so-called wealth effects are examined in the second part, and the doctrine of the static neutrality of money is reexamined. The third part analyzes the effects of the government's activities on the stationary state, in which there is no incentive to capital or wealth accumulation.[25]

The Short Run[26]

In Chapter 5, the conditions of short-period equilibrium were given by three equations (43)-(45), which state the equality between demands for and supplies of goods, labor, and securities, together with the redundant condition, (40), of equality between the demand for and supply of money.[27] The corresponding conditions in the present context are given by[28]

(22) $$X^c \equiv C + I + G - Y^s = 0$$

(23) $$X^L \equiv L^d + L^g - L^s = 0$$

(24) $$X^p \equiv r\,\frac{W}{p} - \left(Y - \frac{w}{p}\,L^d - D\right) - \frac{B^g}{p} = 0$$

(25) $$X^m \equiv \phi^h + \phi^b - \frac{M}{p} = 0$$

These differ from their counterparts in Chapter 5 not only because of the presence of G, L^s, and B^g in the three market conditions but also because of the presence of τ in the household demand and supply functions.

---

[25] Before proceeding, the reader may want to review sections II and III of Chapter 5.

[26] Because the qualitative conclusions of this section were so much a part of the general wisdom concerning government during the period between the collapse of mercantilism and the advent of Keynesianism, it is not possible to give a useful guide to the literature without citing much of the history of thought on public finance. For a brief review of thought on the matter, see Spencer and Yohe (1970, pp. 14–19).

[27] See Equations (43)–(45) on page 112. Equation (40) is on page 107.

[28] Consumption from now on is assumed to include the consumption of banking services. Government money balances are ignored.

It is particularly convenient in analyzing these conditions to treat the public debt as though it consisted of "purchasing power parity bonds," that is, bonds whose coupon payments vary in proportion to the price level. This assumption prevents changes in the price level from creating or destroying wealth by changing the real value of the government debt. The "wealth effects" of changes in the price level can then be introduced as a separate subject. Accordingly, it will here be assumed that changes in p bring about equiproportional changes in B^g, although not, of course, the converse.

The effects of changes in the variables measuring government activity may be examined by analyzing the total differentials of (22)–(25). They are given by

$$(26) \quad
\begin{bmatrix}
\dfrac{\partial X^c}{\partial w/p} & \dfrac{\partial X^c}{\partial r} & \dfrac{\partial X^c}{\partial W/p} & 0 \\[2ex]
\dfrac{\partial X^L}{\partial w/p} & \dfrac{\partial X^L}{\partial r} & \dfrac{\partial X^L}{\partial W/p} & 0 \\[2ex]
\dfrac{\partial X^P}{\partial w/p} & \dfrac{\partial X^P}{\partial r} & \dfrac{\partial X^P}{\partial W/p} & 0 \\[2ex]
\dfrac{\partial X^m}{\partial w/p} & \dfrac{\partial X^m}{\partial r} & \dfrac{\partial X^m}{\partial W/p} & \dfrac{M}{p^2}
\end{bmatrix}
\begin{bmatrix}
d\,\dfrac{w}{p} \\[2ex]
dr \\[2ex]
d\,\dfrac{W}{p} \\[2ex]
dp
\end{bmatrix}
=
\begin{bmatrix}
-\dfrac{\partial X^c}{\partial \tau}\,d\tau - dG \\[2ex]
-\dfrac{\partial X^L}{\partial \tau}\,d\tau - dL^g \\[2ex]
\dfrac{dB^g}{p} \\[2ex]
-\dfrac{\partial X^m}{\partial \tau}\,d\tau + \dfrac{1}{p}\,dM
\end{bmatrix}
$$

The most obvious property of (26) is that the static neutrality of money is preserved by the assumption that the government issues purchasing power parity bonds.[29] Changes in the real debt stem only from changes in the nominal debt, so that dp does not appear in any of the first three equations. This makes their solutions independent of the nominal money supply, which has a proportional effect on the price level.

The remaining dependencies of the system require a more careful examination of the first three equations. From the analysis of Chapter 5, pages 112–114, the pattern of signs on the left sides of the first three equations of (26) is given by

$$(27) \quad
\begin{bmatrix}
\dfrac{\partial X^c}{\partial w/p} & \dfrac{\partial X^c}{\partial r} & \dfrac{\partial X^c}{\partial W/p} \\[2ex]
\dfrac{\partial X^L}{\partial w/p} & \dfrac{\partial X^L}{\partial r} & \dfrac{\partial X^L}{\partial W/p} \\[2ex]
\dfrac{\partial X^P}{\partial w/p} & \dfrac{\partial X^P}{\partial r} & \dfrac{\partial X^P}{\partial W/p}
\end{bmatrix}
=
\begin{bmatrix}
+ & - & + \\
- & 0 & + \\
+ & + & +
\end{bmatrix}
$$

On the right-hand sides, the derivatives of X^c and X^L with respect to τ are negative and negligible,[30] so that the pattern of coefficient signs for the three equations is given by

[29] For earlier discussion of the static neutrality of money, see Chapter 5, pages 107–108.

[30] It is assumed income and substitution effects of τ on the supply of labor, like those of the real wage, virtually cancel one another.

$$
(28) \quad
\begin{bmatrix} + & - & + \\ - & 0 & + \\ + & + & + \end{bmatrix}
\begin{bmatrix} d\dfrac{w}{p} \\ dr \\ d\dfrac{W}{p} \end{bmatrix}
=
\begin{bmatrix} + \\ 0 \\ 0 \end{bmatrix} d\tau +
\begin{bmatrix} - \\ 0 \\ 0 \end{bmatrix} dG +
\begin{bmatrix} 0 \\ - \\ 0 \end{bmatrix} dL^g +
\begin{bmatrix} 0 \\ 0 \\ + \end{bmatrix} \dfrac{dB^g}{p}
$$

Because of the simplicity of the pattern of direct government policy impacts, nearly all effects are clear-cut.[31]

If we recall that the determinant of the coefficients on the left is negative, it is evident that:

1. A rise in the tax rate raises the real wage, lowers the rate of interest, and raises real wealth.
2. A rise in commodity purchases from the private sector has effects that are qualitatively opposite to those coming from a tax increase.
3. A rise in government employment raises the real wage and lowers wealth but has an ambiguous impact on the interest rate.
4. A rise in the public debt raises the real wage, the rate of interest, and real wealth.

All these are comparative static propositions. However, insight into why things work out this way can best be appreciated by tracing through a virtual sequence of events. Consider first an increase in the tax rate. Its proximate effect is to create excess supply of goods. This lowers prices, and in turn creates excess supply of labor, lowering money wages. If wages and prices fall in the same proportion, real profits are unchanged. Coupons on the government bonds are adjusted to keep their real value constant. At given values of the rate of interest, the real value of securities is unchanged. However, real money holdings are now higher, and there is an excess demand for securities. Their real price must rise, and the interest rate must therefore fall. The supply side counterpart to the resulting rise in wealth is an increase in rents owing to the fall in capital costs. The increased wealth lowers the supply of labor, necessitating a higher equilibrium real wage.

The increases in the wage and wealth act to offset some of the impact of higher taxes on consumption. However, consumption must fall on balance. The lower interest rate encourages investment and perhaps reduces commodity production. Since government purchases are unchanged, a fall in consumer demand is the only source of the resources that must be released if investment is to increase. Thus a tax increase shifts resources from consumption to investment.

The effects of a rise in government purchases of goods and services are much like those of a fall in taxes. It lowers real wages, raises the interest rate, and lowers wealth for reasons that are the mirror image of those just adduced to account for the effects

---

[31] Recall the assumption that households measure their expected tax liabilities only by reference to the current tax rate.

of a tax increase. An increase in government purchases is inflationary, and some of the resources to achieve it come at the expense of investment, some at the expense of consumption.

A change in the level of government employment operates directly on the labor market, and only indirectly on the market for commodities. An increase produces an excess demand for labor, and wages rise. One consequence of this rise is an excess demand for goods, so prices rise. However, the real wage must on balance increase. Real profits are reduced, and so is real wealth. The inflation has lowered real money stocks. Whether the interest rate rises or falls depends on the balance between changes in the demand for and supply of real balances. However, the combined effect of the wage, interest, and wealth changes must be to lower the sum of investment and consumption if the process is to stabilize.[32] The rise in wages has reduced commodity supply, and government demand is unchanged.

A change in the government's indebtedness to the private sector has a time dimension that is different from that of spending, hiring, and taxing. Since the debt is a stock rather than a flow, its level cannot change instantaneously unless the government literally gives away assets or steals them back.[33] Hence the effects of increased indebtedness can only be studied by asking the following sort of question. Imagine an economy with given stocks of money, physical capital, and government debt. If it had somehow had a different past, leading to a higher government debt but unchanged money and capital stocks, how would its other economic magnitudes be different?

The answer provided by Equation (28) is that it would have higher wages, interest, and wealth. The higher stock of government bonds would raise the demand for commodities and reduce the supply of labor. Therefore, both wages and prices would rise. On net, wages would have to rise more than prices in order to equilibrate the labor market. Although the value of private securities would be reduced by lower profits, the total supply of real securities would be larger, and the supply of real money would be smaller. Therefore, the interest rate would rise so that asset demands balance supplies. The changes in wages, interest, and wealth would shift the composition of demand away from investment and toward consumption.

Table 7–2 summarizes the results of the separate fiscal actions and facilitates the study of combinations of policies. A particularly instructive combination is a simultaneous increase in G and τ so as, on balance, to leave the commodity market unaffected. A rise in G, taken alone, causes a price increase, destroying real balances, raising the interest rate, reducing wealth, increasing the labor supply, and reducing the real wage. The resources for producing the government's output are squeezed out of the production of private goods by inflation, which dampens both consumption and investment demand. If, instead, the inflation is forestalled by a tax increase, the real

[32] Stability is a definite problem here, since the rise in the real wage augments consumption demand.

[33] If the government held bank balances, it could swap bonds for money. However, this would not change the net indebtedness of the government or the net worth of the private sector.

Table 7-2 Effects of government fiscal actions

Effects of an increase in	Effect on					
	$\dfrac{w}{p}$	r	$\dfrac{W}{p}$	C	I	p
τ	+	−	+	−	+	−
G	−	+	−	−	−	+
L^g	+	?	−	{−}		+
B^g	+	+	+	+	−	+

wage and the rate of interest before taxes are unchanged, as is real wealth.[34] Firms have no incentive to reduce investment demand, so that all the government production comes at the expense of household consumption, which is cut back in response to the income effects of the tax increase.

It is important to note that the tax increase that is sufficient to maintain balance in the commodity market produces a surplus in the government budget. Since income taxation does not affect the market value of wealth, it does not impair the ability of existing wealth to provide for future retirement and bequests. If households were to reduce their current consumption *pari passu* with an increase in their taxes, they would in effect be overproviding for the future relative to the present.[35] Thus part of the impact of increased taxation falls on saving, and the tax increase needed to achieve a given reduction in consumption must exceed that reduction.[36] It follows from this that a balanced increase in the government's budget must lead to excess demand in the commodity market, a price increase, an interest rate increase, and a reduction in private investment.

Similar analyses could be applied to more complicated combinations of government fiscal actions. The lesson to be drawn from each is that any expansion in the government's use of resources must come, one way or another, at the expense of private uses. Even an increase in the debt whose interest payments are matched by a tax increase has its costs because of the "excess burden" effect.[37] Because of the costs imposed by an expansion of the government's fiscal activities, it is not sufficient that these activities be merely valuable. They must be more valuable than the private activi-

---

[34] This may be verified by examining Equation (28). A rise in G and τ that leaves the goods market in equilibrium leaves w/p, r, and W/p unaltered. However, the assumption that the income and substitution effects of $d\tau$ balance out in the labor market is crucial. If this were not so, a rise in τ would disturb the equilibrium of the labor market and ramify throughout the system.

[35] The intertemporal substitution effect of a tax increase calls for redistribution of consumption from the future toward the present.

[36] This is the basis for the celebrated "balanced-budget multiplier theorem." See below, pages 197–198.

[37] See above, page 177.

ties they supplant. This conservative verdict, which short-run equilibrium analysis leads to, is reinforced by a consideration of the longer run. Before turning to the steady state, however, it is necessary to clear up some unfinished business regarding the role of the debt.

Wealth Effects

Up to the present point, the possible consequences of changes in the real value of the government debt arising from price changes have been ignored by treating the debt as though it were a fixed real obligation. Now is the time to explore what happens if the debt is fixed in nominal amount.

Since a given nominal debt has a greater or smaller real value according to the level of prices, policies which change the price level will have indirect wealth effects in addition to their direct effects. These indirect effects are equivalent to those of a change in the nominal debt, prices held constant.

Consider, for example, the impact of an increase in the government's purchases of goods and services.[38] According to the previous argument, such an increase lowers real wages, raises the interest rate, and lowers real wealth. The mechanism by which it works is the following. The higher demand for goods raises their prices. The resultant fall in real wages transmits the excess demand to the labor market, and money wages rise. Such an all-around inflation destroys real money, necessitating a rise in the interest rate and a fall in wealth. The resulting increase in the labor supply implies that the equilibrium inflation cannot be precisely balanced, but that real wages must fall. Consumption and investment decline as a consequence of the lessened wages and wealth and the increase in the rate of interest.

Since the increase in government expenditure is inflationary, it lowers the real value of government interest payments. The capitalized value of these payments, which has already shrunk as a consequence of the rise in the interest rate, shrinks still further because of the inflation. This destruction of real wealth puts additional downward pressure on real wages and offsets some of the upward pressure on the rate of interest. Because of the wealth effect on consumption, the degree of inflation necessary to accommodate an increase in government spending is less than it would be if interest payments were adjusted to keep pace with inflation.

By similarly constructed arguments, the wealth effects of other government policies may be traced. A particularly interesting case is that of money creation. The government debt constitutes "outside wealth," an asset to which there corresponds no immediate private liability. Because money creation raises the price level, it alters the real value of this wealth, and therefore is not neutral with respect to its impact on the real system. The destruction of outside wealth attendant on an increase in the money supply lowers the real wage, the interest rate, and wealth. Demand is conse-

---

[38] Recall throughout that this is entirely a discussion of comparative statics. In this context precise language is very cumbersome, so some sloppiness is to be tolerated in the name of simplicity. In fact, however, what is being talked about is differing levels, not changes.

quently shifted away from consumption in favor of investment. A decline in the money stock has opposite effects.

The extent to which such wealth effects can be expected to operate depends crucially on the extent to which the debt is really outside wealth.[39] If every change in the debt is matched by a change in households' discounted expected tax liability, then the public debt is inside wealth. A rise in the price level lowers the real value of interest payments, and expected real taxes fall as a consequence. The income effects wash out. Whether in fact households perceive this is a matter of controversy, as has already been pointed out. However, it is generally agreed that if part of the government's debt does not bear interest, this part constitutes outside wealth whose real value can be influenced by price changes. If part of the money supply consists of such debt,[40] a change in the price level affects not only the composition of wealth, but also its size.

In summary, the existence of government debt that is outside wealth of fixed nominal value modifies the effects of government policies in two ways. First, it destroys the neutrality of money-bond exchanges between the general public and the banking system. Second, it complicates the impacts of taxing and spending policies through wealth effects that mitigate the direct effects of these policies. It has additional effects that are of importance in Keynesian analysis. These will be discussed in the next major section. First, however, the analysis of equilibrium will be completed by looking at the effects of government fiscal policies on the stationary state.

Government in Long-Run Equilibrium

A full analysis of the role of government in a smoothly functioning market system must extend to the long run as well as to the short. Of particular interest are the effects of the size of the government on wealth and distribution in the stationary state. In order to convey the attitude toward government that is implicit in the neoclassical model, three comparisons will be made. In each case the standard for comparison will be the stationary economy without a government, which was explored in Chapter 5. Contrasted with this economy will be an economy whose government taxes its citizens' incomes and uses the proceeds: 1) to buy privately produced goods and services; 2) to buy labor services; 3) to pay interest on a debt it has previously incurred. It will be assumed throughout that the government uses its goods and labor in ways that are neither competitive with nor complementary to private resource uses.

In each of these three economies, the expenditures must exactly match the proceeds of the tax. If this were not true, the government's debt would be changing; this would obviously be inconsistent with the maintenance of a stationary state. Therefore any increase in one of the three kinds of government expenditure must be accompanied by a sufficient increase in the tax rate, τ, to keep the budget in balance. The

---

[39] Some of the landmarks in the literature on wealth effects are Metzler (1951), Patinkin (1948, 1956, 1965, 1969), and Modigliani (1963).

[40] Debt of this sort consists of hand-to-hand currency and (in some institutional settings) the net reserves which banks hold on deposit with the central bank.

equation of budget balance is[41]

$$(29) \qquad \tau\left(\frac{w}{p}L^s + rK + \frac{B^g}{p}\right) = G + \frac{w}{p}L^g + \frac{B^g}{p}$$

This equation should be thought of as determining τ as a function of government expenditures and the endogenous variables of the system. For this purpose, it is not necessary to pay much attention to the effects of government expenditures on the tax base. It is hard to imagine a fully employed economy in which a rise in real expenditures induces a fully offsetting increase in real tax revenues with no change in the tax rate. Therefore (29) in effect states that τ is an increasing function of the three kinds of government expenditure.

The remaining equations of long-run equilibrium are

$$(30) \qquad S \equiv \rho\left(\frac{w}{p}L^s + rK + \frac{B^g}{p}\right) - C = 0$$

$$(31) \qquad X^L \equiv L^d + L^g - L^s = 0$$

$$(32) \qquad I^n \equiv I - \delta K = 0$$

These state that saving, excess demand for labor, and net investment must all be zero. Government employment appears explicitly in (31). The number of government bonds outstanding appears explicitly in (30) and also implicitly as an argument in the consumption and labor supply functions. The level of government purchases from private firms does not appear directly in any of these relationships, since neither saving, investment, nor the labor market is directly affected by the identity of the purchasers of private product. Like the other government expenditures, of course, G enters indirectly through (29) as a determinant of τ.

The properties of the rather complicated system comprising (29)–(32) are best uncovered by adding together (29) and (30), remembering that $\rho + \tau \equiv 1$. The result is

$$(33) \qquad \frac{w}{p}L^s + rK - C = G + \frac{w}{p}L^g$$

If government interest payments were added to both sides and taxes subtracted, it would state that household saving equals the government deficit. The advantage of replacing (30) by (33) is that its left-hand side is identical in form to that of Equation (72) in Chapter 5.[42] Moreover, if L^g is transposed in (31), it is identical in form to (73) in Chapter 5, and (32) is already identical with (74). Thus the diagrammatic analysis of pages 122–126 in that chapter may be adapted to analyzing the long-run impacts of government policies.

For purposes of this analysis, it will be assumed that the initial levels of government activity are zero, and that each of the three expenditure items is increased while

---

[41] In long-run competitive equilibrium it is assumed that there are no rents, so that rK is the value of property income arising from private business.

[42] See Chapter 5, page 119. Notice that the similarity in form covers up differences in arguments that must be taken account of.

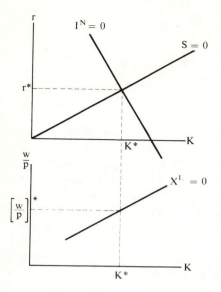

Figure 7-1 Factor returns in long-run equilibrium.

holding the other two at zero and achieving budget balance through increased taxation. This line of inquiry produces some simplifications by comparison with the alternatives without sacrificing anything of substance.[43]

The necessary diagram is Figure 7-1. The bottom panel shows points of labor market equilibrium. The lines in the top panel show points of zero saving and investment, given equilibrium in the labor market. When all activities of the government are at zero levels, Figure 7-1 is identical with Figure 5-4 of Chapter 5.[44] The task of this section is to see how that figure is altered by various balanced changes in the government budget.

These changes have direct effects on (33), the transposed (31), and (32) that may be denoted by

$$(34) \qquad -\Delta S = dG + \frac{w}{p} dL^g + \frac{\partial C}{\partial W/p} d\frac{B^g}{p} + \frac{\partial C}{\partial \tau} d\tau$$

$$(35) \qquad -\Delta X^L = dL^g + \frac{\partial L^s}{\partial W/p} d\frac{B^g}{p} + \frac{\partial L^s}{\partial \tau} d\tau$$

$$(36) \qquad -\Delta I^n = 0$$

These expressions give the government disturbances to the steady state that must be balanced by changes in $w/p, r,$ and K. These responses must satisfy

---

[43] In particular, it eliminates wealth effects and makes the change in the government wage bill equal to the wage rate times any increase in employment.

[44] The reader is referred to pages 122–126 of that chapter for a review of the construction and use of the diagram.

$$(37) \qquad \frac{\partial S}{\partial w/p} d\, \frac{w}{p} + \frac{\partial S}{\partial r} dr + \frac{\partial S}{\partial W/p} dK = -\Delta S$$

$$(38) \qquad \frac{\partial X^L}{\partial w/p} d\, \frac{w}{p} + \frac{\partial X}{\partial r} dr + \left[\frac{\partial L^d}{\partial K} - \frac{\partial L^s}{\partial W/p} \right] dK = -\Delta X^L$$

$$(39) \qquad \frac{\partial I^n}{\partial w/p} d\, \frac{w}{p} + \frac{\partial I^n}{\partial r} dr + \frac{\partial I^n}{\partial K} dK = -\Delta I^n$$

The easiest action to analyze is an increase in purchases from the private sector. If we assume that the income and substitution effects of a tax increase net out in the labor supply function, a rise in G will affect only (37). An increase in the tax rate sufficient to balance the budget will reduce consumption by a smaller amount, since households that are working will want to distribute some of the tax burden over their retirement by reducing saving. Thus dG outweighs $(\partial C/\partial \tau) d\tau$ and $-\Delta S > 0$. In order to maintain zero saving, the interest rate will have to be higher at given levels of w/p and K. Thus the $S = 0$ curve in Figure 7–1 shifts up, and the equilibrium capital stock is lowered. This accords with the result reached above that the short-run impact of a balanced increase in the expenditure budget is to reduce private investment. In the long run, government purchases not only use up output, but also reduce the capital facilities available for producing it.

The effect of an increase in government employment is more complicated. One direct effect is to raise the equilibrium wage at a given capital stock, shifting the curve in the bottom of Figure 7–1 upward. Since a higher wage lowers the incentive to invest and raises the incentive to save at a given capital stock, both curves in the top panel shift down. However, a tax increase equal to the cost of the employment increase reduces consumption by a smaller amount, and $-\Delta S$ in (37) is positive, requiring a higher interest rate to restore a zero saving rate. Since the $S = 0$ schedule is subject to conflicting influences, it might seem that no conclusive results are possible.

However, it can be shown that $S = 0$ must shift up. Suppose that the initial equilibrium (point A on Figure 7–1) were a point on the altered $S = 0$ function. Then at A property income would be unchanged. The change in household income would be given by[45]

$$(40) \qquad dY = L^s d\, \frac{w}{p} - dT$$

where dT is the change in tax collections. Substituting the condition of budget balance, remembering that at the initial equilibrium $L^s = L^d$, and noting that with the labor supply fixed, the changes in public and private employment sum to zero, give

$$(41) \qquad dY = L^d d\, \frac{w}{p} + \frac{w}{p} dL^d$$

[45] Assume throughout that the income and substitution effects of wage and tax changes wash out in the labor supply function.

Since r and K are unchanged, the right-hand side of (41) is the change in income originating in private business. This must equal

$$\frac{\partial Y^s}{\partial w/p} d\frac{w}{p}$$

which is negative. Therefore the wage increase must be smaller than the tax increase, and saving at A must be negative. The $S = 0$ curve therefore cannot run through A, and must be to the left of it. The new capital stock must be smaller than the old. There is no obvious reason why it could not be small enough that the real wage would drop below its initial level.

The reason for all this is that the labor market impact reduces firms' willingness to use capital, whereas the income impact causes a net reduction in households' willingness to own it. By employing more labor, the government effectively impoverishes the system as a whole.

Surprisingly, the effects of a tax-financed increase in the debt are formally quite similar to those of government hiring. An increase in the debt washes out much of the income effect of increased taxation, but the substitution effect reduces labor supply, raising the real wage at any given level of the capital stock. This shifts the bottom curve in Figure 7-1 upward and the two top curves downward. In addition, the "excess burden" of income taxation[46] shifts the $S = 0$ curve upward. By an argument similar to that advanced to explain the effects of an employment increase, it can be shown that on balance the $S = 0$ curve must shift up, and the equilibrium capital stock must fall. Thus the larger is the supply of government securities, the smaller is the amount of productive capital that people will own.

All three forms of government spending and taxation imply a reduction in private incomes and consumption. If this is the case, it seems hard to justify government economic activity unless it confers direct benefits that are of greater value than those of the private activity that is supplanted. This is a source of the distrust of government so widely held by those who believe that the market system works well. However, if the price system works poorly and unemployment is the normal state of affairs, then this verdict on public expenditures cannot be sustained.

III. GOVERNMENT AND KEYNESIAN ANALYSIS

The fiscal and monetary activities of the government enter into Keynesian analysis in ways that are simple and obvious, but not trivial. Indeed, the "action paragraph" of Keynesianism is that such policy can compensate for both short-run instability and chronic deficiencies of the market system. This section examines the basis for this

---

[46] Since a rise in the tax rate encourages the substitution of leisure for market goods, the tax increase at initial income levels must exceed the interest on the debt if the budget is to be balanced ex post. This implies a negative income effect on consumption.

belief. It is divided into four parts. The first covers the way in which the government affects the structure of the system. The second outlines the instruments of stabilization. The third discusses chronic stagnation and the balanced budget multiplier. The fourth outlines some reservations about Keynesianism raised by the "monetarist" school.

The Structure of the System

The fiscal activities of the government enter into the Keynesian model in two ways. First, they influence the effective demands for both goods and money, and therefore the monetary-multiplier equilibrium. Second, government employment and several other variables affect the supply of labor available for private firms, and therefore the level of private production that is possible at full employment. However, none of the activities of the stylized government examined in this chapter influences the conditions of commodity supply.

The forces that are summarized by the IS curve may be written

$$Y = C\left(\frac{w}{p}, r, \frac{W}{p}, L, \tau\right) + I\left(\frac{w}{p}, r, K, Y\right) + G$$

(42)
$$L = L^d\left(\frac{w}{p}, K, Y\right) + L^g$$

$$\frac{W}{p} = \theta\left(r, Y - \frac{w}{p}L^d - \delta K + \frac{B^g}{p}\right)$$

These differ from Equations (5) of the last chapter[47] in the following ways:

1. Government purchases enter directly into the statement of equality between production and effective demand.
2. Taxation affects consumption demand.
3. Government employment must be added to private employment.
4. The real value of government interest payments is part of the property-income argument of the wealth function.

The equation of multiplier equilibrium is therefore[48]

(43)
$$Y = Z\left(Y, r, \frac{w}{p}, K, G, \tau, L^g, \frac{B^g}{p}\right)$$

Any change in a government variable which increases Z at a given level of Y will shift the IS curve upward, since it creates an excess of demand over production that must be offset by a rise in the interest rate. Therefore an increase in G, L^g, or B^g will

---

[47]See Chapter 6, page 133.
[48]This corresponds to Equation (7), Chapter 6.

shift IS up, and an increase in τ will shift it down. In addition, a rise in the real wage will shift it up because it raises the income of government workers without directly reducing the income of anyone else. A rise in the price level shifts it down because it reduces the real value of the public debt.

The government's fiscal activities also influence the relationship determining the LM curve. The equation of balance between the supply of money and the demands for it is[49]

$$(44) \qquad \phi^b \left(\frac{w}{p}, r, K, Y \right) + \phi^h \left(\frac{w}{p}, r \frac{W}{p}, L, \tau \right) = \frac{M}{p}$$

The government influences this relationship directly through the dependence of money demand on the tax rate. It also controls the supply. In addition, it has indirect influences through the presence of government employment in the effective demand for labor and of the public debt in private wealth. Hence the LM curve should be written

$$(45) \qquad \phi \left(\frac{w}{p}, r, K, Y, \tau, L^g, \frac{B^g}{p} \right) = \frac{M}{p}$$

Any change in a government variable that increases ϕ will shift LM upward, since the implied excess demand must be offset by a rise in the interest rate. Therefore a rise in L^g or B^g will shift LM up, and a rise in τ will shift it down. In addition a rise in the real wage will shift it up and a rise in p will shift it down for reasons similar to those just adduced in connection with the IS curve. A rise in the money supply shifts it down.

The overall effects of these changes may be studied with reference to a combined IS-LM diagram. It is assumed that the LM curve is neither vertical nor horizontal and that IS is neither vertical nor more positively sloped than LM. Two configurations satisfying these conditions are presented in Figure 7-2 as an aid to visualizing what follows.

A shift in government purchases from the private sector shifts the IS curve upward but leaves LM unaffected. It therefore unambiguously raises the level of demand consistent with money-multiplier equilibrium. A rise in the real money supply affects only LM, and it therefore has a similarly unambiguous effect on demand. However, changes in employment, taxes, and the public debt shift both IS and LM in the same direction, so that their impact on demand is open to question. In deference to tradition it will be assumed that increases in either government employment or the debt raise demand, and increases in the tax rate lower it. It will also be assumed that an increase in the real wage and hence the income of government employees raises demand, and that a rise in the real value of the debt stemming from a fall in prices does likewise.

The implications of these effects for the Keynesian system as a whole are best appreciated by noticing how they affect the "DD curve" that relates effective demand to

---

[49]This corresponds to Equation (15), Chapter 6.

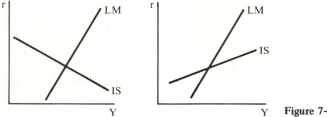

Figure 7-2 IS-LM diagrams.

the price level.[50] The presence of government in the demand generation system has two kinds of effects on this summary relationship:

1. The DD curve may be shifted rightward by an increase in w, G, L^g, or B^g or a fall in τ as well as by an increase in the nominal money supply.
2. The price sensitivity of demand is higher than it would be in the absence of government, since a fall in the price level raises the real debt and the real income of government employees as well as raising the real money stock.

It is interesting to note that the demand increase occasioned by an expansionary government activity may involve an increase in both private investment and consumption. This is obviously true in the case of a money-supply increase in a system with a downward-sloping IS curve: income goes up and the interest rate falls. However, it is also true in more subtle cases. Consider Figure 7-3. The point A is an initial IS-LM equilibrium. Through it are drawn both the IS and LM curves and the loci along which C and I have the same values as they have at A. The slopes of these lines are given by[51]

(46)
$$\left.\frac{dr}{dY}\right]_{dC=0} = -\frac{\dfrac{\partial C}{\partial W/p} \cdot \dfrac{\partial W/p}{\partial Y} + \dfrac{\partial C}{\partial L} \cdot \dfrac{\partial L^d}{\partial Y}}{\dfrac{\partial C}{\partial r} + \dfrac{\partial C}{\partial W/p} \cdot \dfrac{\partial W/p}{\partial r}}$$

$$\left.\frac{dr}{dY}\right]_{dI=0} = -\frac{\partial I/\partial Y}{\partial I/\partial r}$$

Figure 7-3 gives one plausible configuration of these slopes. The shaded region that lies to the right of both of the no-change loci is the region in which both consumption and investment are higher than they are at A. Any government measure that moves the demand-determination system into this region raises both effective private demands. For instance, since the LM curve in Figure 7-3 is relatively flat, reflecting a high interest sensitivity of the demand for money, an increase in government purchases from the private sector will be complemented by increases in the other demands as well.

---

[50] For the construction of the DD curve, see Chapter 6, pages 147–148.

[51] In order to see why, study the derivation of IS on pages 133–135, Chapter 6.

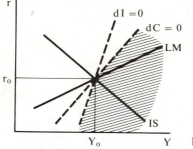

Figure 7-3 Government expenditure and private demands.

Policy measures which shift both IS and LM may have similar effects providing only that the shifted intersection lies in the shaded region.[52]

The effect of government actions on the overall Keynesian system is not limited to shifts in the DD schedule, however. The whole system of relationships that govern the full-employment level of private production is shot through with government influences. This system consists of the equality between the effective demand for and the notional supply of labor, the definition of wealth, and the LM curve;[53] that is

$$L^s \left(\frac{w}{p}, \frac{W}{p} \right) = L^d \left(\frac{w}{p}, K, Y \right) + L^g$$

(47)
$$\frac{W}{p} = \theta \left(r, Y - \frac{w}{p} L^d - \delta K + \frac{B^g}{p} \right)$$

$$\frac{M}{p} = \phi \left(\frac{w}{p}, r, K, Y, \tau, L^g, \frac{B^g}{p} \right)$$

The most obvious and direct influence that the government has on full-employment output arises from the government demand for labor. An increase in government employment directly reduces the supply available to produce private output, and shifts the "FF curve" to the left. However, there are numerous indirect influences operating through the influence of wealth on labor supply

1. An increase in τ reduces the demand for money and therefore the interest rate, raises wealth, and reduces both labor supply and full-employment output.
2. An increase in government employment indirectly raises full-employment output by raising the demand for money and the interest rate, reducing wealth.
3. A rise in the debt directly increases wealth, but indirectly reduces it by raising the demand for money and the interest rate.

In addition, the presence of the government complicates the ways in which changes in prices and wages influence full-employment production:

---

[52] A cut in the tax rate shifts the $dC = 0$ locus to the left as well as shifting IS and LM.
[53] For the derivation of the "FF curve" see pages 149–151 of Chapter 6.

4. A fall in the price level creates wealth not only by increasing the real money supply and lowering the interest rate but also directly by raising the real value of the government debt; this influence is offset in full or in part by the influence of the increased debt on the demand for money.

5. A rise in the real wage stemming from a rise in the money wage or a cut in the price level raises the money demand of government employees and therefore the interest rate; this increase reinforces both the direct effect of real wages on wealth and the direct influence of higher wages on the excess demand for labor.

None of these five influences on the labor supply is central to the argument of Keynesian analysis. They are the stuff that the notes in the backs of journals are made of, and are included here only for the sake of logical completeness. The only government influence on full employment which will be examined in subsequent sections is the direct effect of changes in L^g on the FF schedule.

Keynesian Analysis of Stabilization

A distinctive facet of the *General Theory* and the tradition it engendered is its emphasis on sudden shifts in expectations, scrambles for liquidity, collapses of "animal spirits," and similar shocks to the system determining income and employment. Such shocks overwhelm the endogenous forces of stability and make disequilibrium the normal state of affairs of the market system. A corollary to this line of thought and the analysis of the previous section is that changes in the fiscal and monetary activities of the government can counteract the effects of these shocks and produce a better historical approximation to general equilibrium than could be produced by endogenous market forces alone.

The analysis of stabilization policy has become one of the most technical strands of dynamic literature.[54] No complete analysis of the matter can neglect the lags in perception, decision, and implementation inherent in the problem of responding to a rapidly changing environment.[55] All that this section can do is to attempt to answer the following sort of question: "If the government could foresee the need for compensatory action and react with speed, what ought it to do?"

The government's instruments of control consist of two kinds: the battery of fiscal and monetary measures that influence the effective demand for goods, and its own hiring that influences the effective demand for labor. The first kind shifts the DD curve, the second, both the DD and FF curves. The appropriate combination of these actions depends on the particular disequilibrium configuration with which it wants to cope, the desirability of change, and the intrinsic desirability of changes in the policy instruments themselves.

---

[54] Some of the earliest insights into the dynamic stabilization problem may be found in Friedman (1953) and Phillips (1954, 1957). Other major papers are by Tucker (1966), Holbrook (1972), and Cooper and Fischer (1972b, 1973).

[55] Two widely cited studies of the administrative lags built into the American policy-making processes are those of Ando and Brown (1963) and of Kareken and Solow (1963).

One way to look at the stabilization problem[56] is to see the Keynesian system as a set of relationships whereby the endogeneous variables, say C, I, r, L, and W/p,[57] are linked to the currently ruling levels of wages, prices, the capital stock, the government debt, and the currently controllable government policy variables G, L^g, τ, and M. Such a system might express the endogenous variables explicitly as functions of predetermined and policy variables. A relationship of this sort is the following

$$C = f_1 (w, p, K, B^g, G, L^g, \tau, M)$$
$$I = f_2 (\qquad " \qquad)$$
(48)
$$r = f_3 (\qquad " \qquad)$$
$$L = f_4 (\qquad " \qquad)$$
$$\frac{W}{p} = f_5 (\qquad " \qquad)$$

It might also be possible to express rates of change of prices and wages as functions of these same variables

(49)
$$\dot{w} = f_6 (w, p, K, B^g, G, L^g, \tau, M)$$
$$\dot{p} = f_7 (\qquad " \qquad)$$

Finally, the policy makers might have in mind some objective function, say

(50)
$$V = \chi \left(C, I, r, L, \frac{W}{p}, \dot{w}, \dot{p}, w, p, K, B^g, G, L^g, \tau, M\right)$$

On a formal level, the policy problem is to maximize (50) subject to the set of relationships expressed by (48) and (49). What this amounts to, in effect, is choosing a set of policy variables in such a way as to take account of

1. The desirability of achieving various possible levels of $C, I, r, L, W/p, \dot{w}$, and $\dot{p}$
2. The direct desirability of the levels of the policy instruments, F, L^g, τ, and M
3. The relationships linking the first set of variables to the second
4. The values of the predetermined variables w, p, K, and B^g

Implementation of such a grand design requires both an accurate numerical model of the processes summarized by (48) and (49) and a well-specified social objective function. This is a tall order.[58] Nonetheless, the vision is an impressive monument to rationality.

---

[56] The pioneering work on quantitative policy planning was done by Tinbergen (1956). More modern treatises of note are those of Theil (1964), Johansen (1965), Peston (1974), and Chow (1975).

[57] This list might be longer or shorter. It should contain all currently endogenous variables for which the policy makers have preferences.

[58] See, however, the notable contributions of Cooper and Fischer (1972a) and Holbrook (1974) that indicate how to use such material if it were available.

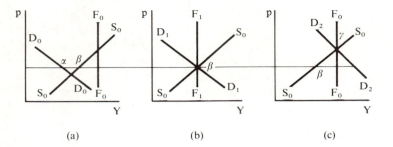

Figure 7-4 Alternative policies to combat excess supply.

Some of the spirit of what is involved may be brought out in a pair of examples of less ambitious scope. Suppose, for instance, that if the government were to select a particular set of policy instruments, the income determination system would be in a disequilibrium such as that indicated by point α in panel (a) of Figure 7-4. At this position, both goods and labor are in excess supply. Suppose further that it wished to reduce unemployment while maintaining price and wage stability. If the only policy instruments that could be altered were its purchases of goods and hiring of labor, then the only fully effective policy prescription would be an increase in government employment sufficient to shift FF to $F_1 F_1$, so as to intersect SS at β, and a shift in government expenditures of a proper magnitude to make the DD curve pass through β.[59] The initial prices and wages would then be at equilibrium levels, as panel (b) indicates. Suppose, however, that the objective function of the policy makers attached a substantial disutility to a change in government employment. It would then not be possible to achieve full employment costlessly. A trade-off would exist between unemployment and increased hiring. One possibility might be to leave government employment alone and to increase commodity purchases sufficiently so as to shift DD to $D_2 D_2$, cutting $F_0 F_0$ at γ in panel (c). The immediate effect would be to move the system to β, with still some unemployment but with less than at α. Since there would be some excess demand for goods, there would be upward pressure on prices. After a period of price increase, the system might end up at γ. This particular policy package would avoid an expansion of government employment, but it would pay a price in terms of prolonged unemployment, price inflation, and a decline in the real wage.

As a second example, consider Figure 7-5. Panel (a) depicts an initial position α, at which there is excess demand both for goods and for labor. If the government's overriding goal were to avoid instability in prices, it might achieve balance of demand and supply in both markets by reducing its employment sufficiently so as to make FF cut SS at β. It could then alter its goods purchases so as to turn the initial prices and wages into equilibrium values, as in panel (b). However, if it wished to protect its initial levels of spending and hiring, it could cut the money supply so as to make DD

[59] Since the increase in L^g itself shifts the DD curve to the right, the appropriate change in G might have either sign or, coincidentally, be zero.

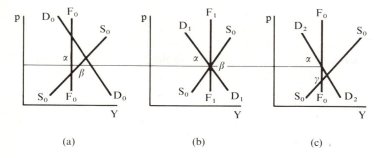

$$(a) \qquad\qquad (b) \qquad\qquad (c)$$

Figure 7-5 Alternative policies to combat excess demand.

intersect FF at α, as in panel (c). At that point effective demand for labor matches notional supply, and effective (and notional) demand for goods matches effective (labor-constrained) supply. Since the notional demand for labor and supply of goods would both be excessive, there would presumably ensue a decline in prices and/or an increase in money wages that, with suitable monetary adjustments, could establish a general equilibrium somewhere between α and γ. This particular policy would end the inflationary pressure without necessitating a change in the government budget. Its cost would be the maintenance of disequilibrium for a period sufficiently prolonged to bring about an increase in the real wage.

Countless similar examples could be constructed. The distinctive theme of this kind of analysis is its stress on the ability of the government to supplant or supplement a market mechanism that fails to achieve equilibrium. Because the government has latitude in its choice of measures with which to make adjustments, it can not only move the system in the direction of equilibrium but also alter the dimensions of the equilibrium itself. This invitation to activity contrasts sharply with the bleak fatalism of equilibrium theory. Small wonder that Keynesianism has such a substantial following among political activists of the meliorist stripe.

Stagnation and the Balanced-Budget Multiplier

The apparent scope for useful fiscal action is not limited to "fine tuning," which offsets short-term fluctuations in private demand. One school of thought led by Hansen, an early adherent of Keynesianism in the United States, argued that mature capitalist economies might expect chronic problems of deficient demand. The reasons advanced, which had to do with an upward drift in the rate of saving and a downward drift in the rate of investment, both measured at full employment, need not be gone into detail here.[60] They were coupled with that brand of Keynesianism that denied the efficacy

---

[60]The most complete statement of the stagnation thesis may be found in Hansen (1941), which is also a basic source for early Keynesian views on fiscal policy. Terborgh (1945) is a well-known conservative attack on Hansen's position. Two works by noted American Marxists, Baran (1957) and Baran and Sweezy (1966) proffer an alternative stagnation thesis deriving from a Marxist analysis of mature capitalism.

of price, wage, and interest rate adjustments.[61] The implication of this "stagnation thesis" was that the market system left to its own devices would lapse into a continual state of depression punctuated by only occasional and accidental bursts of prosperity.

Whether or not the stagnation thesis is substantiable, it is clear that its mere possibility poses a challenge to Keynesianism. Seemingly, if the government were to commit itself to maintain full employment in a stagnant private economy, it would be forced to run nearly perpetual deficits[62] and thereby create an ever-growing ratio of public debt (and debt service) to private income.[63] Such an eventuality could hardly result in anything short of a radical transformation of economic life.

The solution to this dilemma is the famous "balanced-budget multiplier theorem," which states that a balanced expansion in taxes and government purchases has a net expansionary impact on effective demand.[64] The argument, in its simplest form, goes something like this. An increase in government purchases raises private production and income. The tax increase takes away the income increase, leaving households as well off as they were before.[65] Therefore, private consumption demand is unchanged, and effective demand is increased by the amount of the increased government purchases. If firms increase their investment in response to the higher demand, the effect is thereby amplified.

An alternative way of understanding the process is the following. A rise in government purchases increases demand. A rise in taxes reduces it. However, since working households want to defer some portion of the tax impact to their retirement, saving will fall and consumption will be cut by less than the tax increase, so the net impact is expansionary. Because of the multiplier, the direct effect is amplified, and the increase in production is sufficient to restore household income to its initial level.[66] Since the tax increase is fully offset by a rise in pretax income, ex post saving is not reduced. Indeed, if investment responds to the production increase, the accumulation of capital and wealth will be stimulated by the government's action. Any retarding influence from an increase in money demand and the interest rate can always be offset by an appropriate monetary expansion.

The burden of this argument is that a large enough balanced budget can offset any stagnationist tendency. The government can take care of chronic problems as well as short-run instabilities, and it does not really matter that the market system does a poor job of maintaining equilibrium on its own. Foresighted fiscal and monetary policies can assure virtual maintenance of general equilibrium.

---

[61] See Chapter 6, pages 153–154.

[62] The kind of Keynesianism that denies the efficacy of the price mechanism is equally skeptical of the effectiveness of monetary expansion, so that any antistagnation policy would have to be fiscal.

[63] However, Domar (1944) pointed out that in a growing economy, a steady ratio of the deficit to national income leads eventually to a steady ratio of debt to income.

[64] The classic papers on the balanced-budget multiplier are Wallich (1944), Haavelmo (1945), and Baumol and Peston (1955).

[65] This, of course, neglects substitutions and excess burdens.

[66] This statement neglects some niceties that are discussed in Baumol and Peston (1955).

Some Monetarist Misgivings

In recent years there has developed the reaction to Keynesianism which is known as "monetarism." It has already been mentioned above in Chapter 5 in connection with monetary neutrality.[67] It seems fair to say that the monetarists are fundamentally orthodox believers in equilibrium theory, and that they think that Keynesianism is at best irrelevant in the not very long run, and at worst dangerous. However, they also have a number of arguments suggesting that fiscal policy is likely to be a lot less effective in the short run than Keynesians think that it is. To do full justice to the subtlety of their arguments would require another long chapter, perhaps even a book. The intent of this section is merely to add a precautionary postscript to the discussion of Keynesian policy and to provide a spur for further reading.[68]

Some of the arguments advanced by the monetarists are the following:

1. Since the IS curve, properly understood, is highly elastic to the interest rate[69] and the LM curve fairly (or, sometimes, entirely) inelastic, fiscal actions are "crowded out" by monetary reactions and do not substantially influence effective demand.
2. Most government expenditures are so competitive with private demands that they merely supplant them.
3. Households quickly perceive the future tax implications of changes in government expenditures, and as a consequence all expenditures multipliers are effectively of the magnitude of balanced-budget multipliers.
4. Because households understand the budget, tax changes that are not matched by expenditure changes have no effect on capitalized expected tax liabilities.
5. Bond financing creates no net worth, again because of its implications for future taxes.

Since these arguments are partly parallel rather than serial, it is possible to argue that an increase in government demand is contractionary. The only government action that the monetarists will admit to be expansionary is an increase in the nominal supply of money, especially if it takes the form of non-interest-bearing government fiat money. However, they doubt the wisdom of discretionary monetary policy for reasons discussed in Chapter 5 and prefer to rely on monetary rules.[70]

[67]See Chapter 5, pages 107–111.

[68]The place to begin is with the monetary writings of Milton Friedman, many of which are listed in the references at the end of the book. Friedman (1968a) is one of the most impressive and influential addresses ever delivered at the meetings of the American Economics Association. Another important source is the "Symposium on Friedman's Theoretical Framework" in the 1972 *JPE* [see Symposium (1972) in the references]. Two very useful articles, Spencer and Yohe (1970) and Carlson and Spencer (1975), have appeared in the *Review* of the Federal Reserve Bank of St. Louis. They are particularly valuable for their many references. Finally, one should not miss the antimonetarist paper of Blinder and Solow (1973).

[69]The IS curve can be quite flat either because the multiplier is large or because (in this case) small declines in the rate of interest are directly associated with large increases in demand.

[70]See Chapter 5, page 111.

Most of these arguments are still confined to the learned journals; few have filtered through to the popular wisdom, which has not quite grasped Keynesianism yet and is hardly ready for its refutation. The Keynesians wish the monetarists would go home to Chicago, but they keep staying around and spoiling the party. Thus this discussion of government in disequilibrium must have an unsatisfying and vaguely unhappy ending.

IV. SUMMARY AND CONCLUSIONS

This chapter and the two preceding it belong together. They survey the general equilibrium and Keynesian analyses of the market system and of the impact of government upon it. Their wealth of technical detail defies brief summary. What can be summarized is a series of conflicting attitudes toward the market system. These are contained in the following schema, in which seven equilibrium or monetarist (∗) positions are contrasted with the corresponding Keynesian positions.

General equilibrium or monetarist (∗)		Keynesian
1. For practical purposes, markets clear.	vs.	Disequilibrium is the normal state of affairs.
2. There is a substantial harmony of interest between workers and owners.	vs.	There is substantial conflict over distribution.
3. Money is neutral in the long run.	vs.	We live in the short run.
4. In the long run, government resource use competes with private resource use.	vs.	We live in the short run.
5. ∗Money is dangerous in the short run.	vs.	Money is one of the tools of stabilization.
6. ∗Fiscal measures are ineffective in the short run.	vs.	Fiscal measures are the principal tools of stabilization.
7. The system works better by itself. Leave it alone.	vs.	The system needs help if we are to live with it. Get to work.

One might suppose that the controversies implied by these positions would long ago have been resolved, judging from the enormous amount of literature that has been devoted to arguing them out. The fact that there has been little resolution underscores how fundamental and ideological are the differences in viewpoint. What are at issue are perceptions about the effective functioning of the market system that form the basis for the fundamental premises of theory.

The limits of deductive theory for resolving these matters should be apparent. Deduction thought is no more capable of critically examining its own premises than is a child of choosing its parents. Deduction can only explore the implications of premises. It is mute regarding their relevance. Unfortunately, the differences really do matter. The view of thoughtful people regarding both the harmony of interest between labor and capital and the economic impact of government must be fundamentally influenced by their views of the degree to which prices really do clear markets.

The fact that deductive theory is incapable of resolving such issues leads fairly directly to two questions. First, what good is the theory anyhow? Second, what ways are there for rationally choosing between competing bodies of economic thought?

The first question may be answered on many levels. One of the most common answers is constructed around the "empty boxes" metaphor. According to this view of theory it is the necessary handmaiden of empiricism, raising essentially neutral questions the empirical content of whose answers may be pieced together into factual social science. Income effect dominates substitution effect: proceed to point A; substitution effect dominates income effect: proceed to point B. Naturally, this way of thinking provides an answer to the second question: the empirical method of econometrics.

The problems of inference from nonexperimental data are formidable, however. Anyone with extensive experience in econometrics must at one time or another have wondered whether any results are conclusive. Slightly differing approaches to a given body of data often result in diametrically opposed results. The problem is not so much the boxes that are empty as it is the boxes that are stuffed with incompatible findings.

To some extent the proliferation of inconsistent findings is the result of the advocacy system underlying much statistical work in economics. Often the stakes involved in the exploration of a given issue are very much higher than they seem on the surface. For example, the statement that the interest rate may exert a negative influence on the rate of investment seems harmless enough. But what is really at issue is whether the interest rate is an influence sufficiently powerful and quick-acting so as always to maintain equality between investment and full-employment saving. The whole hub of the Keynesian-neoclassical controversey turns on this issue. It is small wonder that the empirical literature on investment is full of inconsistencies and that those who work on this issue hotly dispute not only one another's findings but also one another's integrity.

The source of antagonisms is, of course, the web of ideology that runs throughout both theoretical and empirical economics. The issues of empirical inquiry do not suggest themselves. They have their origins in theoretical constructs, both explicit and implicit. These constructs, in turn, develop from a social matrix. Although there is a line in the logical development of theoretical inquiry, it is crisscrossed with threads leading to the main ideological issues of the society in which it is developed. The pulls and counter pulls of these threads exercise a controlling influence over the direction taken by the line of logical development itself.

It is inevitable that this should be the case. Any explanation of the workings of an economy must of necessity be simpler than the system itself. Theories are therefore simplistic, even to the point of caricature. The theorist seeks to isolate a few crucial aspects of complex reality and to identify them as the genuine essence of the system as a whole. This process of abstracting a limited system of postulates from a complicated reality involves choice. Where there is latitude for choice, preconception and prejudice hold sway. People whose personal and vicarious experiences with the market system have in the main been happy are apt to perceive a smoothly functioning, self-regulating system that consistently rewards ability and effort. Those who are sensitive or sensitized to its faults are apt to perceive a jumble of ill-fitting and contradictory institutions seemingly designed to frustrate and defeat rather than to fulfill. One suspects that ideology creeps into economic analysis mainly at this perceptional level. Once the givens are chosen, of course, all else follows. The process of statement, criticism, and correction that goes in the professional literature will separate the true theorems from the false, but it seldom will expose misleading or sterile premises.

Coleridge told us that there are times when it is productive to exercize a "willing suspension of disbelief" regarding ideas, modes of thought, or means of expression that seem foreign. But it is always dangerous to grant a person his or her premises for the sake of argument. To do so is to grant all that follows, no matter how preposterous or pernicious. Accepting uncritically a set of ready-made preconceptions is a lot like buying a cut-rate encyclopedia on a tie-in contract. The encyclopedia itself is quite a bargain, but part of the deal is to "keep your valuable reference work up to date" by buying the Book of the Year each year for the rest of your life. So every year comes the book, together with a big bill that you must pay whether or not you really enjoy that year's volume. The only way to break the contract is to send back everything, beginning with Volume A.

Unfortunately, it is not always easy to send it back. A person who chooses to work with a system of thought must make a substantial investment to learn it. It then is very hard to treat this intellectual investment as a bygone. The doctrine of sunk costs is good economics but bad psychology. And even if one wants to replace his or her old intellectual capital, it is not easy. As Keynes said in the preface to his *General Theory*:

> The composition of this book has been a long struggle of escape . . . from habitual modes of thought and expression. The ideas which are here expressed so laboriously are extremely simple and should be obvious. The difficulty lies, not in new ideas, but in escaping from the old ones, which ramify, for those brought up as most of us have been, into every corner of our minds.

All this suggests that the development of a world view should be a lifelong occupation. One must read widely in conflicting bodies of thought—not just neoclassical and Keynesian, but classical and Marxist—and keep an open mind until the creep of senility or the rush of events becomes overwhelming.

Abraham, W. L.: "National Income and Economic Accounting," Prentice-Hall, Englewood Cliffs, N.J., 1969.

Ackley, G.: "Macroeconomic Theory," Macmillan, New York, 1961.

——: "Macroeconomics: Theory and Policy," Macmillan, New York, 1978.

Allen, R. G. D.: Some Observations on the Theory and Practice of Index Numbers, *RE Stud* 3:57–66, February, 1936.

Ando, A., and E. C. Brown: Lags in Fiscal Policy, in Commission on Money and Credit, "Stabilization Policies," Prentice-Hall, Englewood Cliffs, N.J., 1963.

Andronow, A. A., and C. E. Chaikin: "Theory of Oscillations," Princeton University Press, Princeton N.J., 1949.

Arrow, K. J.: Toward a Theory of Price Adjustment, in M. Abramowitz (ed.), "The Allocation of Economic Resources," Stanford University Press, Stanford, Calif., 1959.

—— and F. H. Hahn: "General Competitive Analysis," Holden Day, San Francisco, 1971.

Baran, P.: "The Political Economy of Growth," Monthly Review Press, New York, 1957.

—— and P. Sweezy: "Monopoly Capital," Monthly Review Press, New York, 1966.

Barro, R. J., and H. I. Grossman: A General Disequilibrium Model of Income and Employment, *AER* 61:82–93, March, 1971.

——: Are Government Bonds Net Wealth? *JPE* 82:1095–1117, November-December, 1974.

Baumol, W. J.: The Transactions Demand for Cash: An Inventory-Theoretic Approach, *QJE* 66:545–56, November, 1952.

—— and M. H. Peston: More on the Multiplier Effects of a Balanced Budget, *AER* 45:140–48, March, 1955.

Berle, A.: "Power Without Property," Harcourt Brace, New York, 1959.

—— and G. Means: "The Modern Corporation and Private Property," Macmillan, New York, 1933.

Blinder, A. S., and R. M. Solow: Does Fiscal Policy Matter? *Jour. Pub. Econ.* 2:319–37, November, 1973.

Bosworth, B.: "Alternative Models of Investment Behavior," unpublished Ph.D. dissertation, The University of Michigan, 1969.

Brechling, F.: "Investment and Employment Decisions," University of Manchester Press, Manchester, England, 1975.

Brumberg, R.: An Approximation to the Aggregate Savings Function, *EJ* 46: 66–72, March, 1956.

Carlson, K., and R. Spencer: Crowding Out and Its Critics, in Federal Reserve Bank of St. Louis *Review* 75–12:2–17, December, 1975.

Cassel, G.: "The Nature and Necessity of Interest," reprint, Kelley and Millman, New York, 1957.

Chow, G.: "Analysis and Control of Dynamic Economic Systems," John Wiley, New York, 1975.

Clark, J. B.: "The Distribution of Wealth," Macmillan, New York, 1899.

Clower, R. W.: The Keynesian Counterrevolution: A Theoretical Appraisal, in F. H. Hahn and F. P. R. Brechling (eds.), "The Theory of Interest Rates," Macmillan, London, 1965.

Cooper, J. C., and S. Fischer: Simulation of Monetary Rules in the FRB-MIT-Penn Model, *Jour. of Money, Credit, & Banking* 4:384–96, May, 1972.

—— and ——: Stabilization Policy and Lags: Summary and Extension, *Ann. Ec. & Soc. Meas.* 1:407–18, October, 1972.

—— and ——: Stabilization Policy and Lags, *JPE* 81:847–77, July-August, 1973.

Davidson, P.: A Keynesian View of Patinkin's Theory of Employment, *EJ* 77: 559–78, September, 1967.

Deardorff, A., and F. Stafford: Compensation of Cooperating Factors, *Em* 44:671–84, June, 1976.

Debreu, G.: "Theory of Value," John Wiley, New York, 1959.

Dernburg, T. F., and D. M. McDougall: "Macroeconomics," 5th ed., McGraw-Hill, New York, 1976.

Domar, E.: The 'Burden of the Debt' and the National Income, *AER* 34:798–827, December, 1944.

——: The Problem of Capital Accumulation, *AER* 38:777–94, December, 1948.

Duesenberry, J. S.: "Business Cycles and Economic Growth," McGraw-Hill, New York, 1958.

Eichner, A. S., and J. A. Kregel: An Essay on Post-Keynesian Theory: A New Paradigm in Economics, *JE Litt* 13:1293–1314, December, 1975.

Eisner, R., and R. Strotz: Determinants of Business Investment, Research Study Two in "Impacts of Monetary Policy," Prentice-Hall, Englewood Cliffs, N.J., 1963.

—— and M. Nadiri: Investment Behavior and Neo-classical Theory, *RE Stat* 50:369–82, August, 1968.

Evans, G. C.: Maximum Production Studied in a Simplified Economic System, *Em* 2:37–50, January, 1934.

Farrell, M.: The New Theories of the Consumption Function, *EJ* 69:687–96, December, 1959.

Ferguson, J. M. (ed.): "Public Debt and Future Generations," University of North Carolina Press, Chapel Hill, N.C., 1964.

Fisher, F. M.: Embodied Technical Change and the Existence of an Aggregate Capital Stock, *RE Stud* 32:263–88, October, 1965.

——: Embodied Technology and the Existence of Labour and Output Aggregates, *RE Stud* 35:399–412, October, 1968.

——: Embodied Technology and the Aggregation of Fixed and Moveable Capital Goods, *RE Stud* 35:417–28, October, 1968.

—— and K. Shell: "The Economic Theory of Price Indices," Academic Press, New York, 1972.

Fisher, I.: "The Making of Index Numbers," Houghton Mifflin, Boston, 1922.

——: "The Theory of Interest," reprint, Augustus M. Kelley, New York, 1962.

Fitts, J.: "The Identification of Corporate Growth Motivation," unpublished Ph.D. dissertation, The University of Michigan, 1978.

Friedman, M.: The Effects of Full Employment Policy on Economic Stability, in Friedman, "Essays in Positive Economics," University of Chicago Press, Chicago, 1953.

——: The Quantity Theory of Money: A Restatement, in Friedman (ed.), "Studies in the Quantity Theory of Money," University of Chicago Press, Chicago, 1956.

——: "A Theory of the Consumption Function," Princeton University Press, Princeton, N.J., 1957.

——: "A Program for Monetary Stability," Fordham University Press, New York, 1959.

——: The Demand for Money—Some Theoretical and Empirical Results, *JPE* 67:327–51, August, 1959.

—— and A. J. Schwartz: "A Monetary History of the United States," Princeton University Press, Princeton, N.J., 1963.

—— and D. Meiselman: The Relative Stability of Monetary Velocity and the Investment Multi-

plier in the United States, 1897–1958, in Commission on Money and Credit, "Stabilization Policies," Prentice-Hall, Englewood Cliffs, N.J., 1963.
———: The Role of Monetary Policy, *AER* 58:1–17, March, 1968.
———: "Dollars and Deficits," Prentice-Hall, Englewood Cliffs, N.J., 1968.
———: The Optimum Quantity of Money, in Friedman, "The Optimum Quantity of Money and Other Essays," Aldine, Chicago, 1969.
Frisch, R.: Annual Survey of General Economic Theory: The Problem of Index Numbers, *Em* 4:1–38, January, 1936.
Goodwin, R. M.: A Non-linear Theory of the Cycle, *RE Stat* 32:316–20, November, 1950.
———: The Non-linear Accelerator and the Persistence of Business Cycles, *Em* 19:1–17, January, 1951.
Gordon, D., and A. Hynes: On the Theory of Price Dynamics, in E. Phelps (ed.), "Microeconomic Foundations of Employment and Inflation Theory," W. W. Norton, New York, 1970.
Gorman, W. M.: Separable Utility and Aggregation, *Em* 27:469–81, July, 1959.
———: The Structure of Utility Functions, *RE Stud* 35:367–90, October, 1968.
Gould, J.: Adjustment Costs in the Theory of Investment, *RE Stud* 36: 47–56, January, 1968.
Green, H. A. J.: "Aggregation in Economic Analysis," Princeton University Press, Princeton, N.J., 1964.
Grossman, H. L.: Money, Interest, and Prices in Market Disequilibrium, *JPE* 79:943–61, September–October, 1971.
———: Was Keynes a Keynesian? A Review Article, *JE Litt* 10:26–30, March, 1972.
Haavelmo, T.: Multiplier Effects of a Balanced Budget, *Em* 13:311–18, October, 1945.
———: "A Study in the Theory of Investment," University of Chicago Press, Chicago, 1960.
Hall, R., and D. Jorgenson.: Tax Policy and Investment Behavior, *AER* 57:391–414, June, 1967.
Hansen, A.: "Fiscal Policy and Business Cycles," W. W. Norton, New York, 1941.
———: "Monetary Theory and Fiscal Policy," McGraw-Hill, New York, 1949.
Harris, S. E.: "The New Economics," Knopf, New York, 1948.
Harrod, R. F.: An Essay in Dynamic Theory, *EJ* 49:14–33, March, 1939.
Hart, A. G.: "Anticipations, Uncertainty, and Dynamic Planning," University of Chicago Press, Chicago, 1940.
Hicks, J. R.: "The Theory of Wages," Macmillan, New York, 1932.
———: Mr. Keynes and the Classics: A Suggested Interpretation, *EM* 5:147–59, April, 1937.
———: "Value and Capital," 2d ed., Clarendon Press, Oxford, 1939.
———: "A Contribution to the Theory of the Trade Cycle," Oxford University Press, London, 1950.
———: A Rehabilitation of 'Classical' Economics? *EJ* 67:278–89, June, 1957.
Hodgman, D.: "National Monetary Policies and International Monetary Cooperation," Little Brown, Boston, 1974.
Holbrook, R. S.: Optimal Economic Policy and the Problem of Instrument Instability, *AER* 62:57–65, March, 1962.
———: A Practical Method for Controlling a Large Nonlinear Stochastic System, *Ann. Ec. & Soc. Meas.* 3:155–76, February, 1975.
Holt, C. C.: Job Search, Phillips' Wage Relation, and Union Influence: Theory and Evidence, in Phelps (ed.), "Microeconomic Foundations of Employment and Inflation Theory," W. W. Norton, New York, 1970.
Johansen, L.: "Public Economics," North-Holland, Amsterdam, 1965.
Jorgenson, D.: The Theory of Investment Behavior, in R. Ferber (ed.), "Determinants of Investment Behavior," Columbia University Press, New York, 1967.
———: Investment and Production: A Review, in M. Intriligator and D. Kendrick (eds.), "Frontiers of Quantitative Economics," North-Holland, Amsterdam, 1974.
Kareken, J., and R. Solow: Lags in Monetary Policy, in Commission on Money and Credit, "Stabilization Policies," Prentice-Hall, Englewood Cliffs, N.J., 1963.
Keynes, J. M.: "The General Theory of Employment, Interest, and Money," Harcourt Brace, New York, 1936.

Klein, L. R.: Macroeconomics and the Theory of Rational Behavior, *Em* 14:93–108, April, 1946.
——: Remarks on the Theory of Aggregation, *Em* 14:303–12, October, 1946.
——: "The Keynesian Revolution," Macmillan, New York, 1947.
——: Stocks and Flows in the Theory of Interest, in F. H. Hahn (ed.), "The Theory of Interest Rates," Macmillan, London, 1965.
—— and A. S. Goldberger: "An Econometric Model of the United States, 1929–1952," North-Holland, Amsterdam, 1955.
Kregel, J. A.: "The Reconstruction of Political Economy: An Introduction to Post-Keynesian Economics," Halsted Press, New York, 1973.
Lancaster, K. J.: A New Approach to Consumer Theory, *JPE* 74:132–57, April, 1966.
Leijonhufvud, A.: "On Keynesian Economics and the Economics of Keynes," Oxford University Press, London, 1968.
——: Life Among the Econ, *Western Economic Journal* 11:327–37, September, 1973.
Leontief, W. W.: Composite Commodities and the Problem of Index Numbers, *EM* 4:39–59, January, 1936.
——: A Note on the Interrelationship of Subsets of Independent Variables of a Continuous Function with Continuous First Derivatives, *Bull. Amer. Math. Soc* 53:343–50, 1947.
——: Introduction to a Theory of the Internal Structure of Functional Relationships, *Em* 15:361–73, October, 1947.
Lerner, A.: "The Economics of Control," Macmillan, New York, 1944.
Levhari, D., and D. Patinkin: The Role of Money in a Simple Growth Model, *AER* 48:713–53, September, 1968.
Lovell, M.: Manufacturers' Inventories, Sales Expectations, and the Acceleration Principle, *Em* 29:293–314, July, 1961.
Lucas, R.: Optimal Investment Policy and the Flexible Accelerator, *IER* 8:78–85, February, 1967.
——: Adjustment Costs and the Theory of Supply, *JPE* 75:321–34, August, 1967.
—— and E. C. Prescott: Equilibrium Search and Unemployment, *JET* 7:188–209, February, 1974.
McCall, J. J.: Economics of Information and Job Search, *QJE* 84:113–25, February, 1970.
McCulloch, J. R.: "The Principles of Political Economy," 4th ed., Edinburgh, 1849.
Maisel, S. J.: "Managing the Dollar," W. W. Norton, New York, 1973.
Marschack, J.: "Income, Employment, and the Price Level," Augustus M. Kelley, New York, 1951.
Mayer, T.: "Permanent Income, Wealth, and Consumption," University of California Press, Berkeley, Calif., 1972.
Metzler, L. A.: The Nature and Stability of Inventory Cycles, *RE Stat* 23:138–49, August, 1941.
——: Factors Governing the Length of Inventory Cycles, *RE Stat* 29:1–15, February, 1947.
——: Wealth, Saving, and the Rate of Interest, *JPE* 59:93–116, April, 1951.
Miller, M. H., and C. W. Upton: "Macroeconomics, A Neoclassical Introduction," Irwin, Homewood, Ill., 1974.
Modigliani, F.: Liquidity Preference and the Theory of Interest and Money, *Em* 12:45–88, January, 1944.
—— and R. Brumberg: Utility Analysis and the Consumption Function: An Interpretation of Cross-Section Data, in K. Kurihara (ed.), "Post-Keynesian Economics," Rutgers University Press, New Brunswick, N.J., 1954.
—— and M. Miller: The Cost of Capital, Corporation Finance, and the Theory of Investment, *AER* 48:261–97, June, 1958.
——: The Monetary Mechanism and Its Interaction with Real Phenomena, *RE Stat* 45S:79–107, February, 1963.
—— and A. Ando: The Life Cycle Hypothesis of Saving, *AER* 53:55–84, March, 1963.
——: The Life Cycle Hypothesis of Saving, the Demand for Wealth, and the Supply of Capital, *Social Research* 33:160–217, Summer, 1966.

Mortensen, D. T.: A Theory of Wage and Employment Dynamics, in Phelps (ed.), "Microeconomic Foundations of Employment and Inflation Theory," W. W. Norton, New York, 1970.
———: Job Search, the Duration of Unemployment, and the Phillips Curve, *AER* 60:847–62, December, 1970.
Musgrave, R.: "Fiscal Systems," Yale University Press, New Haven, Conn., 1969.
——— and P. Musgrave: "Public Finance in Theory and Practice," 2d ed., McGraw-Hill, New York, 1976.
Muth, J. F.: Rational Expectations and the Theory of Price Movements, *Em* 29:315–35, July, 1961.
Nataf, A.: Sur la possibilité de construction de certains macromodèles, *Em* 16:232–44, July, 1948.
———: Possibilité d'aggrégation de fonctions de production à variable capitale et main-d'oeuvre, *RE Stud* 34:219–26, April, 1967.
Oi, W. Y.: Labor as a Quasi-Fixed Factor, *JPE* 70:538–55, December, 1962.
Patinkin, D.: Price Flexibility and Full Employment, *AER* 38: 543–64, September, 1948.
———: A Reconsideration of the General Equilibrium Theory of Money, *RE Stud* 18(1):42–61, 1950.
———: "Money, Interest, and Prices," Row, Peterson and Co., Evanston, Ill., 1956.
———: "Money, Interest, and Prices," 2d ed., Harper and Row, New York, 1965.
———: Money and Wealth: A Review Article, *JE Litt* 4:1140–60, December, 1969.
Penrose, E.: Limits to the Growth and Size of Firms, *AER* 45S:531–43, May, 1955.
———: "The Theory of Growth of the Firm," Basil Blackwell and Mott, Oxford, 1959.
Peston, M. H.: "Theory of Macroeconomic Policy," John Wiley, New York, 1974.
Phelps, E. S. (ed.): "Microeconomic Foundations of Employment and Inflation Theory," W. W. Norton, New York, 1970.
———: Money Wage Dynamics and Labor Market Equilibrium, in Phelps (ed.), "Microeconomic Foundations of Employment and Inflation Theory, W. W. Norton, New York, 1970.
——— and S. Winter: Optimal Price Policy under Atomistic Competition, in Phelps (ed.), "Microeconomic Foundations of Employment and Inflation Theory," W. W. Norton, New York, 1970.
Phillips, A. W.: Stabilization Policy in a Closed Economy, *EJ* 64:290–323, June, 1954.
———: Stabilization Policy and the Time-Form of Lagged Responses, *EJ* 67:265–77, June, 1957.
Pigou, A. C.: "Wealth and Welfare," Macmillan, London, 1912.
———: "The Economics of Stationary States," Macmillan, London, 1935.
———: The Classical Stationary State, *EJ* 53:343–51, December, 1943.
Pryor, F.: "Public Expenditures in Communist and Capitalist Nations," Allen and Unwin, London, 1968.
———: "Property and Industrial Organization in Communist and Capitalist Nations," Indiana University Press, Bloomington, Ind., 1973.
Rader, T.: "Theory of Microeconomics," Academic Press, New York, 1972.
Raiffa, H.: "Decision Analysis," Addison-Wesley, Reading, Mass., 1968.
Ricardo, D.: "On the Principles of Political Economy and Taxation," 3d ed., P. Sraffa (ed.), Cambridge University Press, Cambridge, England, 1953.
Robinson, J.: The Theory of Money and the Analysis of Output, *RE Stud* 1:22–6, October, 1933.
Rose, H.: Unemployment in a Theory of Growth, *IER* 7:260–82, September, 1966.
Samuelson, P. A.: Interactions Between the Multiplier Analysis and the Principle of Acceleration, *RE Stat* 21:75–8, May, 1939.
———: A Synthesis of the Principle of Acceleration and the Multiplier, *JPE* 47:786–97, December, 1939.
———: "Foundations of Economic Analysis," Harvard University Press, Cambridge, Mass., 1947.
——— and S. Swamy: Invariant Economic Index Numbers and Canonical Duality: Survey and Synthesis, *AER* 64:566–93, September, 1974.
Schelling, T. C.: "The Strategy of Conflict," Harvard University Press, Cambridge, Mass., 1960.
Schneider, H. (ed.): "Grundsatzprobleme wirtschaftspolitischer Beratung," Dunker and Humblot, Berlin, 1968.

Schumpeter, J. A.: Science and Ideology, *AER* 39:345–59, March, 1949.

———: "History of Economic Analysis," Oxford University Press, New York, 1954.

Shackle, G. L. S.: "Expectations in Economics," Cambridge University Press, Cambridge, England, 1949.

Shepherd, W. G. et al.: "Public Enterprise," Lexington Books, Lexington, Mass., 1967.

Slutsky, E.: On the Theory of the Budget of the Consumer, in G. Stigler and K. Boulding (eds.), "Readings in Price Theory," Irwin, Homewood, Ill., 1952.

Smith, W. L., and R. L. Teigen: "Readings in Money, National Income, and Stabilization Policy," Irwin, Homewood, Ill., 1964.

Solow, R. M.: The Production Function and the Theory of Capital, *RE Stud* 23(2):101–8, 1955–56.

Spencer, R., and W. Yohe: The 'Crowding Out' of Private Expenditures by Fiscal Policy Actions, in Federal Reserve Bank of St. Louis *Review* 52-10:12–24, October, 1970.

Staehle, H.: A Development of the Economic Theory of Price Index Numbers, *RE Stud* 2:163–88, June, 1935.

Stigler, G. J.: "Production and Distribution Theories, the Formative Period," Macmillan, New York, 1941.

———: The Politics of Political Economists, *QJE* 73:522–32, November, 1959.

Strotz, R. H.: Myopia and Inconsistency in Dynamic Utility Maximization, *RE Stud* 23(3):165–80, 1956.

———: The Empirical Implications of a Utility Tree, *Em* 25:269–80, April, 1957.

———: The Utility Tree, a Correction and Further Appraisal, *Em* 27:482–88, July, 1959.

Suits, D. B.: Forecasting and Analysis with an Econometric Model, *AER* 52:104–32, March, 1962.

Symposium on Friedman's Theoretical Framework, *JPE* 80:837–950, September-October 1972. (Papers by Brunner and Meltzer, Tobin, Davidson, Patinkin, and Friedman.)

Terborgh, G.: "The Bogey of Economic Maturity," Machinery and Allied Products Institute, Chicago, 1945.

Theil, H.: "Linear Aggregation of Economic Relations," North-Holland, Amsterdam, 1954.

———: "Optimal Decision Rules for Government and Business," North-Holland, Amsterdam, 1964.

Tinbergen, J.: "Economic Policy: Principles and Design," North-Holland, Amsterdam, 1956.

Tobin, J.: The Interest-Elasticity of Transactions Demand for Cash, *RE Stat* 38:241–47, August, 1956.

———: Liquidity Preference as Behavior Towards Risk, *RE Stud* 25:65–86, February, 1958.

———: Money, Capital, and Other Stores of Value, *AER* 51S:26–37, May, 1961.

———: Inflation and Unemployment, *AER* 62:1–18, March, 1972.

Treadway, A.: On Rational Entrepreneurial Behaviour and the Demand for Investment, *RE Stud* 36:227–39, April, 1969.

———: Adjustment Costs and Variable Inputs in the Theory of the Competitive Firm, *JET* 3:329–47, December, 1970.

Tucker, D. P.: Patinkin's Macro Model as a Model of Market Disequilibrium, *SEJ* 39:187–203, October, 1972.

———: Dynamic Income Adjustment to Money-Supply Changes, *AER* 56:433–49, June, 1966.

Wallich, H.: Income-generating Effects of a Balanced Budget, *QJE* 59:78–91, November, 1944.

Walras, L.: "Elements of Pure Economics," trans. W. Jaffee, Allen and Unwin, London, 1954.

Whipple, D.: A Generalized Theory of Job Search, *JPE* 81:1170–88, October, 1973.

Wicksell, K.: "Interest and Prices," trans. R. F. Kahn, Augustus M. Kelley, New York, 1965.

———: "Lectures on Political Economy," trans. E. Classen, L. Robbins (ed.), George Routledge and Sons, Ltd., London, 1934.

Yaari, M.: On the Consumer's Lifetime Allocation Process, *IER* 5:304–17, September, 1964.

NAME INDEX

Abraham, W., 98
Ackley, G., 42, 50
Allen, R., 74
Anderson, A., x
Ando, A., 10, 194
Andronov, A., 145
Arrow, K., 98, 102, 103

Baran, P., 197
Barro, R., 103, 137, 176
Baumol, R., 20, 198
Berle, A., 37
Blinder, A., 199
Bodzin, A., x
Bosworth, B., 45
Brown, E., 194
Brumberg, R., 10, 24, 35

Caprio, J., ix
Carlson, K., 199
Cassel, G., 119
Chaib, A., ix
Chaikin, C., 145
Chow, G., 195
Clark, J., 98, 124
Clower, R., 2, 29, 103, 130
Coleridge, S., 202
Cooper, J., 194, 195
Cross, J., ix

Deardorff, A., ix, 26
Dietrich, S., x
Domar, E., 168, 198
Douglas, M., 91
Driscoll, K., ix
Duesenberry, J., 128

Eichner, A., 129
Eisner, R., 42, 51
Evans, G., 98

Farrell, M., 10
Ferguson, C., 176
Fischer, S., 194, 195
Fisher, F., 74
Fisher, I., 15, 16, 74, 83
Fitts, J., x, 37, 41
Friedman, M., 10, 21, 35–36, 108, 111, 128, 158–160, 163, 194, 199
Frisch, R., 74

Gesell, S., 91
Goldberg, R., 20
Goldberger, A., 128
Goodwin, R., 128
Gordon, D., 69
Gorman, W., 74, 79
Gould, J., 51
Green, H., 75, 78, 79
Grossman, H., 103, 130, 137

Haavelmo, T., 42, 198
Haberler, G., 129
Hahn, F., 98, 102
Hall, R., 42, 173
Hansen, A., 197
Hansen, B., ix
Harris, S., 129
Harrod, R., 168
Hart, A., 103
Hendricks, A., ix
Hicks, J., 76, 98, 103, 124, 128, 130
Holbrook, R., ix, 194, 195

SUBJECT INDEX